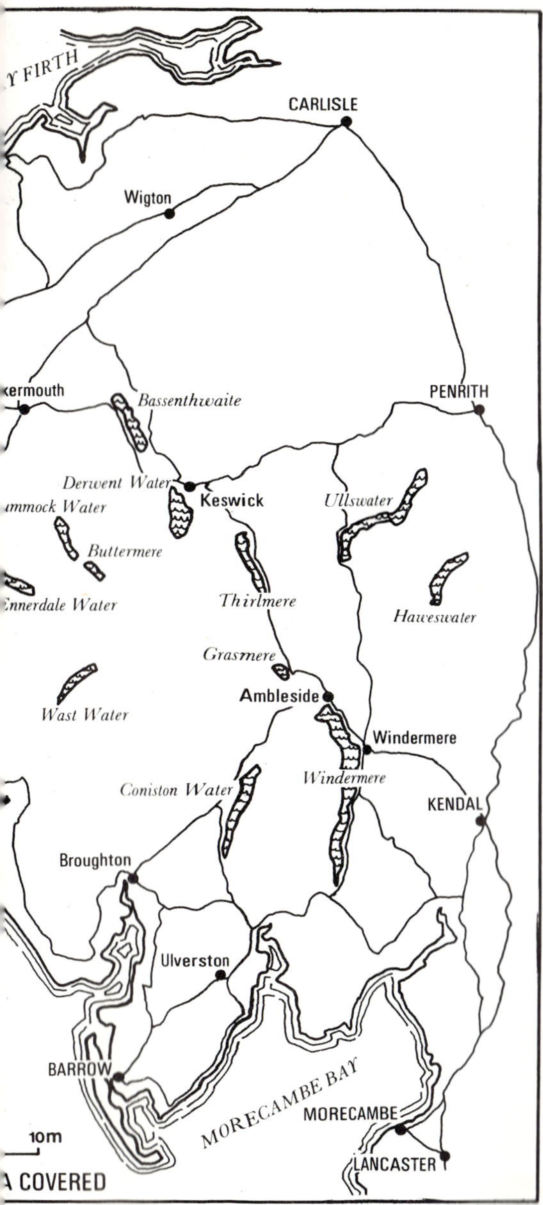
FIRTH
CARLISLE
Wigton
kermouth
Bassenthwaite
PENRITH
Derwent Water
Keswick
Ullswater
mmock Water
Buttermere
Thirlmere
Haweswater
nnerdale Water
Grasmere
Ambleside
Wast Water
Windermere
Windermere
Coniston Water
KENDAL
Broughton
Ulverston
BARROW
MORECAMBE BAY
MORECAMBE
LANCASTER
10m
A COVERED

AF573605

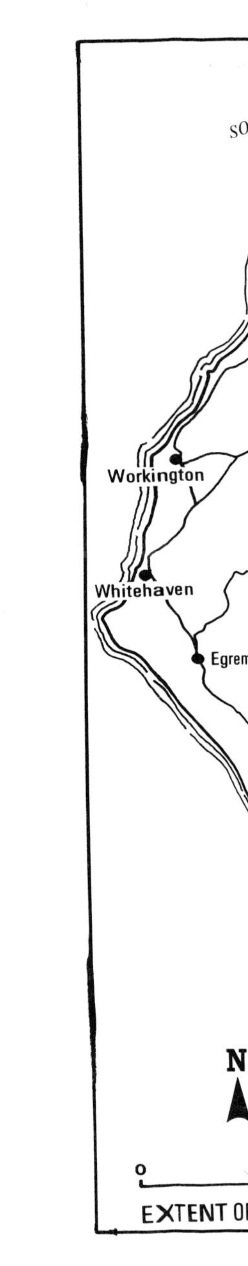

SOLW
C
Workington
Whitehaven
Egremont
N
0
EXTENT OF A

CYCLING IN THE LAKE DISTRICT

Richard Harries

British Library Cataloguing in Publication Data

Harries, Richard
Cycling in the Lake District.
1. Cycling — England — Lake District — Guide-Books
2. Lake District (England) — Description and travel — Guide-books
I. Title
914.27'804858 DA670.L1

Pictures of Derwentwater and Carrock Fell Youth Hostels, and Walna Scar Road were provided courtesy of YHA Lakeland Region. The picture of Patterdale Youth Hostel was provided courtesy of the YHA Head Office at St Albans. Blencathra (p163) and Lake Windermere, near Ambleside (p173) provided by Lindsey Porter. All others including the cover illustrations were supplied by the author.

ISBN 0 86190 107 X

Printed in the UK by
Butler and Tanner Ltd, Frome
for the publishers
Moorland Publishing Co Ltd,
9-11 Station Street, Ashbourne,
Derbyshire, DE6 1DE England.
Telephone: (0335) 44486

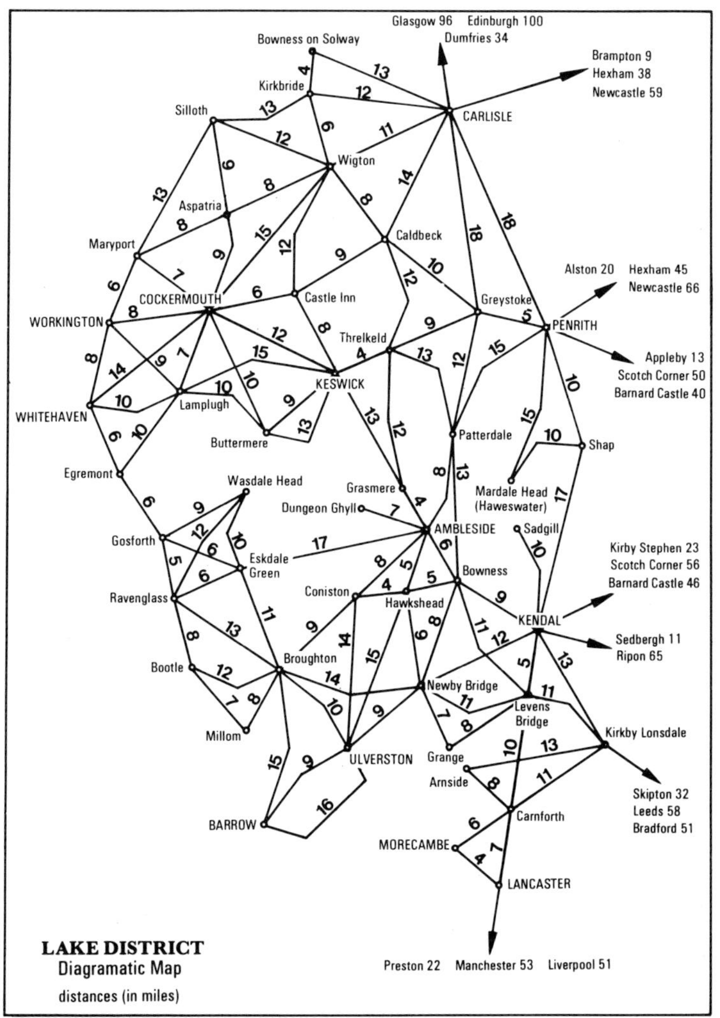

KEY TO ROUTE MAPS	DESCRIBED IN TEXT	OTHER
Tarred roads	━━━	───
Tracks & bridleways (generally rideable)	━ ━ ━	─ ─ ─
Other tracks & paths	• • • • • • •	. . . .

Contents

Preface

Why cycle in the Lake District? The roads are busy, the hills fearsome and it often rains. Surely no-one would choose such a small and mountainous area for a cycling holiday?

In fact, a great number of people do so; I hope that this book will encourage many more. This small corner of England can boast some of the finest scenery in Britain and in many ways the cyclist is better placed to appreciate it than either the walker or the motorist. Roads and tracks pass through the peaceful woods, far from the noise and bustle of modern life; they skirt the lakesides, which mirror the fells in the water; old tracks, with many twists and turns, follow the valleys out of sight and sound of busy motor roads — these are some of the attractions of the cyclists' Lakeland.

Carrock Fell Youth Hostel

Introduction

Cycling in the Lake District

This book has been written to fill a gap. While there are any number of books on the Lake District, the requirements of one group of visitors, cyclists, have been almost totally neglected. Even with a good map, it is difficult to gain the most out of a trip, whether a half-day spin or a week's tour. So in this book I have tried to include information and suggestions of specific interest and value to the cycling tourist, so that he or she may have the greatest possible enjoyment out of a visit to the area.

I have been encouraged by the recent growth in cycling for pleasure, which may be explained in various ways: increased leisure time, concern over health and fitness, and the quest for more environmentally acceptable forms of transport. In addition, the spread of cycle-hire facilities and the popularity of folding bikes that will fit into a car boot have both enabled the cyclist to visit new areas. The policy of British Rail in allowing cycles to be conveyed free on most of its trains has also opened up opportunities.

My intention is to cater for the interests of all cyclists; from the family who may just want to 'potter about' on some quiet byroads for a couple of hours, to the experienced cyclist who is planning a lengthy tour of the district. For the 'rough stuff' cyclist interested in the Lakeland passes, I have given some of the more practicable examples. Also included are a number of short walks complementary to the cycling routes which will add much to any tour.

The area covered by the book is basically the National Park, broadened to include (though in less detail) the immediate approaches and some excursions to nearby places of interest. Virtually all of Cumbria west of the A6 is incorporated in some depth; the eastern part of the county, around the vales of the Eden and Lune, also offers good cycling but it is beyond the scope of this book.

The Lake District certainly has its disadvantages as a cycle-touring area, but in practice these are minor objections. The roads are undoubtedly hilly, but overall no more adverse than those of other parts of Britain famed for scenic beauty such as the West Country or North Wales. Hikers rarely complain that the Lake District is too hilly! That a day's mileage must be less than in flatter terrain also overcomes the objection that the area is too small to provide sufficient scope for a prolonged tour. Though cyclists will occasionally need to retrace their route there is scarcely an uninteresting mile of road in the area; indeed many routes need to be followed in each direction for a full appreciation of their scenery. Above all, the intimacy of the topography demands a leisurely and unrushed exploration.

While the Lake District *is* one of the wettest parts of Britain, there is considerable variation between the central mountain core and the relatively low ground fringing it. Rainfall is invariably quoted for the former, and so the district has a reputation it does not fully deserve. Nevertheless a visitor at any time of the year must expect some wet weather and bear it in mind when planning. In any case, rain or mist need not detract from enjoyment of the scenery: the fells acquire a new and mysterious outline, while the various waterfalls and rivers which contribute so much to the beauty of the area are reinvigorated.

So popular has the Lake District become that the tourist would be well advised to avoid the main summer holiday period if at all possible. Weekends also bring an influx of motor traffic, particularly to the more accessible parts such as Windermere and Ambleside. Scenically, the best time to visit the district is the autumn, as then the leaves and bracken are acquiring their range of russet hues that set off the light-greens of the hills and blue-grey of the lakes so well. The spring months are, of course, even more varied in colour, while some winter days, with snow lying on the higher tops and the air sharp and clear, can be the most memorable.

Touring Suggestions

To prescribe a set tour would be presumptious, as the requirements and tastes of visitors vary so much. As cycling in a hilly area like the Lake District can be hard work, it is advisable to establish short-stay touring bases from which day trips can be made without the encumbrance of all one's luggage. A day's itinerary can then be decided on the spot, rather than be fitted in with the need to reach or arrange fresh accommodation.

With this in mind, a first stop might be Ambleside or one of the neighbouring villages such as Grasmere or Hawkshead. A few days may easily be spent in the surrounding area, while destinations further afield include Furness Abbey and Cartmel. The western dales merit two days' exploration — there are a number of possible centres both inland and on the coast. Keswick is the natural base for Derwentwater, as well as for Thirlmere and Bassenthwaite Lake, while longer excursions may be made to Caldbeck or Buttermere. Ullswater should be approached from the north, but Patterdale, at its head, is much more of a walking than a cycling centre. Both Ullswater and nearby Haweswater may be visited by those returning via Penrith or Shap.

It can be seen that by arranging accommodation at, for example, Ambleside, Ravenglass and Keswick it would be possible to complete a circuit of the Lake District in four days, and the addition of intermediate day trips could readily expand it to a week or more, without the inclusion of other activities such as rambling, boating or sightseeing.

A problem in any guidebook is that descriptions of a route or itinerary in both directions of travel produce considerable duplication of detail, without materially adding to the information provided. With a few exceptions, routes have been described in one direction only. While most excursions are equally profitable in either direction I have included in the introduction to each route recommendations as to the preferable direction of travel. The descriptions themselves include appropriate notes (such as dangerous hills or a viewpoint which may otherwise be missed) for the benefit of cyclists travelling 'the wrong way'. As a rule, all the lakes are best approached from their foot, and so are seen backed by an encircling group of fells. Perhaps the best example of this is Ullswater, the ride up from Pooley Bridge being one of ever-growing interest and beauty.

Equipment

Before starting any cycling tour, particular attention should be paid to two items: tyres and brakes.

Lakeland roads are often bordered or overhung with trees, and their verges become generously carpeted with twigs and thorns. The only defence against punctures is to have both tyres in good condition and correctly inflated.

Brakes are, of course, a vital item of equipment and should be examined for any signs of wear or corrosion in the cables and mechanisms. Any doubtful parts should be replaced, Lake District hills leave no margin for mishaps. Throw away rubber brakeblocks and replace them with those of the composite type, now widely available, which are specifically designed to provide adequate braking in the wet.

For those hiring bicycles who perhaps are not used to cycling any distance I must stress the necessity of finding a comfortable riding position. The saddle should be adjusted so that the leg is just straightened when pedalling and the handlebars raised so that not too much weight is borne by the arms and shoulders. Adjustments are usually very easy to make — do not be afraid to experiment. All loads should be carried on the bicycle in saddlebags and not on one's back. This (with a correct riding position) will not only prevent leg cramp and backache, but also make cycling much easier.

Maps and Rights of Way

A good map is the best guidebook, and for the Lake District everyone should obtain the 1in to 1 mile Tourist Map published by the Ordnance Survey. This shows all roads, bridleways and footpaths. An alternative is the attractive 1in to a mile Tourist Map published by John Bartholomew and Son, and although a little inaccurate in the details of some tracks, it is perfectly adequate for road users. Bartholomews also produce a very useful map on the 1:100,000 scale (sheet 34) covering a much larger area than the 1in maps. It has a larger contour interval (50 or 100 metres), and so gives much less information on the rise and fall of the roads: in this respect it is not so good as its predecessor on the ½in to a mile scale.

The Ordnance Survey also publishes maps on the larger scales of 1:50,000 and 1:25,000 but these are of more use to the walker than the cyclist. A map on a smaller scale such as 1:250,000 may be found useful for covering the approaches to the district and route planning. The key maps contained in this book are intended to complement the Ordnance Survey Tourist Map, but care has been taken to show all the roads in sufficient detail. Also included is a map giving distances at a glance (page 5).

As a number of the routes given in this book utilise minor roads and byways a note on some of the terminology used may be helpful. OS maps used to distinguish between 'tarred', 'metalled' and 'unmetalled' roads. The term 'metalled' dates back to the turnpike days; it refers to the scientific construction of a road surface of broken stone rendered impervious to water by the compaction of traffic. This was the type of road construction advocated by Macadam, hence the term tarmacadam for a sealing layer of tar-coated chippings. Although these days a metalled road is invariably taken to mean one which is tarred, the distinction has been maintained in this book. Lakeland is comparatively well off for byroads which are firm enough for the cyclist, but sufficiently uneven to deter the motorist. Unfortunately, recent OS maps distinguish only between tarred and untarred roads, giving no indication of the practicality of the latter for cycling.

Another difficulty with minor roads (ie those shown uncoloured on the OS map) is that there is no indication whether a right of way exists. This is also true of many old upland tracks, now only passable on foot, which are still technically 'roads', and so cannot be indicated on maps as public footpaths or bridleways. In practice, almost any byroad or path will be a right of way, except for those which obviously are to serve a single house or farm. The classification 'Road used as a public path' given on some maps has been legislated out of existence, such roads now being reclassified either as bridleways or as 'byways open to all traffic'. While the highway authority is not obliged to bring this latter group up to a motorable standard, neither need bridleways be maintained to a standard suitable for cycling.

Bridleways are paths designated for the use of walkers and horseriders, both of which have a right of way. Since the Countryside Act of 1968, this right of way has been extended to *pedal* cyclists, who must however give priority to pedestrians and horseriders. This affirmation of rights long claimed by cyclists was won only after some opposition, and it is therefore appropriate to show due respect for other users, even if this means stopping and dismounting. The fact that a path is a right of way does not give any user or group of users the right to cause a nuisance, and to do so is an offence. Public attitudes to cycling and cyclists are very susceptible to inconsiderate behaviour, both in town and country. At a time when cycling groups are campaigning for improved facilities, inconsiderate behaviour by others is likely to handicap their efforts.

It is perhaps worth mentioning that it is not actually against the law to cycle on a footpath (except where a specific 'No Cycling' ban is in force, or along a footway adjacent to a carriageway) but the cyclist may be liable to a charge of 'reckless, careless or inconsiderate' cycling, as by its very nature pedestrians would be assumed to have uninterrupted use of the path. Further, a cyclist may be turned back by a landowner, as no right of way would exist.

Many of the Lake District bridleways are old packhorse roads and are often of historical interest. Originally well constructed with well-planned gradients, they have suffered from neglect as motor roads took away their traffic and more recently from the sheer weight of use by pedestrians. It is quite common to find a smooth grassy track degenerating into an ugly scar of stony ruts where it steepens and the effects of walking boots and running water have taken their toll. Thus many of these old hill tracks are more difficult to 'cycle' over than in former years, and are likely to deteriorate further.

A selection of the major Lakeland passes is included (Routes 36-42), but careful attention should be paid to the general comments made on pages 17-18.

Distances and Journey Times

After much heart-searching, I have decided to retain the use of miles for distances rather than the alternative metric units — not out of any sentimentality for an obsolete system, but until the general adoption of kilometres for road distances I feel that most cyclists will be more familiar with Imperial units. Elevation are given in both feet and metres in the text, metres only on the maps.

Distances have been measured with the greatest care and are given to the nearest quarter mile, which should be more than adequate. The map giving principal distances at a glance will be found useful for planning.

With the exception of some of the bridleway routes estimates of journey times have been omitted. Such times are dependent on so many factors that to quote averages would mean little to the majority of cyclists. Regular tourers should have no difficulty in planning a day's ride, while for those not used to cycling longer distances, a speed of about 8-10mph between major halts is a reasonable guide. A rule of thumb would be to take a base speed of, say, 12mph on the flat and add 2 or 3 minutes for each 100ft of ascent, but minor roads of the district are often of constantly changing gradient and this can be more tiring than the map might suggest. In any case there are always plenty of other attractions and to cover more than about 40 miles a day probably means that you are missing much of interest.

Train Services

The free conveyance of accompanied bicycles, introduced a few years ago by British Rail on most of its services, should encourage many cyclists to travel to the Lake District by train. The mainline stations are Lancaster, Oxenholme, Penrith and Carlisle, served by inter-city trains on the West Coast route. Oxenholme (just outside Kendal) is the junction for the branch to Windermere, to which a few trains run through from Lancaster, etc. Appleby, on the threatened Settle & Carlisle line, is a useful railhead for visitors from Yorkshire who must otherwise travel to Carnforth or Lancaster on the Leeds-Morecambe line. Carnforth is the junction for the Barrow line, but is not now served by trains to or from the north via Oxenholme. Most Barrow trains start from Lancaster, but some come from Preston and beyond. The section of the line between Arnside and Grange over Sands is most useful in cutting out the long detour via Levens Bridge and the busy A590, while linking with quiet roads to Coniston, Hawkshead, etc.

North of Barrow a local service operates around the coast to Whitehaven and Carlisle. Some stations make convenient railheads but the line is rather remote from the main tourist area. Minor stations on this line and also the Windermere branch are 'request' stops, ie trains set down and pick up only by notifying the guard and signalling to the driver respectively. On Sundays there are no trains between Barrow and Carlisle and in winter no Sunday trains to Windermere, although a Sunday service of two trains each way has been recently introduced between Carlisle and Whitehaven on an experimental basis.

A leaflet giving further information on the conveyance of cycles is available from main BR stations, but a further check before travel is always wise.

DalesRail: This operates on certain summer weekends over the Settle to Carlisle line. Although introduced to open up the Yorkshire Dales National Park, some stations, eg Dent (for Kendal) and Langwathby (for Penrith) as well as Appleby (see above), can be utilised as starting-points for touring the Lake District. Trains run from Leeds, Preston and Blackburn. Cycles are conveyed free, but accommodation for them is limited.

For details of services send a stamped addressed envelope to DalesRail, Metro House, West Parade, Wakefield, W Yorks WF1 1NS.

It is possible that, following recent revisions to the Leeds to Carlisle BR service, some of the DalesRail stations may be reopened to these trains, though at the time of writing the future of the whole line is in doubt.

Lake Sailing and Ferry Services

As well as the point to point services listed below circular trips are operated on Windermere (from Bowness and Ambleside) and Derwentwater (from Keswick). On Coniston Water the restored steam vessel *Gondola* operates a summer service down the lake (Saturdays excepted), but cycles are not conveyed.

Windermere

Sailings operate between Lake Side, Bowness and Waterhead, Ambleside. Cycles are charged half fare. Frequent services operate from the beginning of May to the end of September, and also over the Easter period.

Further details from The Manager, Lake Windermere Services, Lake Side, Ulverston, Cumbria LA12 8AS.

Windermere Ferry (Bowness to Hawkshead road) operates as follows:

Summer service 0650 (Sun 0910) until 2150
Winter service 0650 (Sun 0950) until 2050

The summer service operates April to September. Times above are for westbound journeys, eastbound services start and finish ten minutes later. The ferry runs every 20 minutes, a small charge being made for cyclists.

Ullswater
Services operate between Pooley Bridge, Howtown and Glenridding. Cycles are conveyed, but large parties cannot be catered for. Service runs three times a day from Easter to the end of September, then twice daily until mid-October. The Howtown to Glenridding link is particularly useful to cyclists.

Further details from the Ullswater Navigation and Transit Co Ltd, 13 Maude Street, Kendal, Cumbria.

Cyclists' Touring Club
'The national association devoted to the encouragement of recreational cycling and the protection of cyclists' interests.'
Membership enquiries to CTC National Headquarters, Cotterell House, 69 Meadrow, Godalming, Surrey GU7 3HS.

Membership of this organisation is essential for anyone who is seriously interested in cycling. The CTC has long fought to protect and extend the rights of cyclists and campaigned for better and safer cycling facilities. Many proposed restrictions on cyclists, both national and local, have been successfully opposed by the club, which was also largely responsible for getting cyclists' right to use bridleways recognised by law. There can hardly be a cyclist who has not benefited in some way from its activities.

On an individual level, members receive the bimonthly *Cycletouring* magazine and can obtain the handbook listing approved touring accommodation and other useful information. Membership includes third-party insurance and the club runs a legal aid scheme for members involved in road accidents. The Touring Department offers a wide-ranging information service. Local rides and events are arranged by the various District Associations throughout the country.

Youth Hostels
Membership enquiries to YHA Trevelyan House, St Albans, Herts AL1 2DY.

Youth Hostels provide informal and friendly accommodation for young (and not so young) tourists with a limited budget. They are graded according to the facilities offered and vary from purpose-built hostels such as Patterdale to the remote Black Sail Hut at the head of Ennerdale.

The Lake District can boast the greatest concentration of Youth Hostels in Britain; but those in the main walking areas tend to be full for much of the summer, and advance booking is advised. Hostels on the main hitch-hiking routes are also busy, but room is generally available in those on the fringe of the district such as Arnside, Hawkshead, Cockermouth and the new Carrock Fell hostel near Caldbeck. Hostels on the western side of the district are few but those at Wasdale Hall and Gillerthwaite (Ennerdale) can be recommended. The standard of accommodation for cycles does vary from hostel to hostel.

Cumbria Cycle Way

This provides a 280-mile waymarked route for cyclists round the periphery of the county. It was devised to establish an easy route for cyclists, using minor roads and tracks wherever possible, and keeps close to passenger railway lines to enable it to be covered in stages.

As it nearly all lies beyond the bounds of the Lake District it inevitably misses the finest Cumbrian scenery and necessitates traversing the industrial area between Whitehaven and Maryport. However the majority of the way, especially the section below the western flanks of the Pennines, passes through many little-known areas of great beauty. Some of the coastal stretches of the way are covered by routes in this book, and a plan and description of the way are included in the 'Cycling in Cumbria' leaflet published by the Cumbria Tourist Board and obtainable from Tourist Information Centres.

Some Lakeland Passes
General comments on Routes 36-42

No book on cycling in the Lake District would be complete without a description of the main inter-valley paths which, by virtue of the distance saved, may attract the attention of the cyclist. It must be said, however, that pass-storming with cycles is largely a matter of considerable hard work for comparatively little scenic reward, and invariably no saving in time over going the long way round. To see mountain Lakeland properly one must forsake the bicycle completely and enjoy the freedom of the felltops on foot. The routes included here cover most of the inter-valley tracks, but this is not intended to be a comprehensive guide, which would be a book in itself.

Although elsewhere in this book routes have been included which involve sections of track or path (I have used these words interchangeably) those to be described differ substantially in that the amount of physical effort demanded is much higher and the risk of damage or injury to the cyclist or machine a lot more real. All are well-defined and well-used paths, but they are so rough that progress can be extremely slow. Once off the metalled road the chance of any real cycling is usually nil. While the risk of serious injury is slight the inconvenience arising from, say, a buckled chainwheel or a sprained ankle is obvious.

No specialised equipment is required for these excursions, except a pair of hiking boots or, at the very least stout shoes with good gripping soles. More detailed maps such as the OS 1:25,000 sheets are occasionally useful, but those who cannot find their way with a 1in map should not be leaving the road. I like to carry a compass, not so much for routefinding, but to identify distant landmarks; it adds so much interest to a view if you know what you are looking at. Clothing should be adequate for the windier hill tops and the weather checked beforehand by phoning the recorded Fell Forecast on Windermere (09662) 5151, which gives the local weather outlook and walking conditions. As north-facing slopes can harbour ice and snow, long after southern slopes have cleared, routes are best tackled from the north or worst side outside high summer.

The bicycle should be thoroughly checked beforehand, and en route, to ensure that no parts are likely to work loose. Odd lengths of string and soft wire are handy, as are elastic straps.

In an emergency one should wait, all these routes are well used and assistance should not be long in arriving. Short cuts should not be used to escape from the fells. A reserve supply of food should be carried and the mountain distress signal — six whistle blasts (better than shouting) repeated at minute intervals — should be used when necessary. Every year thousands wander over the Lakeland fells without coming to the slightest harm, but accidents do happen and a few precautions are easily taken.

It is difficult to put the routes included into an order of severity, but the suggested journey times will give some guide. It can be seen that these speeds average about 1-1½ miles per hour, about half typical walking speeds over such terrain.

Motor cycles are not permitted on bridleways.

Those interested in exploring Britain's network of bridleways and old tracks may wish to join the Rough Stuff Fellowship. For details send a stamped addressed envelope to New Membership Secretary, A. John Mathews, 9 Liverpool Avenue, Ainsdale, Southport, Merseyside PR8 3NE.

Approaches from Lancaster 1

Distances from Lancaster: Carnforth 6¾m, Silverdale 11m, Arnside 14¾m, Milnthorpe 14m, Levens Bridge 16¾m, (Hawkshead 31½m, Bowness 28m, Kendal 22m), Burton 11m, Endmoor 16¾m (Kendal 22¼m).

INTRODUCTION

A few notes must suffice to cover the main approaches to the district from the south. The Lancaster to Kendal corridor is notable for the number of transport links that run closely parallel to each other — the old byways, two turnpike roads, the canal, the west coast main railway line and the M6, to which might be added the aqueducts to Manchester.

Fortunately for the cyclist, the motorway has taken much of the traffic off the local 'A' roads and even these may be avoided by a study of the map.

When in Lancaster a visit to the castle (next to the station) may be made, while the popular seaside resort of Morecambe lies only a few miles off the road to the Lakes.

DESCRIPTION

From Lancaster there is little of note until Carnforth, a small industrial town that developed after the coming of the railway. At Steamtown, just west of the station, a number of steam locomotives are maintained in running order.

(a) Carnforth to Kendal via Burton and Endmoor
The original route from Lancaster to Kendal, turnpiked in 1753, is certainly preferable to the A6 at weekends, being much quieter (except where the M6 runs alongside) if slightly more hilly. It is surprising that this road has retained its 'A' road classification as it has been totally superseded for through traffic. Apart from the once-important village of Burton, with its interesting variety of old buildings, it has nothing of note.

Four miles beyond Burton it is joined by the road from Kirkby Lonsdale to Kendal (13m), the main approach from the towns of west Yorkshire and usually busy, though most of the traffic and that from the motorway uses the dual-carriageway link across to the A6. Keeping to the A65, the road continues to Crooklands

1

A591
Staveley
A6
A684
WINDERMERE
BOWNESS
B5284
·94m
Winster
KENDAL
N
Windermere
62m·
Crosthwaite
Oxenholme
10m·
A5074
A65
B6254
Sedgewick
Newby Bridge
·95m
·8m
A591
Endmoor
A591
Crooklands
Heversham
A591
Old
Town
Milnthorpe
·47m
B5282
A65
Lindale
Cartmel
Beetham
Arnside
·57m
GRANGE
OVER
SANDS
A6
Burton
A6070
Silverdale
·5m
B6254
Borwick
Warton
·8m
Morecambe Bay
B6254
CARNFORTH
Hornby
Bolton le Sands
·49m
A683
MORECAMBE
A6
0
5km
0
3m
LANCASTER
ROUTE 1

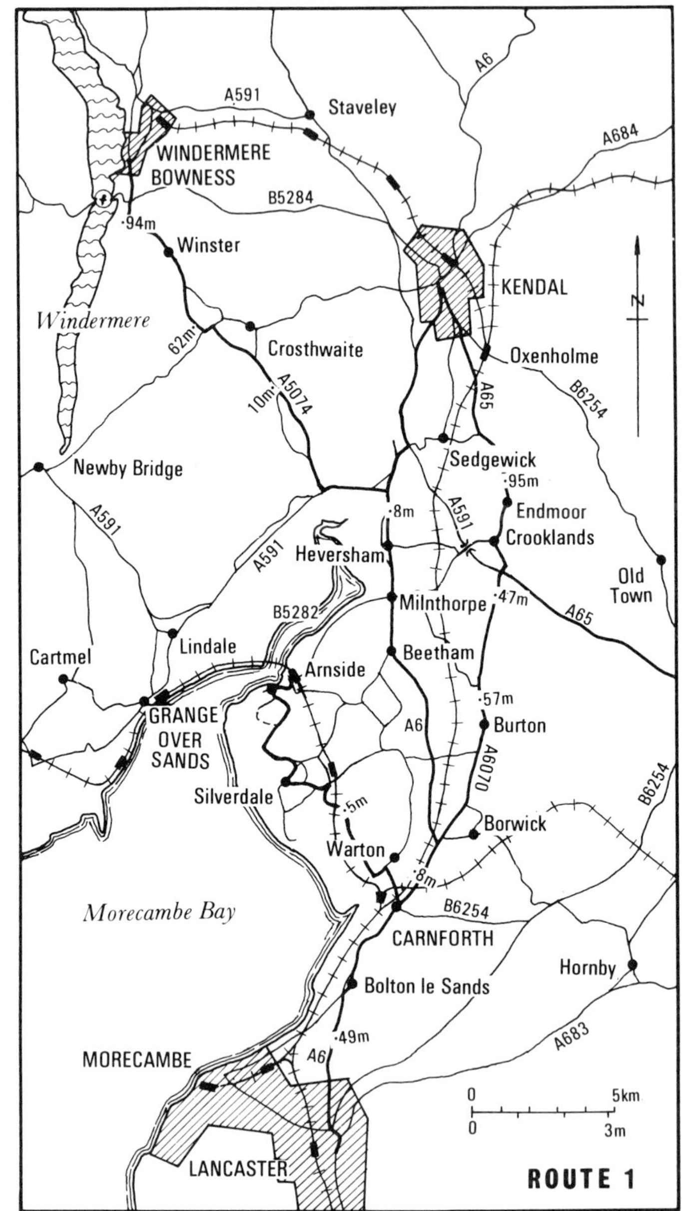

(where a level road branches off to Milnthorpe and Arnside), with a gradual climb through Endmoor and a corresponding descent into Kendal.

The alternative B6254 from Kirkby Lonsdale to Kendal ($11\frac{3}{4}$m) is very much more hilly. In any case, the visitor approaching from this direction should turn off through Kirkby Lonsdale to explore this lovely unspoilt town.

Kendal is the administrative and commercial centre of much of southern Cumbria, including a large portion of the Lake District. The town's history goes back long before its Norman castle. In medieval times it was a prosperous market town, famous for its woollens, and later became an important coaching centre. It now has a variety of industries.

Despite being almost totally bypassed for through traffic the town centre still suffers from road congestion and retains a somewhat drastic one-way system. The main street, comprising Kirkland, Highgate and Stricklandgate, is one way northbound for a total length of nearly a mile, though the cyclist can short-circuit it by turning right into the market place and down the cobbles. Southbound traffic is obliged to use Aynham Road on the east side of the river. A side turning off this (Parr Street) leads up to the scant remains of the castle overlooking the town.

Apart from the castle one should visit the Abbot Hall Museum, off Highgate, near the fine old church.

Although Kendal has its own station, Oxenholme, on the main line 2m south of the town, is the better railhead.

(b) Carnforth to Milnthorpe, Bowness and Kendal

The A6 is the easier but busier of the two main Kendal roads. Built in 1820, it superseded the old road to Beetham through Warton and the Yealands, now a delightful country lane. Beetham is an attractive village, as is Milnthorpe, which was formerly the port of Kendal. The main part of the village lies a little way along the Burton road. Milnthorpe is $9\frac{1}{2}$m from Kirkby Lonsdale, $3\frac{1}{2}$m from Arnside.

Kendal

There is a slight hill out of Milnthorpe, after which one can turn off through Heversham to rejoin the A6 near Levens. Just past Levens Hall (page 34) the routes to Kendal and Bowness via the Lyth Valley divide. The Kendal road is good and level, rather busy between the M6 link and the foot of the bypass, but with a quiet alternative through the villages of Sedgewick and Natland. For Kendal see above.

For Bowness and Windermere the best route is to turn off at Levens Bridge on to the A590, taking the A5074 after 1½m. This road, leading up the Lyth Valley, was once popular as a route avoiding Kendal, but since the opening of the Kendal bypass most motor traffic has reverted to the A591. The Lyth Valley is famous for damson growing and is particularly beautiful in May when the trees are in bloom.

After about three or four miles the hills close in and the road becomes more undulating with some short steep ascents. Soon after the attractively situated hamlet of Winster the long descent to the shores of Windermere commences, though the lake is mainly concealed behind high walls. If proceeding to Hawkshead (31m) there is no need to enter Bowness, but most visitors make the detour. For a description of Bowness see pages 47-9.

(c) Carnforth to Arnside (for Grange over Sands)

The railway between Arnside and Grange provides a useful link between quiet lanes on either side of the Kent estuary. Check train times at Carnforth, as the exploration of this delightful limestone area may then be made to fit in.

The most interesting way to Arnside is via Silverdale, where byways may be taken down to the shores of Morecambe Bay. North of the village the road runs along the top of former seacliffs — now half a mile inland — and past Arnside Tower, a substantial 'pele'. There are several examples of these defensive towers in Cumbria and adjoining border counties, most of them incorporated into later buildings. There is a long descent into Arnside.

Arnside may also be reached by turning on to a well-surfaced bridleway opposite the lane to the tower. This runs up through the woods to the car park below Arnside Knott (a good viewpoint), and the village is entered by Redhills Road, passing the Youth Hostel.

Approaches via Grange over Sands & Newby Bridge 2

Distances from Grange: Cartmel 2¼m, Newby Bridge 7¾m, Bowness 15½m (Ambleside 21½m, Windermere 16¾m), Hawkshead 16½m (Ambleside 21¾m).

From Grange to Newby Bridge direct (B5271 & A590) saves half a mile but a visit to Cartmel should not be omitted.

INTRODUCTION

Grange, the first stop on the coastal railway line north of the Kent estuary, makes an excellent starting point for cyclists arriving by train or using it as a short cut from Arnside. As the routes described below do not coincide with the main traffic arteries, the roads — mostly unclassified — are very quiet even in summer, an advantage over the usual approaches via Levens or Kendal.

The countryside here is varied and pleasant enough, but it lacks the grandeur and beauty of the Lake District proper, and the views are rarely extensive. The roads themselves are the attraction, winding their way unhurriedly along secluded valleys and between rich hedgerows.

As well as natural charms there are several man-made places of interest that can be visited, such as Cartmel Priory, Holker Hall, the Lakeside & Haverthwaite Railway (steam operated), Rusland Hall (a museum of cameras and mechanical instruments), the home of Beatrix Potter at Sawrey, and Hawkshead, with its quaint old buildings and associations with Wordsworth.

Grange over Sands, too, is a pleasant spot to linger. Nicely placed below limestone hills overlooking Morecambe Bay, its sheltered and south-facing position makes it a favourite home for the retired. The town is proud of its floral gardens and promendade, between the railway and the shore. The sand of the bay is of a brown, silty type which strangers are apt to mistake for mud.

The various approaches from Grange have for convenience been put into two groups — those via Newby Bridge, and the shores of Windermere, and those via Haverthwaite to Coniston or up through Grizedale Forest to Hawkshead. (These latter

2

Great Langdale
Little Langdale
Skelwith Bridge
AMBLESIDE
Troutbeck
N
A593
B5286
A591
41m
HAWKSHEAD
B5285
WINDERMERE
CONISTON
Esthwaite Water
BOWNESS
B5284
205m
A593
Grizedale Forest
Torver
90m
170m
Winster
68m
Coniston Water
Satterthwaite
Windermere
105m
A5084
60m
93m
Bowland Bridge
A592
Rusland
50m
Oxen Park
Newby Bridge
Bouth
A590
Spark Bridge
70m
A590
A590
Haverthwaite
High Newton
50m
6m
170m
Greenodd
A590
B5281
100m
8m
50m
Lindale
A590
B5278
CARTMEL
35m
100m
GRANGE OVER SANDS
ULVERSTON
B5278
Cark
Flookburgh
0
5km
0
3m
ROUTES 2 & 3

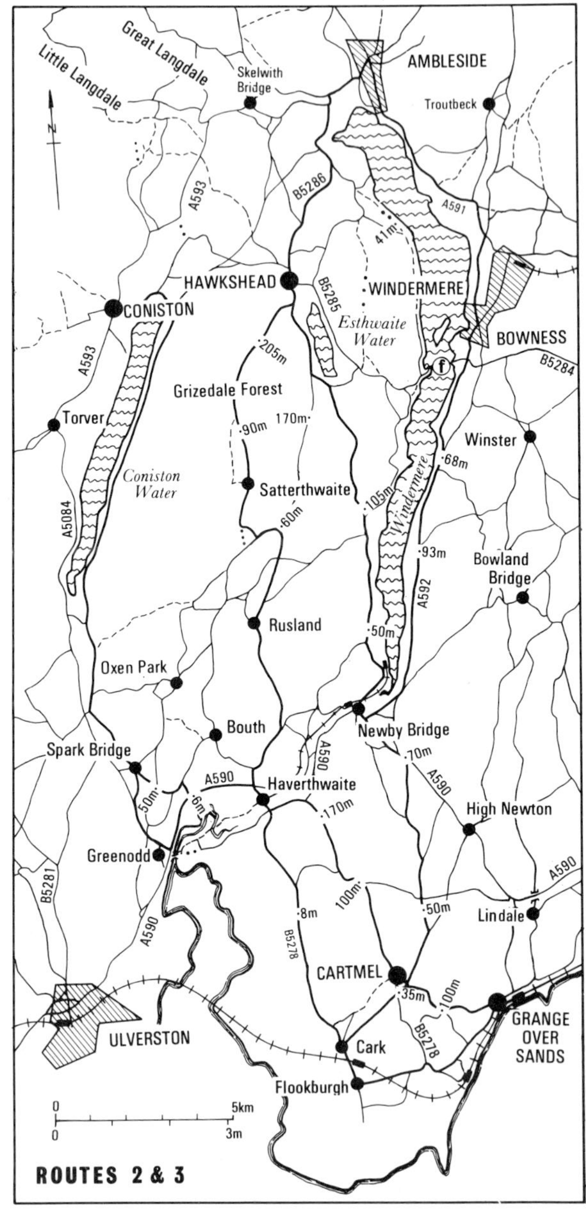

approaches are given in Route 3 following.) As the area around Grange and Cartmel is not on the 1in tourist maps, directions are given in more detail than usual. All the roads are well signposted, a credit to the former Lancashire County Council.

DESCRIPTION

From Grange railway station, follow the road westward into the main street of the town, turning up by the clocktower into Grange Fell Road. There follows a steep one-mile ascent to surmount the ridge between Grange and Cartmel. After the summit (400ft, 120 metres) turn right at the crossroads and the village and priory of Cartmel come into view, lying in a broad and pleasant vale. At the foot of the hill the road up the valley from Cark to Newby Bridge is reached: this will be taken later on. For Cartmel turn right then left. On entering the village note the old milestone at the next junction, giving the distances to Lancaster and Ulverston across the sands of Morecambe Bay — two routes not to be found in this book! The fording of the bay from a point near Lancaster was the main route to the Furness district until the development of the turnpikes, and, later, the railways, made such hazardous crossings unnecessary.

Cartmel Priory, commenced in 1188, survived the Reformation as it was in part used as the parish church. It was later restored at the instigation and expense of George Preston of nearby Holker. Its most unusual feature is the upper tower placed diagonally to the earlier, lower, part. The interior of the church is noted for its fine carvings and early glass, as well as its variety of architectural styles.

Newby Bridge

Cartmel is also famous for its racecourse, tucked away at one end of the village and easily missed — unless, of course, a meeting is taking place.

2

After looking round the village return to the Newby Bridge road, and there turn left, to follow a broad gently-ascending valley. In a mile, bear left again at an old guide stone, where the roads to Kendal and Hawkshead diverge (the Kendal road - via High Newton and Cartmel Fell — is briefly described under Route 5). The Hawkshead road (and it is instructive to notice that it is the ancient town, rather than the more modern Bowness or Windermere, which appears on the old guidestones) continues almost imperceptibly uphill to reach the main A590 road a mile or so short of Newby Bridge, to which there is a steady descent. If bound for Bowness by the A592 the corner may be cut by turning off through Staveley but Newby Bridge is such a lovely spot that it should not be missed. From here either side of Windermere may be followed northwards.

(a) Newby Bridge to Bowness and Ambleside

This is a straightforward run up the A592, a road not too busy by 'A' road standards. As far as Beech Hill (4m) it will be found much more hilly than might be supposed from its running alongside a lake. In fact, Windermere is largely concealed behind dense woodland or high walls and is only revealed at intervals. A little north of Newby Bridge is Fell Foot Country Park, (National Trust) with an information centre and access to the lake. The best roadside views are from the car park and picnic area at Beech Hill.

Bowness, with its narrow streets, is always alive with tourists. For a description see pages 47-9. For Ambleside the road continues northwards, passing, in half a mile, the steamboat museum. It then climbs Miller Brow (good viewpoint) to join the main road from Kendal 1½m north of Bowness. The road to Ambleside is busy, but very attractive when the lakeside is regained.

(b) Newby Bridge to Hawkshead and Ambleside

For Hawkshead cross the fine old bridge over the Leven, and then the road turns right for Lake Side. Here is the northern terminus of the Lakeside & Haverthwaite Railway and the pier for the steamers to Bowness and Ambleside. After a brief glimpse of the lake the road leaves the waterside to climb through densely-wooded country, very pretty, but rather enclosed. In the dip below the junction of the Hawkshead and Finsthwaite roads are the Stott Park Bobbin Mills. Wood-turning was once an important local industry in the low well-timbered fells, with their abundant supply of fast-flowing streams to provide water power. Several other mill buildings which survive in the Lake District have been converted to other uses. Stott Park, however, has been restored to working condition as a water-powered mill and is now open to the public. 2

After visiting Stott Park, a steep but rewarding diversion may be made to High Dam, a romantically situated tarn in the hills. The footpath leaves the Finsthwaite road just before the village. The stream fed the water-wheel of the mill. High Dam has been compared to the better-known Tarn Hows but it lacks the distant views of the latter. (It also lacks the hordes of motorists.)

The road to Hawkshead runs through more wooded country for 2m to Graythwaite Hall (gardens open to the public in summer). A little further on, a hilly side-road winds via Cunsey to the ferry and Bowness, the latter being 8¼m from Newby Bridge by this side of the lake. The views from this road are particularly fine, Windermere being seen at its best.

The Hawkshead road crosses an intervening ridge before dropping steeply to the banks of the Cunsey Beck, the outfall from Esthwaite Water. Either side of the lake may be taken for the final few miles to Hawkshead — each is attractive.

Hawkshead is an interesting little town (for a description see page 44) set in pleasant, if not spectacular, countryside. The direct Ambleside road — B5286 — runs through the same sort of hilly wooded scenery with few distant views. A diversion may be made to Tarn Hows (which should be included in any holiday in Lakeland), but perhaps the best way to Ambleside is to turn off at Outgate, a mile north of Hawkshead, on to the narrow road running over to Skelwith Fold. Here, a little way down the turning to Skelwith Bridge, is Spy Hill, which offers one of the finest views in the Lake District and certainly one of the best from a road. The richly wooded slopes seem to pile up on top of each other, the Langdale Pikes towering on the skyline. A cottage or two dotted about, with perhaps a plume of wood smoke, add a touch of serenity to the scene. As a first sight of the mountain core of Lakeland, it will never be forgotten.

Ambleside may be reached by returning to the minor road that follows the south bank of the river Brathay, or by dropping down to Skelwith Bridge and picking up the main road from Coniston. Both offer scenery of the highest order. Skelwith Force is a cascade a little way above the bridge.

Skelwith Bridge is 4¼m north of Hawkshead, 2½m from Ambleside and 4½m from Dungeon Ghyll, Great Langdale. For continuation to Great Langdale see Route 11.

3 Approaches via Grange over Sands & Haverthwaite

Map — see Route 2

Distances from Grange: Flookburgh $3\frac{1}{2}$m, Cark 4m, Haverthwaite $9\frac{1}{4}$m, Spark Bridge 12m, Coniston (via east side of lake) $22\frac{1}{4}$m, Rusland $12\frac{3}{4}$m, Satterthwaite 16m, Hawkshead 20m.

NB The most direct way from Grange to Haverthwaite — $7\frac{1}{4}$m — is via Cartmel (Route 2), and then by a narrow road which turns right at the far end of the village square and gradually climbs to nearly 600ft. (180 metres). There is a steep descent to the Leven Gorge at Haverthwaite. An easier way from Cartmel is by a level road to Cark ($1\frac{3}{4}$m) where the route described below is joined.

INTRODUCTION

The route, or rather routes, described here, complement those given from Grange via Newby Bridge under Route 2. There are many variations available to the cyclist depending on his ultimate destination: they all have the merit of following byroads which provide a quiet and secluded approach to the finest Lakeland scenery by avoiding the main traffic arteries. The first part of the journey might profitably be varied to include Cartmel, a most interesting village (see pages 25-6), and then proceeding to Haverthwaite either direct or via Cark (see above).

DESCRIPTION

From Grange station the B5277 is taken into the town centre, after which the road rises steadily to give an extensive view over Morecambe Bay. After dropping into Allithwaite the road briefly rises again before a gentle descent to Flookburgh. To the south of the road is Wraysholme Tower, a pele, now incorporated into a farmhouse.

Flookburgh now presents a rather sleepy appearance, but it was formerly quite important. Fishing for flukes (flounders), cockles etc is still carried out around this part of the coast, extensive sands being exposed at low tide.

From Flookburgh the road heads north to Cark and Holker, passing Cark and Cartmel station. This provides an alternative railhead to Grange, but the latter is more convenient if visiting Cartmel. A little further on is Holker Hall, open to the public in summer. The gardens are the home of the annual Lakeland Rose Show, held in July. The hall itself is mainly nineteenth century and contains some excellent wood carving. Holker also houses the Lakeland Motor Museum.

The journey from Holker to Haverthwaite calls for little comment, the road taking a level course along the foot of the fell. The Barrow monument above Ulverston is occasionally in view. Haverthwaite is a dispersed village amid the fine scenery of the Leven gorge. The old station, half a mile east of the village, is the southern terminus and main depot of the Lakeside and Haverthwaite Railway.

Haverthwaite is the parting of the ways for the routes to Hawkshead and Coniston. Newby Bridge may also be reached in an easy 2½m.

(a) Haverthwaite to Hawkshead

The main A590 is crossed to head up the Rusland valley, a sheltered vale rarely visited by the tourist but offering the cyclist an interesting and leisurely entrance to the busy resorts further north. The road up to Grizedale also presents a case study in geology; the cyclist will notice that the valley is formed from a number of level stretches linked by short but fairly steep hills at Rusland, Thwaite Head and the gorge above Force Mills. The first indicates a former position of the coastline, while it requires little imagination to picture a lake in the level valley bottom between Satterthwaite and Grizedale, similar to Esthwaite Water just over the hill.

As one enters the valley, the woodlands reaching down the road from the heights of Yew Barrow present an especially fine scene, with the village of Rusland seen ahead on a slight rise. Rusland Hall contains a selection of bygones, including early cameras and mechanical musical instruments. Beyond, the valley closes in a little but the road is still level and easy. The hillside on the right is terraced in appearance and ahead on the left a bracken-clad slope marks the entrance to the upper valley containing Satterthwaite.

At Thwaite Head, a peaceful spot alongside Ashes Beck, a steep hill brings one to this upper level and to a road junction. The right fork leads over to Hawkshead via Dale Park and Esthwaite Water, the easier of the two roads but rising through woods to 524ft (170 metres). The recommended way is to the left, leading to Force Mills, where the road from Ulverston to Hawkshead is joined. Southbound traffic to Rusland is signposted down this road.

3

Ulverston to Hawkshead

15m via Greenodd (3½m), Oxen Park (7m) and Satterthwaite (11m)
This is unlikely to be used as an approach other than from Furness, but it is a convenient route to or from Furness Abbey. Although now just an obscure country byway, this was an important road in medieval times, as the abbey had extensive land and property at Colton and Oxen Park and also held a manorial court at Hawkshead. A longer but easier route from Ulverston is via Haverthwaite crossroads to Rusland (9m).

Main route continued

At Force Mills (not named on some maps) the Hawkshead road turns north to climb alongside the river, which here forms a cascade over the rocks. Though not a true waterfall, it is an impressive sight and sound after rain. At the top of the winding hill the valley opens out again to reveal another beautiful and sequestered scene. Ahead is the trim little village of Satterthwaite in the green valley bottom, while the low surrounding hills are richly wooded. There is an inn and a shop in the village, the only one between Haverthwaite and Hawkshead.

From Satterthwaite it is an easy and pleasant run to the hamlet of Grizedale, the road entering the limits of Grizedale Forest on the way. There is an alternative route by a cart-track skirting the west side of the valley. Half a mile west of Satterthwaite, where this track to Grizedale turns right, the left branch soon descends to some waterfalls (rather hard to reach) in a gorge below the two bridges.

The Forestry Commission is very active in this area, but as there is a considerable amount of deciduous planting, the

Satterthwaite

scenery is by no means dominated by conifers. There is an information centre in Grizedale hamlet as well as numerous waymarked footpaths in the vicinity. Grizedale also boasts the 'Theatre in the Forest' which has a programme of plays and musical recitals in the summer months.

3

Beyond Grizedale the valley closes in once more, as the road climbs to the watershed, 675ft (205 metres), beyond which a steep and twisting descent brings one out overlooking Esthwaite Water and Hawkshead a little south of the village. For Hawkshead see page 44; for the roads on to Langdale and Ambleside Route 2.

(b) Haverthwaite to Coniston

On reaching the main A590, turn left and follow it for a level couple of miles to the village of Greenodd. The old railway between Haverthwaite and Greenodd is used as an unofficial footpath and is quite wide enough to form a useful cycle route. It connects with the Leven footbridge at Greenodd. The busy town of Ulverston lies about three miles to the south. From Greenodd to the foot of Coniston Water is 5m, and roads along either side of the river Crake may be followed, the best course probably being to take the main road for a mile and then cross to the quieter road on the east side at Spark Bridge. Here a short cut from the Haverthwaite road comes in over the hill.

Of the roads up the lake itself, the unclassified road following the east bank is much preferable, although it carries its fair share of tourist traffic. It is never far from the lake side, occasionally wandering off into the woods but always drifting back to the water's edge. Across the lake the Coniston Fells present an impressive front with the Old Man most prominent, though the rugged cliffs facing him over the intervening hollow are likely to attract equal attention.

Presently signposts announce Brantwood, the final home of the artist, critic and writer John Ruskin (1819-1900), who is buried in Coniston churchyard. The house is open to the public.

The road from Brantwood to Coniston, 2½m, starts with the only appreciable hill along the lakeside. From the top there is a particularly fine view of the village seen across the lake with its mountain backcloth. After rounding the head of the lake, the shore of which is often as crowded as a seaside beach, and with one last view down its length, a level road leads into Coniston.

The main road (described in Route 14) from Greenodd to Coniston via Lowick and Torver, although pleasant enough in its own right, is not recommended. The lake is only occasionally in view and the mountains are concealed by their high foreground. For a description of Coniston see page 55.

4

Kendal to Newby Bridge, Ulverston & Broughton via Levens Bridge

Distances from Kendal: Levens Bridge 5¼m, Lindale 11½m (Grange over Sands 13¾m), Newby Bridge 16½m, Haverthwaite 19m, Greenodd 21½m, Ulverston 25m, Broughton in Furness 30½m.

Lancaster to Levens Bridge 16¾m (Route 1); Kirkby Lonsdale to Levens Bridge 11m via A65/A591.

INTRODUCTION

The main motoring approach for all long-distance traffic to the southern and western parts of Cumbria, the road is busy at all times, particularly at weekends. Upgrading of this trunk road is progressing and it has been almost totally rebuilt between the motorway link north of Levens and Greenodd, the junction for Ulverston and Barrow.

The road west from Levens Bridge, constructed in 1818-20, provided a much needed alternative to the direct road from Kendal to Newby Bridge (Route 5), with its precipitous hills, as well as avoiding the hazardous approach from Lancaster across the sands. By skirting the various north-south-running ridges, severe gradients were almost avoided, the exceptions being at Lindale and west of Greenodd. The problem reappears in miniature near Broughton where the saw-tooth profile of the road has led to the encouragement of a detour via Foxfield.

As a cycling route it will be found easy going apart from the two main hills, and is scenically quite varied and pleasant. If coming from Lancaster, however, the approach via Arnside and the railway to Grange is much preferable.

DESCRIPTION

From Kendal the A6 Milnthorpe road soon joins the bypass coming over the hill behind the town. A few miles of busy dual carriageway follow but the road is level and fast. On the right, not seen from the road, is Sizergh Castle, the ancient home of the Strickland family, a very interesting old

KENDAL
Coniston Water
A592
Windermere
Crosthwaite
0
5km
0
3m
N
:51m
Brigsteer
Rusland
BROUGHTON
Lakeside
A6
A5084
A595
Newby Bridge
:47m
Bouth
Spark Bridge
A5092
:200m
:36m
:70m
:5m
A591
50m:
:50m
:6m
:138m
A590
Grizebeck
Haverthwaite
Heversham
High Newton
Kirkby
Broughton Beck
Greenodd
:125m
:7m
B5281
Milnthorpe
Lindale
A595
A590
B5278
ULVERSTON
:6m
CARTMEL
Arnside
ROUTE 4
GRANGE OVER SANDS
A6

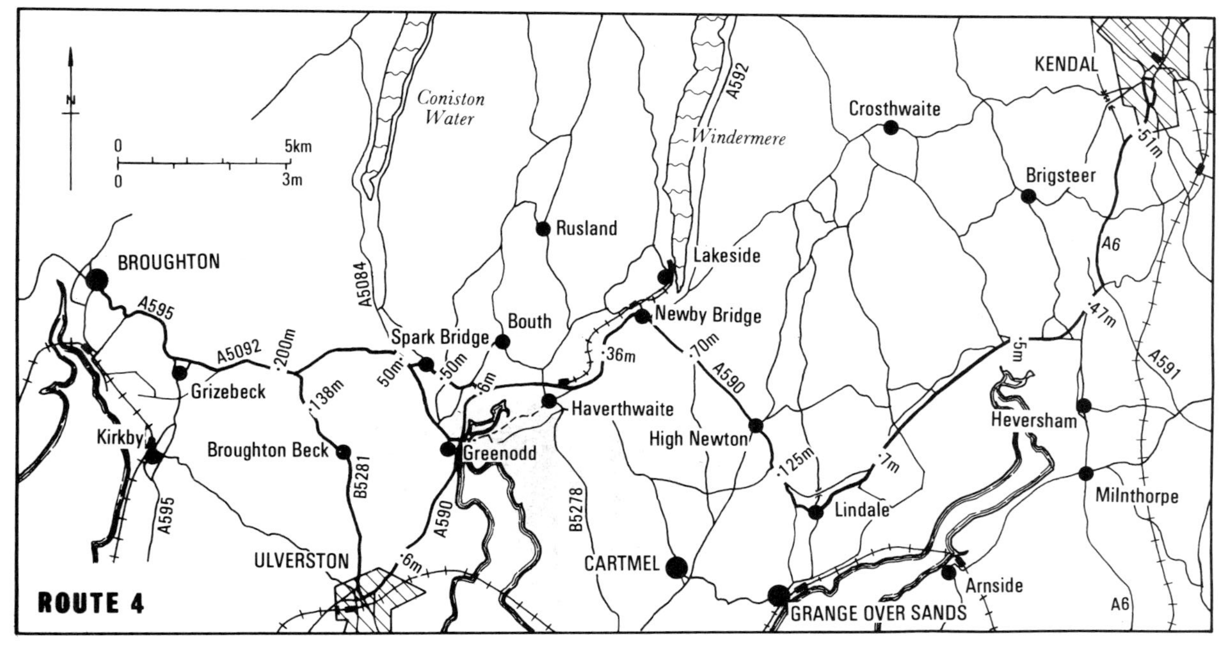

4

building containing a number of historical items and open to the public on certain weekdays in summer. There is no vehicular access from the A6 immediately adjacent.

Turning off at the roundabout, the A6 and A590 soon fork, the latter bearing off right on a new section of road. It is worth continuing a little along the Milnthorpe road to Levens Hall, another old building based, like Sizergh, on a pele tower but much altered and extended. The gardens are famous for their topiary work and formal seventeenth-century layout. The house and gardens are open most days throughout the year.

From Levens Bridge the road runs westward across the flat coastal mosses with the limestone cliff of White Scar ahead. At Sampool (or Gilpin) Bridge the road bears left to keep to the low ground and commences a new stretch opened in 1981. The former A590, running parallel on the right, may be followed; it is reached by turning off just past the A5074 junction (no signpost) and regains the new road in 2½m where the dual carriageway resumes (signposted Witherslack coming east). This then need only be followed for a mile to where a roundabout marks the start of the Lindale bypass, curving impressively over the tip of Newton Fell. In all the road rises 400ft (120 metres). Most cyclists will probably prefer the old road through the village, steeper though it is.

Grange over Sands
This attractively situated resort lies about two miles south of Lindale and makes a pleasant diversion which can profitably be extended to include Cartmel, Flookburgh, etc. The various places of interest are mentioned in Routes 2 & 3.

From the top of Lindale Hill the road is undulating as far as High Newton, where the outline of the Coniston Fells may be seen ahead. A gradual descent brings one to Newby Bridge. The scenery grows in beauty all the way, the wooded slopes that enclose Windermere bringing a welcome richness of colour. The hill ahead is topped by Finsthwaite Tower, which may be reached by a steep public path from Newby Bridge.

Newby Bridge is a small but most delightfully situated hamlet, its famous bridge spanning the river Leven about a mile below its outlet from Windermere. The nearest access to the lake is at Fell Foot, on the Bowness road (p 26).

West of Newby Bridge the road runs down the ice-carved Leven Gorge. The approach to Backbarrow provides a surprise in the site of the former ultramarine works, but this locality has a long and varied industrial history. The first blast furnace in Cumbria was established here in 1711 and iron making continued until 1967. There were also cotton mills and gunpowder works in the valley. Backbarrow now shares in the development of Lakeland's latest industry of tourism.

A little further on is the southern terminus and depot of the Lakeside and Haverthwaite Railway, which has accompanied the road from Newby Bridge. A steam shuttle service is operated in summer. Haverthwaite village lies on a loop to the south of the present A590.

It is possible to leave the main road and cut over the hill to Spark Bridge, picking up the A5092 to Broughton at Lowick Green. However it is perhaps preferable to continue for a level run of a few miles to Greenodd, pleasantly placed at the confluence of the rivers Crake, flowing out of Coniston Water, and the Leven. Shipbuilding was once carried on here in a small way in the days before the railway killed off the coastal trade. The village bypass involved diversion of the river Leven so that the road could be routed along its old bed. The direct road from Greenodd to Broughton is described below, but a brief mention must first be made of Ulverston, only a few miles off the main route.

Ulverston is 3½m south of Greenodd by a level and busy road. On Hoad Hill overlooking the town is a monument, appropriate in style, to Sir John Barrow, onetime secretary to the Admiralty. The town is an important and busy centre, better placed than the larger Barrow in Furness, and the market town for a wide area. Stan Laurel was born in Ulverston and there is a Laurel & Hardy Museum in Upper Brook Street where their films are shown. A few miles south of the town is Conishead Priory, a nineteenth-century mansion on a much older site, now occupied by the Manjushri Institute; the house and gardens are open to the public in summer. Ulverston (and surrounding areas of Low Furness) was an early centre of Quakerism; Swarthmoor Hall, just outside the town, has connections with its founder, George Fox. For Ulverston to Furness Abbey, Barrow etc see Route 13.

(a) Ulverston to Broughton, 10m

Ulverston is in some ways a better railhead for south and west Cumbria than Foxfield station, just south of Broughton, as the rail route between them involves a considerable detour via Barrow and often a change of train. Little time is thus lost by cycling from Ulverston. From the station turn right into Princes Street and carry straight on to and through the town centre. The road (B5281) gradually ascends an uninteresting valley to meet the A5082 from Greenodd just short of its summit. For continuation see below.

There is an alternative road, with good views, west from Ulverston to Kirkby to Furness (4¾m), but this is much more hilly, rising to 850ft (260 metres). From the market cross head up
4 Daltongate, taking the next turning right.

(b) Greenodd to Broughton, direct

North of Greenodd the Broughton road, despite its trunk road status, is much quieter and attractive, as it runs up the leafy valley of the Crake through Penny Bridge to Lowick Green, where the A5084 Coniston road (Route 14) bears right. To the north the Coniston Fells appear in apparent isolation. The Broughton road heads west and climbs, slowly at first but then steeply — a most dreary hill — to emerge on the open fell above Gawthwaite. Here is a welcome view over the distant Coniston Water to the central fells of Lakeland.

After a few ups and downs near the 650ft (200 metres) contour the long descent of Grizebeck Hill commences. Ahead is the sandy estuary of the Duddon backed by sprawling Black Combe. Grizebeck Hill was formerly notorious for its twists and turns but now holds no terror for the cyclist — in this direction.

Beyond Grizebeck village, now bypassed, a short rise is encountered before the road runs across the flat coastal plain. Main road traffic is now signposted round via Foxfield to miss the narrow streets of Broughton but the cyclist should turn right for the village, in spite of the hills.

Kendal to Newby Bridge & Ulverston via the Old Road

5

Distances from Kendal: Crosthwaite 5m, Bowland Bridge 7½m, Newby Bridge 11½m, Bouth 15m, Penny Bridge 17¼m, Greenodd 18m, Ulverston 21½m, Spark Bridge 17¼m, Broughton in Furness 25½m.

The recommended diversion via Finsthwaite, between Newby Bridge and Bouth, adds 2½m.

INTRODUCTION

This follows the old turnpike road of 1763 that led from Kendal to Newby Bridge and thence via Bouth to Ulverston. It continued on to Kirkby Ireleth, where the sands were crossed for Millom and the west coast. Unlike the later turnpike roads, which were usually totally new, this was an ancient packhorse route improved, and no measures were taken to avoid steep hills. Further west, the marshy coastal area was skirted by a devious course through Bouth.

In 1818-20 the new road (now A590) from Levens Bridge was opened, offering a much more easily graded route and, though five miles longer to Newby Bridge, there is little difference in cycling time. West of that point the new road is much quicker.

For the cyclist the long and steep gradients of the Old Road are a deterrent but scenically it is more interesting and quieter than the very busy Levens route. It also features some fine old roadside hostelries. The two principal climbs are of 550ft (160 metres) between Kendal and Crosthwaite and 700ft (200 metres) between Bowland Bridge and Fellfoot.

DESCRIPTION

From Kendal the road turns up opposite the Town Hall and climbs steadily out of the town. A dip follows where the bypass is crossed before another steep ascent to the summit, 700ft (210 metres), alongside the TV mast. There is a good view back over Kendal (concealed in the valley) to the fells above Sedbergh and Dent. Underbarrow Scar, the northern end of which is skirted by the road, is a bare limestone escarpment, reminiscent of the Craven dales. There then follows a sharp

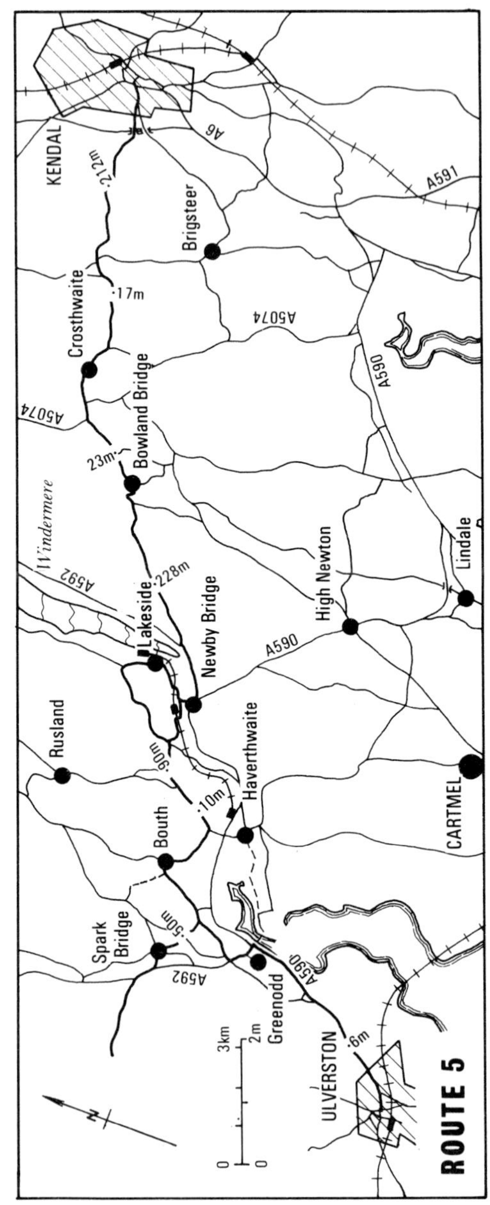
KENDAL
·21½m
A6
A591
Brigsteer
Crosthwaite
·17m
A5074
Bowland Bridge
A5074
A590
23m·
Windermere
A592
·228m
Lakeside
Newby Bridge
High Newton
Lindale
A590
Rusland
·90m
·10m
Haverthwaite
CARTMEL
Bouth
·50m
Spark Bridge
A592
Greenodd
A590·
·6m
ULVERSTON
0
3km
0
2m
N
ROUTE 5

descent to Underbarrow, a scattered village of white cottages and farms, nicely situated in the valley of the little river Pool. A mile or so further on is Crosthwaite, another spread-out village with a neat Victorian church. Hereabouts are views down the broad Lyth Valley to the Kent estuary.

Beyond Crosthwaite there is a gradual ascent, at the top of which the A5074 from Levens is joined and followed westward until the point where it turns north for Bowness. The Newby Bridge road continues straight on, descending between low wooded hills that contrast with the bare rock-dotted fields.

An extremely worthwhile diversion may be made just before Bowland Bridge by turning off for Cartmel Fell Church, a mile south of the road, passing on the way two interesting old buildings, Cowmire Hall and Hodge Hill. Cartmel Fell Church is noteworthy for its fine seventeenth-century woodwork and the glass in its eastern window, fragments of which were probably removed from Cartmel Priory. The church is situated in truly sylvan surroundings and a more peaceful or secluded situation can hardly be imagined.

Cartmel Fell Church may be reached from Bowness (8m) via Winster and from there the quietest of country lanes.

From below the church pleasant minor roads run south via High Newton to Cartmel (7m) and via Lindale to Grange over Sands (7½m). The former is the more hilly but offers fine eastward views.

For Newby Bridge the steep road up past the church is followed to rejoin the road up from Bowland Bridge at Strawberry Bank.

The second major climb from Kendal begins from Bowland Bridge with the road rising 700ft (200 metres), mostly in the next mile. There is a dip before the second, higher, summit, where a view opens up over the foot of Windermere. Nearby Gummers How (15min from road) is a worthwhile walk.

Returning to the road there is a long straightforward descent to the lake at Fellfoot, a mile north of Newby Bridge. The grounds of Fellfoot are owned by the National Trust and run as a country park.

From Newby Bridge the cyclist will probably choose the easy course of the A590 through Haverthwaite and Greenodd to Ulverston (8½m, Route 4). The discerning, historically-minded or just plain stubborn tourist will cross the fine old bridge and turn left on to the old road again.

Diversion via Lake Side & Finsthwaite

This adds much of interest for comparatively little extra effort. Turning right after the bridge, the road runs through woods to Lake Side, whence the steamers sail for Bowness and Ambleside. There is a good view up the lake from the jetty, but elsewhere the road is too well screened by walls and buildings. A little further on, the Finsthwaite road bears left above the old Stott Park bobbin mills (see pages 26-7), now restored. A short climb brings one to the village, a delightful cluster of buildings situated in a secluded side valley. The road winds along this valley before dropping to meet the direct road up from Newby Bridge.

The direct road from Newby Bridge rises to cross the railway and in a dip meets the loop road round from Finsthwaite. Avoid the mistake of taking the road down to Backbarrow. The Bouth road continues through the woods before reaching a steep drop into the Rusland Valley, one of the quietest corners in Lakeland. A little way down the hill, near a turning to Rusland (not signposted), is an old milestone — the thirteenth from Kendal — reminding one that the present quiet country lane was once an important through road.

From the foot of the hill there is an easy run across the valley bottom to the bridge over Rusland Pool ('Pool' here signifies a slow moving stream). The main road runs parallel on the left, usually with plenty of traffic. Bouth now has a sleepy air, but could once boast a market.

Beyond Bouth the road soon drops into another side valley and an important junction about a mile west of the village. The turning to the left leads down to the A590 and provides the nearest route to Greenodd and Ulverston: the right turn cuts over the hill to the Crake valley for Broughton and Coniston. The old turnpike road runs this way, bearing left in ¼m (no signpost) for Penny Bridge and Greenodd. This last section still seems to retain an air of its former importance. There are fine views, first back to the Rusland Valley and then of Penny Bridge. A few yards east of the bridge is the seventeenth milestone from Kendal.

Cyclists heading for Broughton or the Coniston direction will probably keep to the road straight on from the above-mentioned junction, dropping down to the Crake at Spark Bridge, another old industrial site. A variation from Bouth is via a cart track through bluebell-carpeted woods to Colton and then by an 'uncoloured', but perfectly good, lane over the intervening hill.

For Broughton see Route 4, Coniston Route 3 or 14.

At Penny Bridge turn left for Greenodd and Ulverston (the road straight on is steep and offers no distant views). The main road is very busy but is level and soon traversed.

Kendal to Bowness & Hawkshead

6

Distances from Kendal: Crook 4m, Bowness 8¾m, Hawkshead (direct) 12½m, Coniston 16½m, Bowness to Hawkshead 5m.

INTRODUCTION

A hilly road, but one with much to commend it, as it enables the cyclist to avoid the much busier A591 between Kendal and Windermere. Besides forming the most direct approach to Hawkshead and Coniston, it also makes an interesting alternative route to Ambleside, if, after crossing the ferry, the lakeside road north to Wray is taken, as described below. Hawkshead is an excellent centre for touring southern Lakeland as well as being an historic old town and might well be made a base for the first few days of any holiday. Some notes on the roads beyond Hawkshead to Coniston, Langdale etc are included for the convenience of cyclists proceeding to those places, though fuller descriptions are given elsewhere.

DESCRIPTION

From Kendal there is no escape from the long and initially steep ascent to and beyond the bypass. The Hawkshead road, B5284, winds down to the hamlet of Crook, with occasional views of the high fells to the north. The steep Cockpit Hill brings one to St Catherine's Church, with the ruins of the earlier church visible to the south of the road. Another two undulating miles follow, across a rather uninteresting upland, before, on rounding the golf course, a welcome descent leads down through woods to the ferry. For Bowness, which is well worth the slight detour involved, bear right opposite the Linthwaite Country House Hotel.

Bowness always presents a picture of activity, with its twisting and congested streets and throngs of visitors. For a description of the town see pages 47-9.

Following the Newby Bridge road south soon brings one to the ferry turning and the joys of cycling past the signs proclaiming 'approx 45 minutes wait', 'approx 30 minutes wait'

6

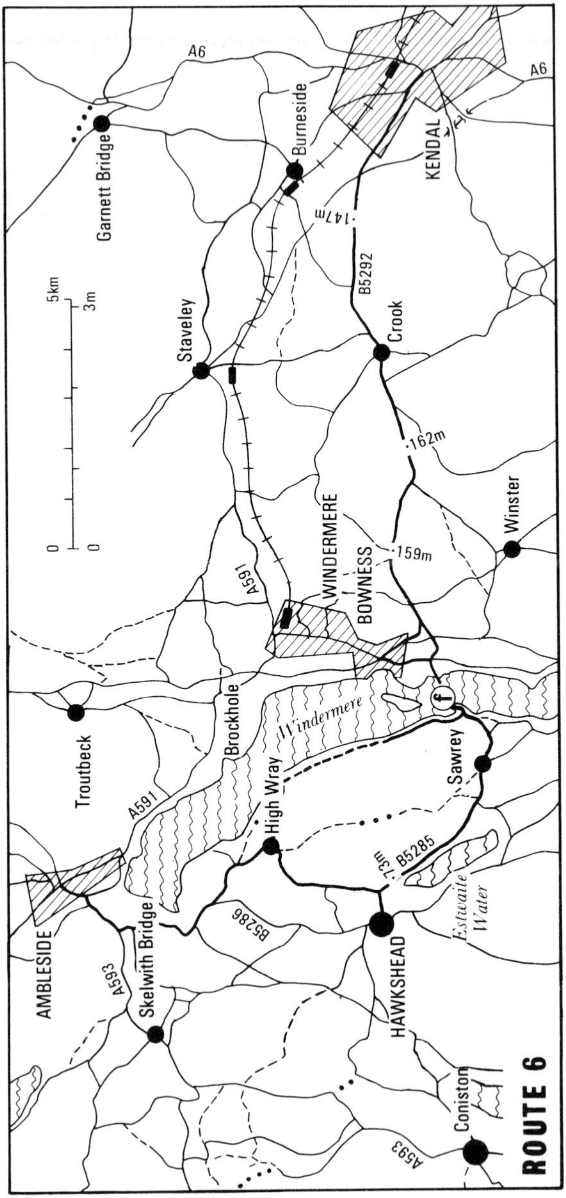

ROUTE 6

Garnett Bridge
Burneside
KENDAL
A6
A6
147m
B5292
Staveley
Crook
5km
3m
0
0
162m
WINDERMERE
BOWNESS
159m
Winster
A591
Troutbeck
Brockhole
Windermere
High Wray
Sawrey
A591
B5285
73m
AMBLESIDE
Skelwith Bridge
B5286
HAWKSHEAD
Estwaite Water
A593
Coniston
A593

Cyclists leaving Windermere ferry

erected for the benefit of queuing motorists. The ferry operates every 20min throughout the day, with the last crossing about 9pm (see pages 15-16). 'Asses and cyclists' were once listed together on the toll board!

Bowness to Hawkshead (7m) or Ambleside (8½m) via the west side of Windermere

This makes a delightful digression on the way to Hawkshead, especially if time does not allow a prolonged acquaintance with Windermere. It also provides an interesting and traffic-free approach to Ambleside or the return leg of an Ambleside to Bowness circular tour of about fourteen miles. The route involves the 'uncoloured' road along the western side of the lake: this is a little rough in parts but quite rideable.

At the end of the promontory from the west side of the ferry, turn right along the unsignposted road. The first mile or so is tarred and is a truly beautiful ride, the wooded islands and boats on the water adding so much to the scene. Later, the road deteriorates into a loose stony-surfaced lane, still practicable for cycling; after wandering off into the woods, it returns to the lakeside.

2m north of the ferry, the tarred road resumes at a fork, beyond which it climbs to High Wray with good views over the lake. From High Wray, twisting roads lead round to either Hawkshead (2¼m) or north to Ambleside (3¾m). If aiming for

Ambleside the margin of the lake may be followed by continuing past the car park at the fork mentioned above. This track (just about rideable) eventually comes out on the Ambleside road near the entrance lodge to Wray Castle, a Victorian mansion now used as a training college by the Merchant Navy. The grounds, maintained by the National Trust, are open to the public.

Main route continued
After first winding along the western shore of Windermere, the Hawkshead road, B5285, soon begins a steep ascent of some 250ft (70 metres). The views, first back over the lake to the white villas of Bowness and then onward into the lush green valley into which the road descends, are beautiful. The road wanders through the hamlets of Far and Near Sawrey, the latter famous for being the home of the authoress Beatrix Potter. She moved here from London to find the inspiration for her children's books in the surrounding countryside. Her home, Hill Top, is now owned by the National Trust and maintained as a museum of her life and works.

A little side excursion is that to the pretty Moss Eccles Tarn, about a mile north of Near Sawrey. The lanes up to it can get rather muddy. The continuation of the track, over to Wray, traverses an area which can only be referred to politely as swamp, before it meets a good forestry road.

From Sawrey on to Hawkshead is an easy run of about two miles with the choice of following the east or west shore of Esthwaite Water. Elsewhere this lake would be a foremost tourist attraction, but here it is rather overshadowed by the grandeur of the larger lakes and the alpine settings of many of the smaller ones. It nevertheless presents a most peaceful scene, nestling in the vale below the wooded hills.

On approaching Hawkshead, the town at first appears to consist of one large car park, but this impression is soon dispelled. The town — and town it still feels, although now ranking in size and importance as no more than a village — consists of a narrow main street along which buildings are arranged in a most haphazard manner with no apparent thought for the convenience of either motorised or horsedrawn traffic. From it, little alleyways and courts lead off to serve the jumble of houses. Fortunately, extraneous traffic has been removed by the construction of a bypass, one length of new road in the Lake District that has been unanimously welcomed.

Hawkshead's roots are claimed to lie with the founding of a settlement by the Viking Haukr in the ninth century, but its later prominence was due to its establishment as a chapelry under the control of Furness Abbey. Hawkshead Hall, just north of the town, was used for the manorial courts. In later years, wool became the staple trade and Hawkshead became the market town for a large area. The railway age passed by the town and it fell into relative unimportance as Ambleside and Bowness expanded, but in so doing preserved its old-world character. Hawkshead also boasts an association with Wordsworth, who was educated at the old Grammar School.

From Hawkshead the watershed may be crossed to Coniston, either direct (4m), or, preferably, via Tarn Hows (see Route 30). Great Langdale is best approached by following the Ambleside road north to Outgate, and then cutting across by the 'Drunken Duck' and Skelwith Fold to Skelwith Bridge ($4\frac{1}{4}$m, Route 2). The direct road, very rough and not recommended, from Hawkshead to Little Langdale is by an untarred and stony road from near Borwick Lodge across to the summit of the Coniston to Ambleside road at Oxen Fell. It passes near Tarn Hows but the particular beauty of the place is not seen.

Hawkshead

7 Kendal to Windermere & Ambleside

Distances from Kendal: Staveley 4¾m, Ings 6¼m, Windermere Station 8½m, (Bowness 10m), Troutbeck Bridge 10m, Ambleside 13½m.

Add 2m if coming from Oxenholme station.

INTRODUCTION

This is probably the most used of all the approaches to the Lake District, certainly from the south. The road itself has little to commend it; there is a long hill out of Kendal and some trying shorter ones before Windermere, and it is only then that typical Lakeland scenery is entered. The finest part of the run is from Troutbeck Bridge to Ambleside along the northern fringe of Windermere.

The road has heavy traffic, paricularly north of the junction with the Kendal Bypass. The first part of the journey, as far as Staveley, may be made by the quiet back lanes described in Route 8, while a more interesting approach to Ambleside, via Bowness and the west side of Windermere, is given in Route 6.

DESCRIPTION

From Kendal the road begins with a long hill out of the town, rising for nearly two miles. Only the first half-mile is steep. There follows a good and fast stretch of road to Staveley, with extensive eastward views. Here are the first indications of the nearing mountainous scenery. Beyond Staveley there is a gentle rise to Ings.

Ings to Troutbeck (4½m)

This involves slightly more hillclimbing than the main road, but it has better views and little traffic. After a steady climb from the A591 for 1¼m, a little after bearing right at a fork, a magnificent view is revealed over the basin containing Windermere to the mountains beyond. The view is broadly similar to that from Orrest Head (described below) but not as extensive. Windermere lake is not visible.

About half a mile further on a stony road on the right doubles round to Kentmere by the Garburn Pass. Keeping to the Troutbeck road the village comes into sight across the valley, into which the lane drops steeply. At the main road turn right, then left just before the church for the village.

7

Beyond Ings the main A591 rises to nearly 600ft. From a second summit the mountain-girt basin of Windermere is revealed, with a first glimpse of the lake. A winding descent brings one to Windermere railway station, beside which is the turning to the town centre and down into Bowness; opposite is the footpath to Orrest Head.

Orrest Head: This famous viewpoint provides perhaps the finest easily-accessible vista in the Lake District. All visitors entering the district for the first time should make the climb, the path leaving the road a little below the station and on the opposite side. After various turns it emerges on the open fell, where there is a wide view over the full length of the lake and across to the Cumbrian fells.

As this will be the first sight for many of the Lakeland peaks it may be worth picking them out in detail. (There is a direction indicator naming the principal points of interest.) Beyond the lake are the low wooded hills of Grizedale Forest that separate it from Coniston Water. Behind rise the Coniston Fells, the Old Man on the left with the ridge swinging north and east to Wetherlam. Next comes the gap indicating Little Langdale, which leads up to the Wrynose Pass. To the north of this gap the ridge rises to the aptly-named Crinkle Crags and the majestic Bow Fell. Between them peers the distant Scafell Pike (or, more accurately, Pikes), the highest mountain in England. Below Crinkle Crags is the symmetrical Pike o' Blisco, in front of which is Lingmoor Fell. To the right of Bow Fell appear Great End and Great Gable, at the watershed of Borrowdale and Wasdale, many miles away.

The Langdale Pikes are unmistakable, towering over Great Langdale. Further north is the low, but distinctive, Helm Crag above the vale of Grasmere and then the mighty ridges of the Fairfield range, partly hidden by the nearer Wansfell. North is the deep Troutbeck valley bordered by the characteristic summits of the ridge leading up to High Street. Althogether the combination of the winding lake, with its wooded shores, the low intermediate heights and the shapely fells stretching to the horizon present an unforgettable sight.

Windermere — the town — owes its existence to the railway, extended here in 1847. The main buildings astride the road to Bowness, all in the local slate, still retain a solid Victorian air. Windermere and its older neighbour, Bowness, have expanded to become more or less contiguous and together constitute one of the most popular tourist resorts in the Lake District.

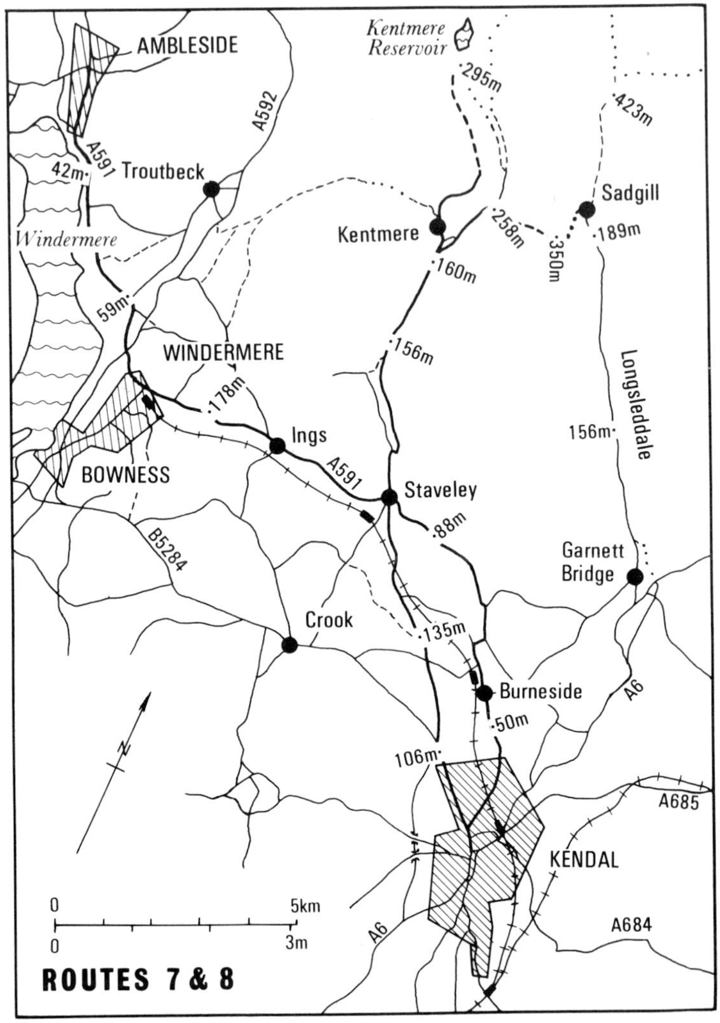

The attention of most visitors is concentrated on the lakeside at Bowness, an extremely colourful scene as the boats on the water wind in and out of the islands that make this middle reach of Windermere so attractive. From the pier steamers run up and down the lake, and there are various other scenic trips available, as well as boats for hire.

The dense traffic in the town's narrow streets detracts much from the ambience of the place. A haven of quiet in this turmoil is St Martin's Church, which contains a number of old features and items of interest. Half a mile north of Bowness is the Steamboat Museum, illustrating a past age of transport almost unique to Windermere. There are a number of steam-powered vessels, all beautifully restored. This road meets the direct road from Kendal a mile further on.

Lake Windermere (the tautology being necessary since the development of the town) is the largest lake in England. Over ten miles long, it is mostly less than a mile in width, giving it the appearance of a great river. As the most accessible of the Cumbrian lakes, it is under extreme pressure from the various water-related sports and activities. There are different speed limits on different parts of the lake to reduce conflict between motorboats and other lake users. Windermere station is $1^3/_4$m from the lakeside and 300ft (90 metres) *above it.*

Main route continued

Below Windermere station, the road continues to descend to Troutbeck Bridge, crossing the road from Bowness to Patterdale on the way. Here the level lakeside fringe is reached and the road, a good broad highway, soon passes the National Park Centre at Brockhole. This is well worth a visit and the time spent will be repaid in a better understanding of the area. The centre covers the geology, geography and natural history of the National Park by means of exhibitions, displays and photographs. The grounds reach down to the lakeside.

The next few miles, alongside the lake, are most pleasant. Opposite are the square towers of Wray Castle (page 44). At Waterhead, a mile short of Ambleside, the road for all through traffic bears left and soon passes the steamer and boat-hiring piers. The direct road leads into Ambleside but the one-way system necessitates dropping down to the other road before entering the town.

Ambleside forms the ideal base for the visitor intent on seeing the southern half of the Lake District. From the town roads radiate to Bowness, Hawkshead, Coniston and the Langdales, while the town is situated on the main spine road through the National Park to Grasmere and Keswick. Even Ullswater is near enough for a day trip, though few would fancy tackling the Kirkstone Pass twice.

Ambleside is constructed entirely in the traditional slate, which, if a little sombre, is very pleasing when after rain the sunlight brings out its blue and green tinges. The tourist season here lasts more or less the whole year round, and the town sets out to cater for them. From its central position it has the disadvantage that in wet weather it ends up full of bedraggled hikers who wander round dejectedly in dripping cagoules, poking each other's eyes out with their packframes.

Ambleside is excellently placed not only for a number of mountain ascents but also for several delightful short strolls. A few are suggested below; even the most dedicated cyclist will find ample reward in them.

Stockghyll Force: A fine waterfall $\frac{1}{2}$m east of the town, reached by a steep lane on the south side of Stock Ghyll (not the Kirkstone road). A path turns out of this lane and up to the fall.
Scandale: Due north of the town. A charming lane, with views over Ambleside and Rydal, leads up to High Sweden Bridge ($1\frac{3}{4}$m).
Jenkin Crag ($1\frac{1}{2}$m): A fine viewpoint overlooking Lake Windermere, reached by a path from Ambleside to Troutbeck skirting Wansfell.
Loughrigg Fell: This undulating height provides the freedom of a mountain top without as much exertion. It can be gained from the bridge over the Rothay, just west of Ambleside.

Foot of Windermere

Kendal to Staveley & Upper Kentdale

8

Map — see Route 7
Distances from Kendal: Burneside 2¼m, Staveley 5⁵⁄₄m (4¾m direct via A591), Kentmore (church) 9¾m, Kentmere (Reservoir) 12½m.

INTRODUCTION

The valley of the Kent above Kendal provides a pleasant foretaste of the more dramatic scenery of the Lake District. Quiet byroads follow the river all the way from Kendal to its source in the reservoir above Kentmere.

The river Kent has long been harnessed to satisfy the needs of industry; indeed, Burneside and Staveley were primarily industrial villages. Even the reservoir at the head of the valley was built to ensure a reliable supply of water for the mills, although man was only completing what the work of ice had all but achieved. The natural lake that gave its name to the nearby village of Kentmere was drained early last century.

Scenically, the route falls into three distinct sections — the wandering valley to Staveley, with the river gliding between low rounded hills, the straight-sided valley from there to Kentmere, and finally the concealed upper valley, out of the reach of the motor-borne. Of the various tracks out of the dale from Kentmere, only that to Sadgill, in Longsleddale, can be regarded as practicable for the touring cyclist and this is justifiably included below.

DESCRIPTION

This way to Staveley via Burneside adds about a mile to the distance via the main road, and, despite avoiding the long hill out of Kendal on that road, will take a lot longer. Its advantage lies in its avoidance of traffic and the loveliness of the approach to Staveley.

As far as Burneside, the road is not particularly interesting, being largely built-up. A mile beyond the village an unsignposted road on the right is taken across the river Kent. As low hills hem in the valley at this point, the views are not extensive,

8

Upper Kentdale from Stile End

but the road itself is delightful — a narrow single-track lane twisting between meandering walls and wooded slopes. The first indication of Staveley is a large packaging factory, but the fine view from the bridge up the valley of the Kent should encourage those with time to explore this area further.

The four miles from Staveley to Kentmere provide easy and quiet cycling, but the best scenery of Kentdale lies beyond the end of the road. The lane runs broad and straight alongside the river, crossing to the east bank in half a mile. The valley scenery is pleasantly pastoral, mainly devoted to sheep grazing. The first view of Kentmere is very sweet, the cottages and church dotted over the lower slopes of a crag-topped hill. In the bottom of the valley can be seen Kentmere Hall, with its ancient pele tower, and above it the Garburn Road climbing over to Troutbeck. Nearing the hamlet the road forks, the left turn signposted Troutbeck, the right Longsleddale. Neither is accessible by motor car, and both involve plenty of hard work for the cyclist!

Kentmere marks the end of the public road but the best of the scenery is yet to come. The village is situated on an obvious geological boundary, the character of the landscape 'stepping up a gear' as the upper reach of the valley is revealed. The boundary is between the Borrowdale-series volcanic rocks to the north and the sedimentary Silurian slates, and is roughly marked by the Garburn Pass into the Troutbeck valley and the old road into Longsleddale at Sadgill, where the same transition can be noted. This road will be described after some comments on upper Kentdale.

Upper Kentdale: Beyond the rocky spur over which the houses spread, the valley broadens out again, while on all sides hills rise precipitously.

Although there are only rights of way on foot in this upper section (other than the track over Nan Bield to Haweswater) there is a private road as far as the reservoir. No one is likely to object to its use by the occasional cyclist. Follow the road past Kentmere church which climbs up towards Nook and, where this turns left, continue straight on through a gate. The road is tarred as far as Hartrigg Farm and this section is especially beautiful, running beneath richly wooded crags. Above Hartrigg, the road continues as a metalled track to the quarries a little below the reservoir. This part of the valley, although more bare, is made attractive by its isolated groups of trees.

The return to Kentmere may be varied by fording the river at the quarries and taking a footpath on the opposite bank to Tongue House and then down the lane to the end of the public road at Overend, a mile north of the village. Strictly speaking, this way back has only footpath status.

Kentmere to Sadgill (Longsleddale) 2¾m. Allow 45-60min
This link, by an old and disused road, is a convenient outlet from the two valleys and presents no difficulty to the ordinary cyclist. The road — 'unsuitable for motor vehicles' — is a stony cart track, most of it easy for cycling and well-defined throughout. In Victorian times this and the adjacent Garburn Pass formed a popular touring route for light carriages, an indication of how much both have deteriorated. As motor vehicles are not actually banned, it is popular with motor cyclists, though they cause further damage to the surface.

From the bridge below Kentmere church follow the road up the east side of the river, turning left at the T junction at the top of the hill. The road rises until, in a dip, a signpost points the way to Sadgill. The track is rideable in the reverse direction, but the combination of gradient and bumpiness precludes much cycling eastbound. A gradual rise leads to the summit, 1,120ft (350 metres), marked by a lone cairn. The surrounding hills are featureless, the interest of the route being confined to the two valleys.

The descent into Longsleddale is initially steep where it runs alongside the stream and this part must be wheeled, but lower down the path improves for the remainder of the way to the bridge at Sadgill. In the reverse direction, turn left on crossing the bridge and go through the gate above the farm.

The head of Longsleddale has some impressive mountain scenery, but the lane north from Sadgill is barely rideable. It is an easy ten miles down the valley to Kendal, entered either by the A6 or through Burneside. The return to Staveley via Garnett Bridge is also ten miles.

9 Ambleside to Coniston & Broughton

Distances from Ambleside: Skelwith Bridge 2½m, Coniston 7¾m, Torver 10¼m, Broughton 16¾m, Foxfield station 18¼m.

Torver to Greenodd 8¼m, Ulverston 11¾m, see Route 14.

INTRODUCTION

This very attractive road, particularly in the vicinity of Coniston, provides a useful link to the coast road at Broughton and the railway at Foxfield. Although basically a valley road, it is surprisingly hilly beyond Torver, and this section is rather hard going. If intent on visiting Tarn Hows, the alternative way to Coniston (Route 30) should be taken.

DESCRIPTION

From the centre of Ambleside the road descends to cross the Rothay and then runs along the foot of Loughrigg Fell through Clappersgate. As far as Skelwith Bridge the valley rises only gently and offers easy cycling in pleasant surroundings.

An alternative route from Clappersgate is to cross the Brathay bridge (1m from Ambleside) and continue via a narrow lane running along the south side of the river. The combination of wood and water is very beautiful. At Skelwith Fold turn right, and in a few yards an excellent view is revealed from Spy Hill. On the descent, turn left in half a mile to join the main road coming up from Skelwith Bridge.

From Skewith Bridge (for falls see page 64) the A593 climbs steeply for almost a mile. The views opening up northwards to Great and Little Langdale are very good, the road running along a terrace above the valley. Beyond the turning to Little Langdale and the Wrynose Pass, the Coniston road climbs again to a height of 500ft (150 metres). Just before the summit, tracks lead off to Tilberthwaite (right) and Hawkshead (left). The Hawkshead track, although passing near Tarn Hows, offers no views of the lakes and is very rough. The turning to the right is tarred as far as High Oxen Fell, whence it continues as a cart

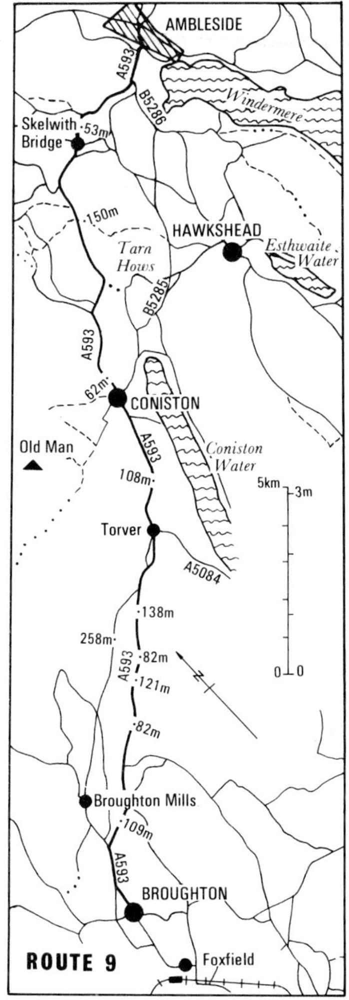

track to Hodge Close and Tilberthwaite (pages 143-4). Coniston may then be reached by either side of Yewdale Beck. This little corner of Lakeland is a maze of side valleys, old slate workings and inviting tracks, fully meriting a leisurely exploration.

From the main road summit a long descent brings one past Yew Tree Tarn, artificial, but no less attractive for that. A little further on a steep footpath left provides a pedestrian route to Tarn Hows. The remaining two miles to Coniston are of great beauty, the richness of the foliage and grace of outline of the fells being as fine as any in the Lake District. The road winds down a gently-descending vale, Yewdale, with a tranquil scene revealed at every turn.

Coniston village does not live up to the standard of its surroundings, a consequence of its industrial past. Slate and copper mining were extensively carried out in the vicinity, but the remains do not intrude too drastically into the views. Slate is still quarried locally.

The lake is reached by crossing the bridge and taking the next turning left, which leads in half a mile to the boat landings. Motor or rowing boats may be hired here. The steam yacht *Gondola,* rescued from the bed of the lake and restored to its original glory, operates a service down the lake in summer.

Coniston Water is often compared with Windermere, but it lacks the graceful curves and more varied surroundings of the larger lake. Nonetheless, seen backed by the Old Man or the

Coniston

wooded hills that line its eastern shore, the views of the lake are quite charming. Coniston Water is just over five miles long and the circuit of it by road about thirteen miles, better taken anticlockwise.

Coniston is the natural starting point for the ascent of the Old Man (2,631ft, 803 metres), to which half a day or more should be devoted. One may also explore the Coppermines valley north-west of the village: the mines themselves are unsafe.

From Coniston the Broughton road climbs with good views across the lake to Grizedale Forest. Woods then close in most of the way to Torver, a small village where the road to Ulverston turns off, taking most of the traffic with it. After a new straight stretch built along the old railway, the road becomes winding and hilly, hardly recognisable in character as an 'A' road. Indeed, heavy vehicles are prohibited beyond Torver. This section of road, a switchback of steep and unexpected hills, is a rather trying one for the cyclist. The parallel railway, now abandoned, had a much easier gradient with a single summit of 345ft. (Its conversion to a public path from Torver to Broughton would be a great boon to cyclists.) The scenery is an anticlimax after Coniston, the road being shut in by low and rather uninteresting fells.

At the top of the last and longest hill, a fine view is revealed over the Dunnerdale Fells, with the coastline discernable beyond. A gentle descent then leads to Broughton, past the park-like grounds of Broughton Tower. Foxfield station is 1½m south of the village.

If proceeding west of Broughton, a short cut may be taken, but the village is worth the extra distance. It can boast a fine Georgian square and an old market hall, which now houses a motorcycle museum.

Ambleside to Ravenglass via Wrynose and Hardknott Passes

10

Distances from Ambleside: Skelwith Bridge 2½m, Little Langdale (Three Shires Inn) 5m, Top of Wrynose 7¾m, Cockley Beck Bridge 10m, Top of Hard Knott 11m, Boot 14¾m, Eskdale Green 17¼m, Ravenglass (via Irton & Saltcoats) 23½m.

At Eskdale Green Route 16, from Broughton to Wasdale and the coast, is crossed.

Distances from Ambleside: Seascale 24¾m, Gosforth 22¾m, Wasdale Head 26¾m.

INTRODUCTION

A famous and historic route across the heart of the Cumbrian Mountains. The two passes — Wrynose and Hard Knott (both 1,290ft or 393 metres) — are steep but low in relation to the elevation of the surrounding fells, and their value in communications has long been appreciated. The Romans utilised them for their road between Ambleside and their port at Ravenglass and in more recent times this formed the packhorse route between Kendal and Whitehaven. Woollens and other products were exported and on their return the packs often contained smuggled goods landed on the coast. The turnpikes and railways gradually killed off through trade, but in the latter part of the last century growing numbers of tourists, among them the early cycling pioneers, caused it to be improved to cater for wheeled traffic. It long provided a challenge to the sporting motorist until Wrynose was properly surfaced in the thirties; Hard Knott was not so treated until after the Second World War. Since then the route has grown in popularity and it seems that no motoring holiday in the Lakes is complete without an assault on Wrynose and Hard Knott. Traffic jams are not uncommon at the height of the summer: patience, not performance, is all that is now required. How long the use of this road can remain unrestricted is a matter of conjecture. Cyclists should certainly endeavour to avoid any summer weekend for making a crossing if the solitude of the fells is to be enjoyed.

The other problem for the cyclist is the severity of the descents from the two principal summits. These are very steep — about 1

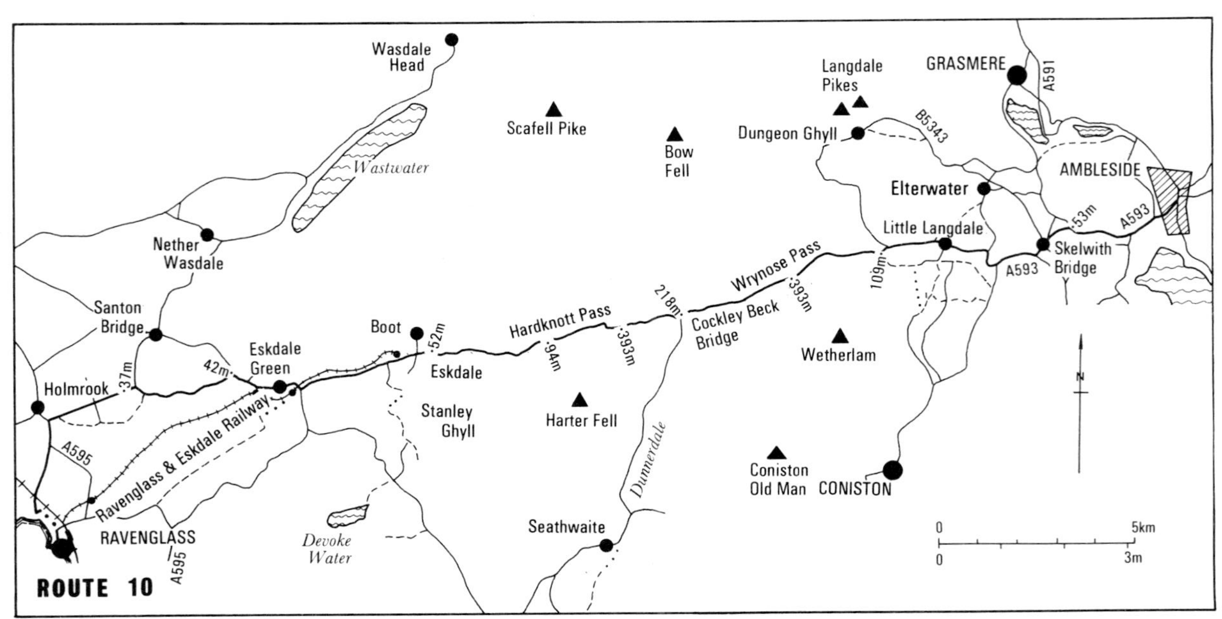
Wasdale Head
GRASMERE
A591
Langdale Pikes
Scafell Pike
Bow Fell
Dungeon Ghyll
B5343
Wastwater
AMBLESIDE
Elterwater
Nether Wasdale
Little Langdale
53m
A593
Skelwith Bridge
A593
Wrynose Pass
109m
Santon Bridge
Hardknott Pass
218m
393m
Cockley Beck Bridge
Boot
52m
393m
Eskdale Green
42m
Wetherlam
94m
Eskdale
Holmrook
37m
Stanley Ghyll
Harter Fell
Ravenglass & Eskdale Railway
Dunnerdale
A595
Coniston Old Man
CONISTON
N
RAVENGLASS
Devoke Water
Seathwaite
0
5km
0
3m
A595
ROUTE 10

in $3\frac{1}{2}$ (30 per cent) at their worst — requiring sustained period of full braking. This is an obvious safety hazard, particularly in wet weather when it is advisable to walk down the steepest pitches. Hillclimbing, it should be noted, is not confined to the two watershed passes, the Brathay valley beyond Skelwith Bridge containing some sharp ascents.

The landscape traversed is a contrast between the sheltered and fertile vales of the Brathay and Esk and the bleak terrain that forms the gathering grounds for the river Duddon. The Duddon valley, into which the road dips between the two passes, has its softer, romantic side, but to appreciate this the traveller needs to follow the river downstream to Ulpha. As viewpoints of the surrounding mountains the two passes are rather disappointing.

The initial part of the journey may be varied by travelling up Great Langdale, crossing from Dungeon Ghyll on the road passing Blea Tarn, but Great Langdale deserves better than to be the first (and probably rushed) stage of an arduous but enjoyable day.

DESCRIPTION

The one-way system of Ambleside has to be unravelled before the cyclist emerges on the Coniston road, A593. There is a pleasant 2m run alongside the river Brathay to Skelwith Bridge (for falls see page 64). Here the river, which will be followed to its source, is crossed. There then comes a steady climb for a mile or so to the turning for Little Langdale and Wrynose, the junction is almost midway between Ambleside and Coniston, about four miles from each. A sharp descent leads to a recrossing of the Brathay after which a left fork is taken (coming east one must give way at the foot of the hill). A little way up the river is Colwith Force, a charming cascade reached by a path on the left. This part of the road is attractive, running along a densely-wooded hillside, but includes some short steep pitches.

The hamlet of Little Langdale shelters below a hill spur reaching out into the valley and enclosing beyond it the yet unseen tarn. Opposite a side valley leads past Tilberthwaite to Coniston and provides an alternative route from that village (see Route 30). A climb up this spur reveals the upper part of the valley, bordered by the unbroken northern flanks of Wetherlam and Swirl How — two noble peaks. Ahead, the top stage of the climb to Wrynose can be seen — a little offputting from this angle. The course of the Roman road may also be discerned, slanting up the hillside slightly above the modern road. In the foreground is Little Langdale Tarn, which unfortunately fails to live up to its surroundings, being somewhat shallow and reed-filled. Coming in on the right at this viewpoint is a short-cut from Elterwater, in Great Langdale — one of those characteristic and charming old Lakeland roads, now no more than a cart-track at its northern end.

After passing the tarn the road forks, the turning to the right climbing over the watershed into Great Langdale. The Wrynose branch drops a little way to Fell Foot, the last farm in the valley and, in former days, an inn. Fell Foot marks the point of transition from the cultivated valley bottom to the open fellside. The road climbs, levels off, then rises again in earnest, as the way ahead is seen flanking up the hill. The total rise from Fell Foot to the top of the pass is 920ft (280 metres) in 1½m, the gradient increasing to 1 in 4 in parts. Wrynose Bridge, about halfway up, provides an opportunity for a cooling splash from the stream. As the road ascends, there is a fine view back down Little Langdale, with both Wansfell (above Ambleside) and the conical Ill Bell prominent. By the side of the road just before the summit is the Three Shire Stone, marking the former meeting point of Cumberland, Westmorland and the Furness district of Lancashire. They were merged into the new county of Cumbria in 1974.

From the top of the pass a limited view westwards is revealed, hemmed in on both sides by bare fellsides. Straight ahead is the Hard Knott Pass, blocking the way to the coast. The descent is steep at first, requiring care, but soon eases as the road runs alongside the river to Cockley Beck Bridge, across the Duddon. Near here can be caught a glimpse of Scafell Pike, viewed up Mosedale.

From Cockley Beck Bridge a most attractive road runs down the Duddon valley to Ulpha (7¼m) and Broughton (11¾m). The finest scenery is in the vicinity of Seathwaite. The valley is described under Route 16.

On the far side of the bridge, a track leads to Dunnerdale (Black Hall) Youth Hostel. This is the only approach which can be recommended to the cyclist.

The first part of the climb to Hard Knott — about half a mile — is not too steep, but then the fearful zigzags commence. At their foot a grassy track from Black Hall joins. The gradient increases to almost 1 in 3 in places, although overall this part of the ascent is surprisingly no steeper than 1 in 7. For most cyclists this is academic and it will be a case of dismounting and pushing.

The total rise from Cockley Beck Bridge is nearly 600ft (175 metres) — less severe this way than Wrynose, but nevertheless a long climb, only relieved by occasional glimpses down the Duddon valley.

The summit, like that of Wrynose, presents a confined view, looking down the winding Esk to the sea. The descent on this side is dangerously steep in places and, extending to a thousand feet, considerably longer than the eastern ascent. Additionally, the surface is most uneven where rutted by motor traffic, and this makes for unsteady riding. A very steep left-right zigzag near the top will require full braking power or dismounting in wet weather.

Lower down the hill, a finger post points the way to the Roman fort of Mediobogdum, an outpost protecting their road from Galava (Ambleside) to Glanoventa (Ravenglass). The fort, more usually known as Hard Knott Castle, straddles the ridge on the right overlooking the wilds of upper Eskdale. Only bare walls remain of the buildings, but the fascination of the place lies in its magnificent location in these bleak foreign hills. North-east of the fort is the Roman parade ground, a level area of approximately three acres. The visitor should not fail to walk a little way north of the fort to the top of some crags for the sake of the fine mountain panorama across to Sca Fell, Scafell Pike and Bow Fell.

Wrynose bottom looking up the pass

After descending steeply again with another tricky zigzag, the road reaches the comparatively level valley bottom, which then provides some glorious cycling. Indeed, after the tribulations of the mountain passes there is the risk that the 5m of open road to Eskdale Green will be raced over, and that one will be through the most scenic part of the valley without realising it. Resist the temptation to press on, as Eskdale can offer much to linger over, particularly along the banks of its river.

Travelling down the valley a long cascade called Birker Force can be seen threading down between the crags on the left. Passing the Woolpack Inn the quaint hamlet of Boot is reached. It lies along a short side road, at the end of which is the old cornmill. A little further down the valley road is Dalegarth station, the upper terminus of the Ravenglass & Eskdale Railway. Originally built to carry iron ore and slate, it is now exclusively a tourist line and after past vicissitudes is enjoying great popularity. There is a souvenir shop and cafe at the station.

Stanley Ghyll and Force: This diversion should not be omitted by any visitor to Eskdale. The waterfall, also known as Dalegarth Force, is not in itself as impressive as some others in the Lake District, but the walk up to it is most beautiful, particularly when the rhododendron bushes lining the path are in flower. Turn up a side road opposite the school, a little way from the railway terminus. The river Esk is crossed where it reveals an attractive rocky bed and a metalled lane is then followed up the hill. Dalegarth Hall, an interesting old building with huge cylindrical chimneys, is seen on the right before a gate is passed through. Keeping to the wall on the left the entrance to the ghyll is reached and cycles must be left here. The falls are gained by following a path up the side of the stream which soon leads one into a narrow ravine, its steep sides draped from head to foot with every variety of fern and tree. Two rustic bridges as crossed and from a third the falls are revealed in a deep cleft. The whole excursion is delightful and unforgettable.

The road that leads to the ghyll, if continued upwards, brings one out on the Eskdale Green to Ulpha road on Birker Fell. The going, rough at first, gradually improves. Allow an hour from Eskdale over to Ulpha. For a fuller description see Route 16.

Below Boot the valley gradually broadens out, with the road accompanied by the river and railway. The two and a half miles to Eskdale Green provide an opportunity to race the trains on the 'Ratty'. At the King George IV Inn a choice of roads leads to Ravenglass. The less interesting but slightly shorter way ($6\frac{1}{2}$m) is to turn left and then right in $\frac{3}{4}$m. The road runs along the south side of the Esk. (The bridge across the Esk between Forge House and Muncaster Head Farm is private. The rough road down the north side of the valley must be gained from near Irton Road station.) In crossing from the Esk valley to Ravenglass there is a climb of 250ft (80 metres) along the main road past Muncaster Castle.

The recommended way to Ravenglass is through Eskdale Green and past Irton Hall to the coast road near Holmrook, and then through Saltcoats. Eskdale Green, reached by a short hill, is most sweetly placed overlooking the Esk and Mite valleys, the latter river being crossed a little further on. After the Bower House Inn, the turning to the right leads to Gosforth on the road up the coast and is also the way to Wasdale. Both are described in Route 16. The branch to the left leads to Holmrook (for Seascale) and Ravenglass.

A pleasant run now follows as the road is parallel with the river Mite: a train may be heard across the valley. In 1½m the grounds of Irton Hall are reached, and here our road turns left to head for the coast. This section dates from the enclosure of Irton Moor, the old road (not recommended) loops round to the south. On the way a turning leads up to Irton Church, on an escarpment overlooking the valley of the Irt. There is an old cross, believed to date from the ninth century, in the churchyard.

The main A595 along the coast is reached about 2½ miles north of Ravenglass and a little south of Holmrook (cafe). The main road runs past the restored Muncaster Watermill and then climbs round the western tip of Muncaster Fell before descending to Ravenglass. The better way is first to follow the A595 and then take the fork to the right, signposted Saltcoats. This road leads to the old ford across the mouth of the Mite and, of more practical use, the footbridge alongside the railway to Ravenglass.

To many cyclists who have toiled westward up hill and down dale, Ravenglass will come as a disappointment. Nowadays it is the fashion of guidebooks to picture everywhere in such eulogistic prose that this must lead to the visitor's disillusionment in many cases and nowhere has been more overpraised than Ravenglass. True, the village street is full of old cottages, but there is not much else in the place despite its past importance.

At least one cannot miss its nautical links. At the far end of the street a gate opens on to the tidal waters of the Esk which, augmented by its sister streams the Irt and the Mite, has created a sandy estuary winding out to the open sea. The scenes at sunset over the mixing waters are glorious, and there is much of interest to the ornithologist and nature lover. Railway enthusiasts will of course be drawn to the museum and souvenir shop of the 'Ratty'. Muncaster Castle, just east of the village, is a popular venue for family outings.

The main street of Ravenglass lies on the old road (such as it was) along the coast, which forded the rivers Esk and Mite west of the present A595. Just south of the village was the Roman fort of Glanoventa. Part of a bathhouse ('Walls Castle') still stands 12½ft high, and is regarded by most authorities as one of the best-preserved Roman structures in the North of England.

11 Ambleside to Great Langdale

Distances from Ambleside: Skelwith Bridge 2½m, Elterwater 4m, Chapel Stile 5m, Dungeon Ghyll 7m, Little Langdale (3 Shires Inn) 11m, Ambleside 16m.

INTRODUCTION

One of the most popular short excursions in the Lake District, this is a beautiful run throughout, the scenery building up steadily to the glorious mountain horseshoe guarding the head of the valley and the distinctive outline of the Langdale Pikes. By keeping to the main road, no real hills are encountered, but this cannot be said of the branch turnings.

The round of the Langdales — travelling up Little Langdale and returning via Great Langdale or vice versa — is a popular outing from Ambleside of some sixteen miles. For cyclists it will be found hard going through Little Langdale and in crossing the watershed between the two valleys.

DESCRIPTION

From Ambleside, the Coniston road is taken, a lovely ride up the Brathay valley for a few miles to Skelwith Bridge, which is not crossed. Skelwith Force is about 300yd from it and reached by a path through the slate works. The fall is inferior to many in the district but is nevertheless a popular attraction. The river rushes through a cleft in the rocks with a drop of about 12ft (4 metres). The fall can also be reached from the Langdale road, which runs alongside. A gap in the wall marks the spot, but there is nowhere to leave cycles.

The road onwards leads in ¾m to the reedy banks of Elterwater, an irregularly shaped lake amid woods. This part of the road, from Skelwith Bridge to Elterwater village, was built in 1895, just before the motor age; even in those days the valley had its traffic problems! The old road runs higher up past the secluded Loughrigg Tarn and is very much more hilly, but might be considered as a variation for the return journey.

Elterwater village lies just south of the road up the valley. Visitors are surprised to learn that one of its principal industries was gunpowder making, a little incongruous in these rural

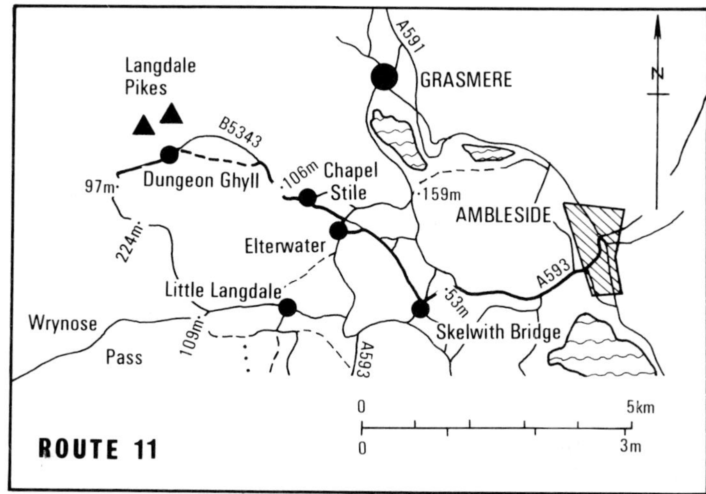

surroundings until one remembers that in this area charcoal was plentiful and the river provided ample waterpower. The site of the works is now a caravan and chalet park.

Chapel Stile, a mile further, is the last village in Langdale. The valley here is rather enclosed but soon opens out again, affording a marvellous view. Ahead is Bow Fell and on the right the Langdale Pikes rise majestically.

Old road: A mile from Chapel Stile the old road, keeping to the centre of the valley, strikes off left. This section fell into disuse after 1925, when the road up the valley was improved. The imposing sign proclaiming 'No Motors' is alas no more and the only indication of the turning is now the letter box on the wall. The views are excellent, the Pikes more advantageously seen than from the present road which runs closer to their foot. The two roads unite in a mile near the New Dungeon Ghyll Hotel and Stickle Barn Cafe.

The southern aspect of the Langdale Pikes is one of the most striking mountain profiles in Britain. Strangely, the Pikes themselves are no more than a facade, being the southern limit of a high and generally uninteresting fell range running north to Keswick.

The ascent of the Pikes is generally made from the foot of Dungeon Ghyll, but a description of the various routes is outside the scope of this book. Well within the range of the occasional walker is the climb to Stickle Tarn, below the cliff-like Pavey Ark, or up the edge of Dungeon

11

Loughrigg Tarn

Ghyll itself, a deep rift at the bottom of which can be heard the unseen stream. There are several paths leading up the hillside, and care must be taken in setting off — the intricasies of this compact area cannot be fully appreciated from the map, or time easily related to distance.

The road along the valley bottom continues a little way to end at the Dungeon Ghyll Old Hotel. The only exit for cyclists is via the steep hill over by Blea Tarn into Little Langdale, by which a return to Ambleside may be made. It is described in the reverse direction in Routes 10 and 30. The hill paths out of the head of Langdale to Borrowdale, are definitely only for walkers, the ascent of Rossett Gill being reckoned one of the most difficult in the Lake District.

Ambleside to Keswick

12

Distances from Ambleside: Grasmere 4m, Dunmail Raise $6^3/_4$m, Wythburn Church 8m, Thirlspot 11m, (Threlkeld 16m), Keswick $16^3/_4$m.

INTRODUCTION

This, the principal link between the south and north of the district, is one of the busiest Lakeland roads, though heavy vehicles are banned north of Grasmere and sent round via Penrith. The scenery is of the highest order throughout, particularly the waterside stretches between Rydal and Grasmere and along Thirlmere. The road is well-graded but there are two main summits — Dunmail Raise (782ft, 238 metres) and Castlerigg (702ft, 214 metres) enclosing the Thirlmere basin (580ft, 175 metres). The longest climbs are thus out of Grasmere northbound and out of Keswick southbound.

DESCRIPTION

From Ambleside the road runs up the beautiful valley of the Rothay, beneath the long ridges thrown out by the Fairfield range. As far as Rydal there is an even more pleasant road, a lane running along the west bank of the river from the bridge on the Coniston road. Rydal is delightfully situated where the valley first closes in. Rydal Mount, a little way above the road, was the home of William Wordsworth for the latter part of his life, and contains period furniture and mementoes of the poet. Although now primarily known for his poetry, Wordsworth wrote one of the earliest and most definitive guidebooks to the Lake District, setting a trend which shows no sign of abating.

A little further on, the road runs along the north shore of Rydal Water, a lovely tree-girt lake. Above Rydal, the road bends with the valley, winding through woods until suddenly opening out on Grasmere. The lake with its single island presents a fine picture with its irregular backcloth of encircling fells. Ahead, dividing the valley, is the prominent Helm Crag, also variously known as The Lion and the Lamb, or The Old Lady at the Organ, from the curious combination of rocks crowning its summit. On the right is the long and rather ominous line of the

12

KESWICK
Threlkeld
A66
214m
Derwentwater
A591
156m
B5322
169m
Thirlspot
215m
Thirlmere
A591
Helvellyn
Wythburn
179m
238m
Dunmail Raise
A591
Fairfield
GRASMERE
65m
Rydal
0
5km
0
3m
AMBLESIDE
ROUTE 12

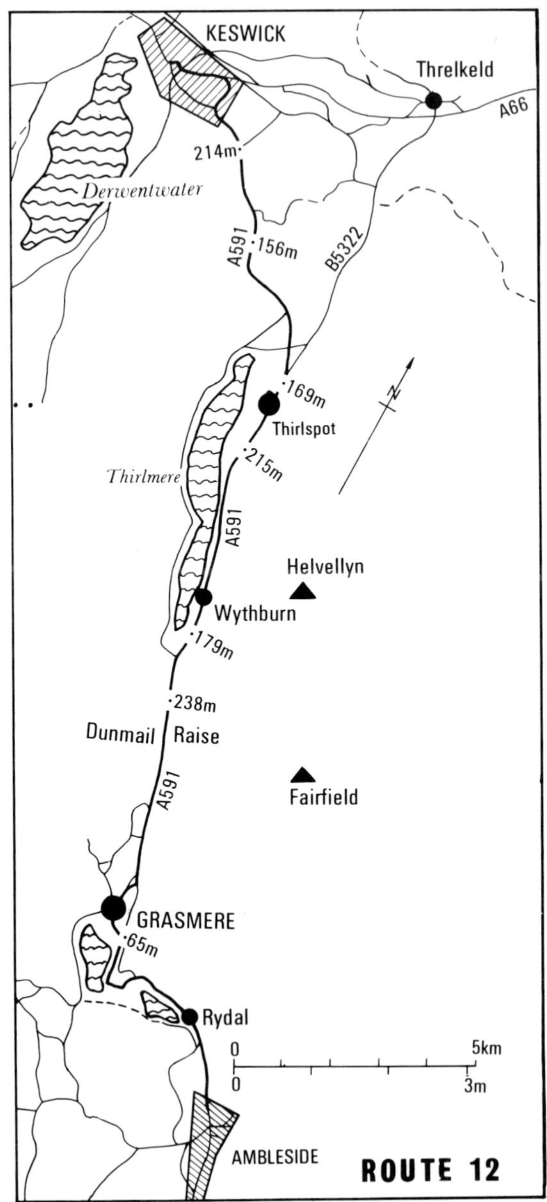

road up to Dunmail Raise.

Excellent though the view is, it cannot compare with that from Red Bank, on the road over from Langdale, or the higher old road from Rydal, to name but two available to the cyclist. The lake is a gem but its setting is best appreciated from a higher viewpoint.

After a short run the road forks, that to the left, which should be taken, passing through Grasmere village. At this junction, a little back up the old road, is Dove Cottage, home of William Wordsworth, his wife Mary and sister Dorothy from 1799 to 1808. The cottage and nearby barn contain memorabilia of the poet and his family.

Grasmere village is not without charm, but has been so given over to catering for the tourist trade that commercialisation has rather spoilt it. The sheer number of visitors detracts from what they all come to see. The real attraction of the place, apart from its literary associations, lies in its beautiful surroundings, and these at least are unimpaired. A short walk in any direction leads to fresh and surprising views at every corner.

Grasmere church, between the village and the lake, is an unpretentious, but not uninteresting, building. Its main object of pilgrimage is, of course, the grave of Wordsworth in the churchyard.

Two pedestrian excursions may be recommended before the cyclist moves on to tackle Dunmail Raise. Easdale Tarn, situated in a wild upland valley, is a popular round walk of about five miles from the village, while Easdale itself will surprise many who think of Grasmere as only embraced by the valley traversed by the main road. Helm Crag may be ascended in under an hour by a well-defined path leaving the road up Easdale a mile north of the village. One can cycle as far as this, a lovely ride.

The road over Dunmail Raise must eventually be faced, and though the return to the A591 may be postponed by keeping to the back lanes, the long climb is inescapable. It lasts for about two miles and rises to 782ft (238 metres), ie about 550ft (170 metres) above the village and lake. Taken in the reverse direction, there is a climb of 200ft (60 metres) from Thirlmere. The summit is bleak, and contrasts strongly with the sheltered vale left behind. Ahead is the depression containing Thirlmere, although the reservoir is all but concealed by the encircling plantations. The view north, hemmed in by the long mountain ridges on either side, extends to the Skiddaw range beyond Keswick.

The Raise formerly marked the boundary between Westmor-

12

Dunmail Raise

land and Cumberland, now both incorporated into Cumbria. There is still a strong sense of a border about it, for as well as being an obvious watershed, it, along with the nearby Kirkstone Pass, separates the southern part of the Lake District, centred on Ambleside and Windermere, from the northern lakes of which Keswick is the principal focus.

The road descends steadily for ¾m to a road junction a little before the lake. Here an unclassified road turns off and runs round the western side of Thirlmere to rejoin the main road five miles nearer Keswick. This road and the vicinity of the lake are described in more detail in Route 31. The main road along the east bank is a good one, part of it constructed when the water level was raised. Of the hamlet of Wythburn nothing but the little church and a farm now remains. The road eventually leaves the lakeside to pass behind an intervening knoll (a good viewpoint), and no more of the lake is seen.

A little beyond Thirlspot the road down St John's Vale bears away right, followed by the stream issuing from Thirlmere. The first mile or so of this road is most attractive, as indeed are all the environs of the northern end of Thirlmere. The main Keswick road runs along a winding vale which eventually broadens out into a depression drained by the Naddle Beck. The Ice Age, responsible for the many sheets of water that grace this part of England, must take the blame for some of the less attractive features when the result is, instead, an infertile basin of badly drained land. The standard of the scenery drops momentarily, and then the road attacks the final ridge blocking the way to Keswick. Northbound there is a climb of 200ft (60 metres), coming the other way it is 450ft (130 metres).

On the descent into Keswick the view is transformed into one of great beauty, with Skiddaw soaring majestically above the shores of Bassenthwaite Lake. The town is in the foreground and to the left one can glimpse Derwentwater, backed by the soon-to-be-familiar ridge of Catbells and Maiden Moor.

Keswick is the unrivalled capital of northern Lakeland. The view from the higher parts of the town, looking over Derwentwater into Borrowdale, the most romantic valley in Britain, is justly famous, while to the north the town is dominated by the sprawling mass of Skiddaw. No visit to the Lakes is complete without a halt at Keswick; indeed such a stay would be difficult to avoid.

But Keswick is much more than a mere overnight halting place; it is a worthy resort in its own right. It can boast two fine parks, the Century Theatre, a cinema and an interesting museum. A first stop should be at the information centre in the old Moot Hall. This building, with its rather Tyrolean air, is the one feature of architectural interest in the town, the narrow streets of which, usually thronged with visitors, are somewhat mundane. There is an abundance of accommodation to suit all pockets and the usual line in Lakeland tourist shops. The layout of the place can be a little confusing, especially as the road signposts route traffic round the town wherever possible.

Keswick and Derwentwater enjoy a close relationship, as the best approaches to the lake, that is from its foot, must be made from the town. The nearest way is via Lake Road, continuing as Borrowdale Road, which leaves the market place at its SW corner, then doubling back at the roundabout. At another roundabout turn left to regain Lake Road. Pedestrians may save a little distance by using the underpass. The road leads to the boat landings, then continues as a footpath only to Friar's Crag. Here one looks straight up the island-studded lake into the heart of the mountains enclosing the distant Borrowdale. It is one of the best-known and -loved scenes in the Lake District.

From the boat landings, circular tours of Derwentwater operate at frequent intervals. Nearby is a bathing spot, but this end of the lake is very shallow.

There are many fine viewpoints in the vicinity of Keswick and indeed the road routes given in this book mention several. Of the heights accessible on foot Latrigg (1,203ft, 367 metres), just north of the town, is probably the most rewarding. The way is across the bypass by the footbridge (signposted Skiddaw), then along a green lane up the western flank of the fell. This doubles back to lead to the open grassy summit. The view is magnificent in all directions.

13 Ulverston to Furness Abbey & Barrow

Distances from Ulverston: Bardsea 2½m, Baycliff 4½m, Aldingham 5½m, Rampside 10m, Roa Island 11¼m, Roose 14½m, Barrow in Furness 16½m, Furness Abbey 18½m, Dalton 20½m, Ulverston 25½m.

Omitting the continuation down the coast to Roa Island saves 2½m; the direct road from Roose to the abbey saves 2m.

INTRODUCTION

Although this route turns its back on the attractions of the Lake District, there will be found sufficient interest along the coast and in the ruins of Furness Abbey to occupy half a day or more. For those merely wishing to visit the abbey, the most convenient railhead is Dalton, only 2m distant.

The route described is taken along the shores of Morecambe Bay to Roa Island, a good run, then inland to Barrow and Furness Abbey. The coastal road, now the A5087, was built in the 1920s to provide work for the unemployed. The old lanes were widened, bypasses built and a totally new section of road constructed from Aldingham to Rampside along the sea wall. The return route given is via the busy A590 through Dalton, with the inclusion of the road from Dalton to Broughton for those proceeding up the west coast. As the area is not included on the Tourist Map directions are given in more detail than usual. It is unfortunate that the Bartholomews 1:100,000 map of the Lake District excludes the area south of Ulverston which could conveniently be included on an inset.

DESCRIPTION

For Ulverston see page 35. The road south of the town passes under the railway a little east of the station. It is a good, well-graded road, passing Conishead Priory (see p 35) and gaining the coast below Bardsea. The view extends across the shining sands of the bay to Morecambe, backed by the Forest of Bowland, and south to Fleetwood and Blackpool. The beach along this side of the bay is mainly pebble and shingle with extensive sands revealed at low tide. Bardsea village, bypassed

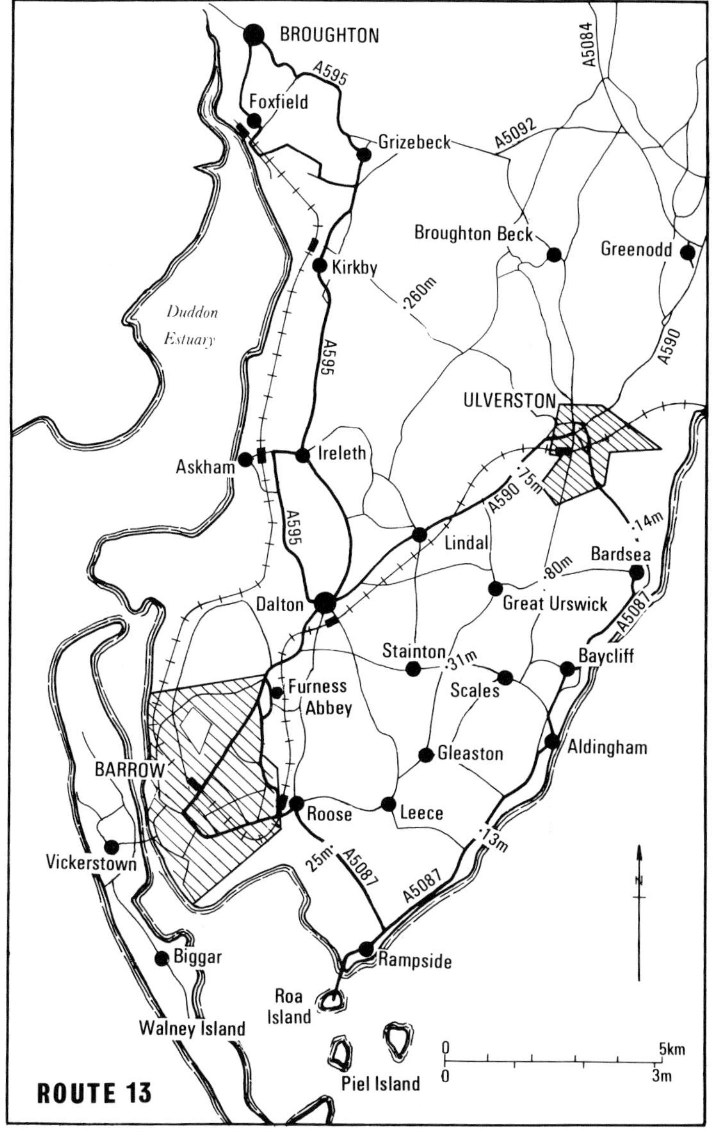
BROUGHTON
A595
Foxfield
Grizebeck
A5092
A5084
Broughton Beck
Greenodd
Kirkby
260m
Duddon Estuary
A595
A590
ULVERSTON
Askham
Ireleth
A590
75m
A595
Lindal
14m
Bardsea
80m
Dalton
Great Urswick
A5087
Stainton
31m
Baycliff
Furness Abbey
Scales
BARROW
Gleaston
Aldingham
Roose
Leece
13m
Vickerstown
25m
A5087
A5087
N
Biggar
Rampside
Roa Island
Walney Island
Piel Island
0
5km
0
3m
ROUTE 13

by the main road, is quite attractive, some way above the shore.

Beyond Bardsea the road soon turns inland again, climbing to the modest height of 190ft (57 metres) in the vicinity of Baycliff. Aldingham, a little further on, consists of not much more than the fine hall and the church, the waves practically beating against its walls. Formerly the village extended much further to the east, but centuries ago the sea encroached over it. Now, with just the cawing of the rooks and the lapping of the tide it is a melancholy spot.

After Aldingham the road for a while leaves the shore, then hugs it for the remainder of the way to Rampside. The seafront forms a popular promenade with Barrow folk at weekends and on summer evenings, while a more recently-developed pastime is windsurfing.

Before entering Rampside the main road turns inland for Barrow, but a continuation along the coast for a mile or so is of some interest. Rampside is just a bungalow village, at the far end of which a causeway leads to Roa Island. This was briefly the terminus of the steamer service from Fleetwood and the railway up the coast until the later development of Barrow, becoming a forgotten outpost of Victorian enterprise. Today it is a popular boating centre, with innumerable small craft to be seen on all sides. A mile away is Piel Island with the remains of its fourteenth-century castle.

For Barrow the road is retraced through Rampside, after which a level run of two miles leads to Roose, on the outskirts of the town. The easiest way then to Furness Abbey is to turn right just after crossing the railway at the station. This is Flass Lane, continuing via Rating Lane to the abbey (2m). However, having come this far it is worth first visiting the centre of Barrow, a town very much a product of the second half of the nineteenth century, being developed along with the exploitation of the local iron ore deposits. It is still best known for the production of warships and armaments. The town centre is well laid out, on the standard Victorian grid pattern. The main road out of the town, Abbey Road, leads past the railway station and in another mile or so a turning right leads down to Furness Abbey.

The abbey was founded in 1127 by Stephen, later King of England, the monks soon adopting the Cistercian order. The power of the abbot was immense, having virtual rule over a large area of what is now Cumbria. The ruins, of red sandstone, exhibit a variety of architectural styles reflecting the different periods of construction. As a whole the remains are low and unimpressive, but they contain a number of beautiful features. Perhaps the finest is the set of three recessed arches, leading to the chapter house.

NB If travelling from the abbey into Barrow care must be taken to find the correct road. Leading up from near the entrance (Manor Road) it meets Rating Lane at the top of the hill. Turn left for Roose, right then left (into Abbey Road) for Barrow station and town centre.

Continuing north from the abbey past the hotel into the main A590, a few hilly miles lead to Dalton, a small industrial town. It was the administrative centre of Furness until overtaken first by Ulverston and later Barrow. A tower alone remains of the castle built by the abbot of Furness Abbey.

Dalton to Ireleth (2½m), Sandside (6m), Grizebeck (8m) and Broughton (11m)

As far as Ireleth there is a choice of roads, the A595, or the old road from the north end of the town (left at Tudor Square). They are equally hilly. Beyond Ireleth the road descends gradually to Soutergate, beyond which a loop road should be taken through Sandside (Kirkby in Furness). Across the Duddon Sands is seen the long whaleback outline of Black Combe, rising abruptly from the coastal plain. Keep straight on at Kirkby station to regain the A595 via Marshside.

After following the main road north for a quarter-mile to Chapels, it is preferable to turn left on to a narrow track marked by the weight-restriction sign and Cumbria Cycle Way sticker. This provides a short cut to Foxfield. Beyond the bridge it becomes a metalled road. Turn right in ¼m to run via Waitham Hill to the railway, which is crossed and recrossed to join the main road just south of Foxfield station. Although it is a little further to Broughton than the main road via Grizebeck, this way avoids the steep hills and traffic of the latter.

The Ulverston road from Dalton is good and gently-undulating. It is usually busy, as it is the principal route to and from Barrow. Between it and the coastal road lies an area of some interest, and those with time to spare might profitably resort to the back lanes through Stainton and Great Urswick. These lie in a limestone country that might have been transported from the Yorkshire Dales. Great Urswick contains a number of buildings of character and backs on to a small tarn. Birkrigg Common, to the east, is a popular spot for picnics.

14 Ulverston to Coniston & Langdale

Distances from Ulverston: Greenodd $3\frac{1}{2}$m (Spark Bridge 5m), Blawith $7\frac{1}{2}$m, Torver $11\frac{3}{4}$m, Coniston $14\frac{1}{4}$m, Elterwater 20m, Dungeon Ghyll (Gt Langdale) 23m, Skelwith Bridge $19\frac{1}{2}$m, Grasmere $22\frac{1}{2}$m, Ambleside 22m.

INTRODUCTION

Nearly all of this route is covered elsewhere in this book but in a rather disjointed fashion. The main road from Greenodd to Coniston, up the west side of the valley and lake is given here, although the unclassified road to the east is preferable. This road is best reached by turning off through Spark Bridge, via which it is 15m to Coniston (Route 3). The main road from Ulverston to Greenodd can be avoided by taking the B5281 to Broughton Beck and crossing the hill to Lowick, but this is much hillier (see map).

Ulverston is the most convenient southern railhead for Coniston, although the approach from Grange over Sands adds interest.

DESCRIPTION

For Ulverston see page 35. If coming from the station, carry straight on at the first traffic lights to include the town centre en route. The busy A590 is taken out of the town, a level road running below Hoad Hill. Beyond Greenodd the road, now winding and shady, traverses the beautiful valley of the Crake through the hamlets of Lowick and Blawith. The road is undulating without any long hills, the Coniston Fells intermittently showing themselves ahead.

The lake is not revealed until some way past its foot and for a mile or so this most attractive road is never far away from the shore. Beyond Oxen Park Bay the road turns away from the lake and points towards the Old Man, climbing up to the little village of Torver. For a while both mountain and lake are hidden until the splendid descent into Coniston. For Coniston and surroundings see page 55-6.

The road north of Coniston is most beautiful, even for

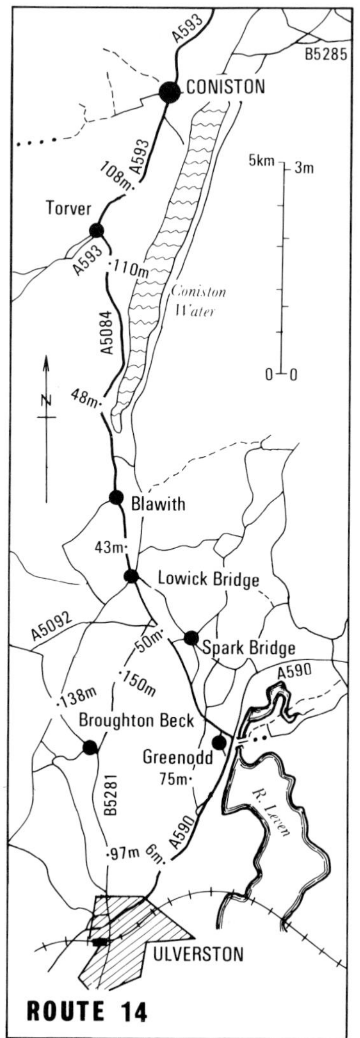

Lakeland, winding up sheltered Yewdale. Eventually the road climbs over Oxen Fell (500ft, 150 metres) to descend towards the magnificent mountain and valley scenery of Great and Little Langdale, a wonderful mixture of wood, rock and water. Four miles from Coniston, the road drops down left to Colwith Bridge (for nearby falls see page 59), beyond which the road for Langdale leads through woods to Elterwater, crossing a low rise on the way.

From Elterwater village it is an easy and beautiful run up to Dungeon Ghyll, at the foot of the majestic Langdale Pikes. For description see Route 11.

From Coniston, Grasmere may be reached either via Elterwater, as above, or by continuing along the Ambleside road to Skelwith Bridge. Either way, the distance is the same and both involve the long climb to the top of Red Bank (page 146) before the final descent to Grasmere. There is nothing to choose between the two routes as both run through most delightful scenery.

15 Broughton to Bootle & Ravenglass

Distances from Broughton: See below. If coming from Foxfield station add 1½m.

INTRODUCTION

For the cyclist eager to get to Ravenglass or the western dales to the north of the town, the road from Broughton via Ulpha and over Birker Fell is recommended; the routes described below are more appropriate for those wishing to work their way leisurely up the coast. It must be admitted that this far-flung corner of Cumbria is more traversed by through traffic than visited for its own sake.

The main A595 offers the easiest road of all and should be considered if the weather is really bad, but the fell road from Duddon Bridge to Corney saves 7m and will be as quick, despite rising to 1,300ft (397 metres). The less energetic will possibly resort to the railway.

DESCRIPTION

(a) via A595 Broughton to Whicham (A5093 jc) 7½m, Bootle 11¾m, Broad Oak 16¼m, (Eskdale Green 21¾m), Ravenglass 20m.

This will be described first for convenience rather than as a recommendation. A hilly road for some miles beyond Duddon Bridge, it eventually drops into the broad Whicham Valley. Even here there are some nasty surprises in the shape of some short steep pitches. Silecroft village, just off the Millom road near Whicham, leads down to the sea where there is a long empty beach.

Millom (7½m from Broughton, 7½m from Bootle) is unlikely to be visited unless one leaves the train there. It is a small industrial town, formerly based on iron-making, to which its folk museum is devoted.

North of Whicham the road to Bootle is excellent, running below the towering bluffs of Black Combe. Views of the sea are largely cut off by a low ridge, in this coastal strip the valleys run north/south.

The road shown on some maps looping round the coast

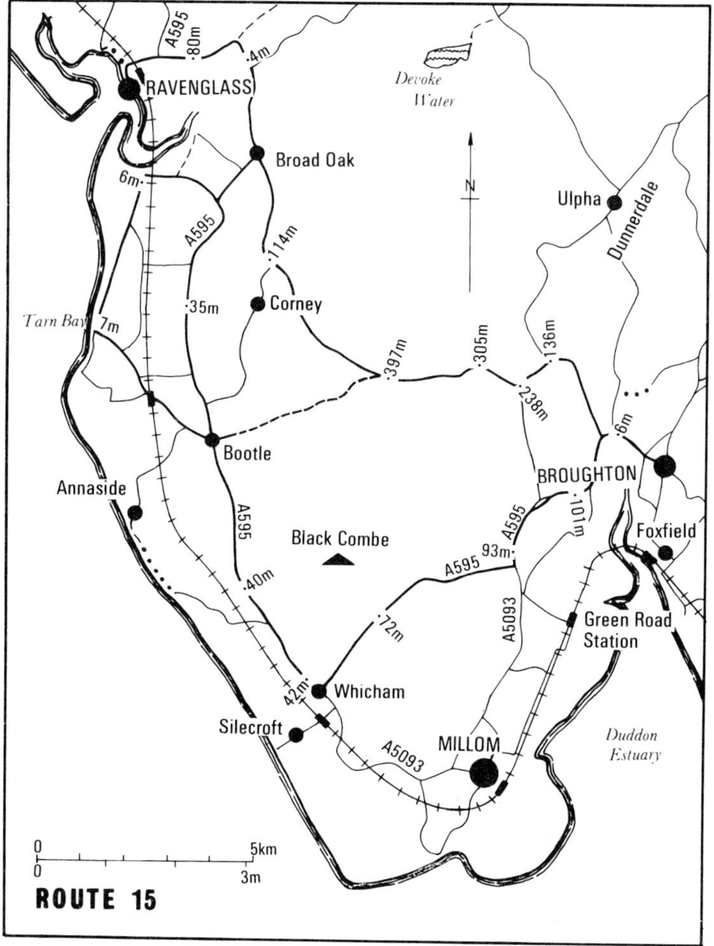

between Gutterby and Annaside is no longer passable except on foot, a ¼m section having been washed away some time ago. Elsewhere it is very muddy and cannot be recommended. The OS map marks it only as a public footpath.

There is nothing of particular note in Bootle, though the village is pleasant enough. Northwards, one may either continue on the main road or turn off to the coast (see below). The A595 remains a fast, gently-undulating road, rising in about three miles to meet the road down from Corney Fell at the hamlet of

Broad Oak. The greenery of the Esk valley and the wooded slopes of Muncaster Fell provide a welcoming scene. The prominent peak visible from the Esk bridge is Bow Fell — a shapely profile from any angle. Across the valley a steep climb leads past the wooded grounds of Muncaster Castle before a corresponding descent brings one into Ravenglass. For the village see page 63.

Bootle to Ravenglass via Eskmeals
This adds 2½m. The road winds down to Stubb Place and the edge of the sea — a point not made apparent on the OS Tourist Map. There is plenty of good castle-building sand and pebbles of every colour, while all the normal trappings of a seaside resort are conspicuously absent. Turning north, the road runs inland again, separated from the coast by the M.O.D. Proof & Establishment Station, a rather depressing series of buildings. Eventually the banks of the Esk are reached, and the road ducks down under the railway viaduct. The road under the bridge is very low-lying and impassable at high tide.

Beyond the railway, a pleasant prospect opens up of the Esk valley and the distant fells, a most peaceful scene. The lane winds its way through Newbiggin to join the main road at Waberthwaite Lane End, 4½m south of Ravenglass.

(b) Via the Fell Road
Broughton to hill summit 5¼m, Bootle (direct) 8¼m, Broad Oak 9½m, Ravenglass 13¼m.

This is the shortest route from Broughton to Ravenglass, and, although scenically inferior to that via Ulpha and Eskdale (about sixteen miles), it has the better distant views, first of the Lakeland fells on the long ascent, and then, westwards, to the sea.

Ravenglass

From Broughton the intervening hill is crossed before the road dips down to the fine old bridge over the Duddon. Turning right after the bridge (signposted Corney) the road soon passes the remains of Duddon Furnace, one of the most important industrial archaeology sites in Cumbria. The charcoal-fed furnace was in operation from 1736 to 1867, and it is hoped to undertake some restoration work on the buildings.

The road onwards rises steadily through the woods that border the river, the gradient gradually steepening as the road swings up a tributary valley, but easing on emerging above the trees. Pulling up the open fell, a grand and extensive prospect of the Cumbrian mountains opens out above Dunnerdale. Ahead, the road strikes determinedly up the moor, with the rocky height of Buckbarrow Crag providing a contrast with the smooth grassy hills around. An intermediate ridge, a thousand feet (300 metres) up, is eventually crossed before a gentler slope resumes.

The final summit comes suddenly, with the sea seemingly at one's feet. Ahead can be seen the Isle of Man, behind which are the Mountains of Mourne in Northern Ireland. Northwards are the Galloway Hills in Scotland. Looking up the coast the cooling towers of Sellafield are visible, and beyond are the red cliffs of St Bees Head. Southwards, the view is totally shut in by the sprawling mass of Black Combe. A stroll may be taken to the little tump of Stoneside Hill, half a mile from the road, but the view is not appreciably wider.

Direct road to Bootle

This is signposted as 'unfit for cars' but is quite suitable for cyclists, if not too heavily laden. It is all rideable, with a little care, but rather bumpy. For those who like to 'get away from it all' it will be found ideal. For routes north of Bootle, see above.

The right fork just beyond the summit drops steeply, a real slog coming up, but holding no problems when descending. Further on, the fall is more gradual, with one or two steep pitches. Eventually, enclosed fields are re-entered as the road levels out to become a pleasant country lane. On the way, there is an unexpected but unmistakable view of Great Gable, framed between the 'wrong' side of the Wasdale Screes and Sca Fell. The main A595 is joined at Broad Oak, about four miles short of Ravenglass. Before reaching the village the road rises to 250ft (80 metres) in crossing the intervening ridge past Muncaster Castle.

16 Broughton to Eskdale & Wasdale

Distances from Broughton: Ulpha 4½m, Eskdale Green 11½m, Santon Bridge 14m, Gosforth (direct) 17m, Strands (Nether Wasdale) 16¼m, Wasdale Head 21m.
Add 1½m if coming from Foxfield station.

INTRODUCTION

A feature of the western dales — Dunnerdale, Eskdale, Wasdale and Ennerdale — is their limited accessibility from the central and eastern part of the Lake District. Apart from the road over Wrynose and Hard Knott passes, there are no practicable routes between Broughton in the south and Keswick in the north. Although the route from Ambleside is, despite various shortcomings, the most direct approach, this alternative way round via Broughton may find favour with some cyclists. Foxfield station, just south of Broughton, provides a starting point for those arriving by train, although Ulverston (page 35) is almost as convenient.

The scenery is attractive all the way, apart from a rather plain section over Birker Fell — a climb of about 700ft (200 metres). In the reverse direction there is a similar climb out of Eskdale.

DESCRIPTION

From Broughton there is a climb up through the town's narrow streets to the crossroads at the top of the hill, after which the road plunges down to the coastal levels of the rivers Lickle and Duddon. In a little way the road on the right to Ulpha is taken. This soon begins a very steep climb through woods, emerging from which the cyclist is greeted with a fine view up the valley, though none of the higher fells can be seen. The road now runs along the hillside beneath some impressive crags before dropping to the scattered hamlet of Ulpha. The rocky river bed here is a lovely green hue. There is a shop cum post office at Ulpha, but the nearest inn is at Seathwaite, a little further up the valley.

Upper Dunnerdale: So inviting is the view up the Duddon valley that many cyclists will be keen to explore it more closely before girding their loins to tackle Birker Fell. Not a few will find themselves completing the

16

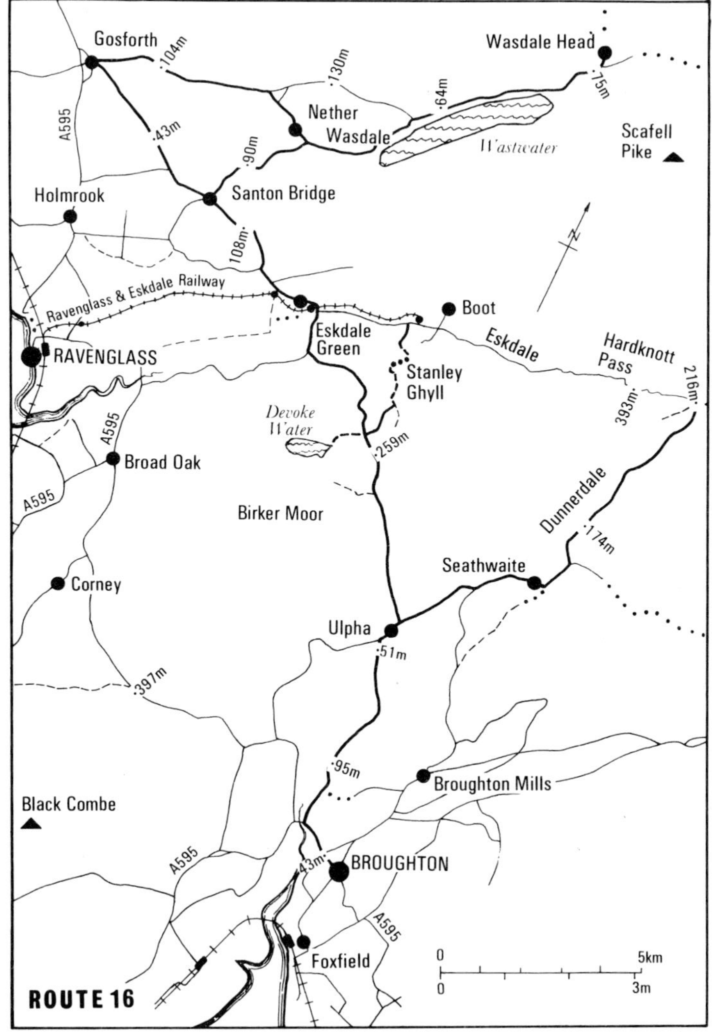

seven miles from Ulpha to Cockley Beck Bridge, where the road from Ambleside is reached and continuing into Eskdale via the Hard Knott Pass; such is the attraction of Dunnerdale.

From Ulpha an easy run of about two miles brings one to Seathwaite, a charmingly situated hamlet near where the river Duddon emerges from a deep gorge. Various paths lead down to the stepping stones by the river, a most lovely spot below Wallowbarrow Gorge. Above Seathwaite the road climbs to the divergence of the track via Walna Scar to Coniston, drops briefly, then climbs again finally to come out on the open fellside high above the Duddon. The valley closes in once more as the river is rejoined but the gradients are gentle for the remainder of the way to Cockley Beck. Birks Bridge, with the river flowing deep below, is the starting point for various Forestry Commission waymarked footpaths and also for a boggy track to Dunnerdale (Black Hall) Youth Hostel. The youth hostel is best reached by a track from Cockley Beck Bridge, a couple of miles further on. Cockley Beck marks the end of scenic Dunnerdale, the valley towards Wrynose Pass being rather desolate. Ambleside to Eskdale via Wrynose and Hard Knott is described in Route 10.

Main route continued

The climb from Ulpha is initially very steep, requiring care when descending in the reverse direction. As the open moor is reached the gradient eases, the road becoming undulating and rather uninteresting for a few miles until quite suddenly the foreground falls away to reveal a grand mountain panorama ahead. These are the fells that border Eskdale with, at its head, the finely-shaped pyramid of Bow Fell. Sca Fell presents a somewhat bulky profile. To its left are Kirk Fell and Pillar, on the far side of Wasdale. Progressing a little further, Eskdale itself comes into view, a fertile green valley dotted with farmsteads. On the descent a signpost is reached at a crossroads.

The turning to the left (rough at first but soon improving) leads in about half a mile to Devoke Water, a sizeable tarn in bleak surroundings. The road down to the right leads to Boot, and is tarred as far as High Ground Farm and metalled from there to Low Ground. Thereafter, following a short boggy patch, it descends to the top of a wood with good views ahead to Sca Fell. Crook Crag and Green Crag provide a rugged eastern skyline. The descent through the wood is too rough to cycle but improves at the bottom. Watch out for a gate on the right, leading to Stanley Ghyll and the waterfall, one of the main attractions of Eskdale (see Route 10).

The road on to Eskdale Green descends steeply in places, but on the whole is an exhilarating cycle run. The bracken-clad slopes are a blaze of colour in late autumn. With remarkable abruptness the flat valley bottom is reached as the road turns up the dale a little way. On the left, a turning leads down to the coast at Ravenglass (5¾m) and ¾m further, after crossing the Esk, the road down from Hard Knott and Boot is joined at the King George IV Inn. The detour up Eskdale to the foot of Hard Knott

Wastwater

is a most pleasant and worthwhile digression and can readily be recommended. For a description see Route 10. From the inn it is a short uphill ride to the small village of Eskdale Green, crossing the Ravenglass & Eskdale Railway on the way. The village is charmingly situated on a low wooded hill, dividing the valleys of the rivers Esk and Mite. The upper part of Miterdale is very secluded but a narrow road leading up it may be followed for a mile or two from a turning just west of Irton Road station.

The road on to Wasdale and the coast descends to, and crosses, the Mite, and soon bears right to climb a steep wooded hillside, to wind among leafy knolls and slopes before dropping steeply to Santon Bridge.

The highest of these knolls, Irton Pike, presents an excellent all-round view at the cost of 10-15min walk up from the road. This should be left a little west of the car park entrance, by the FC sign. Crossing a forestry road the path runs straight up the hillside to emerge on the open summit. The views extend over Wastwater to Great Gable.

At Santon Bridge the road ahead leads in three easy miles to Gosforth on the main coast road, but few cyclists will have come this far and not wish to visit Wastwater. The road to the lake and Wasdale turns right just before the bridge. From the top of the following hill the cyclist is rewarded with a first sight of the famous screes and a tiny glimpse of the lake. A gentle descent leads to the bridge over the Irt, with the trim little village of Strands (or Nether Wasdale, as it is now referred to) seen on the left. A little way along the Strands branch road is the War Memorial shelter, a useful refuge for anyone caught in the rain. The road forward to the lake winds beneath a fine avenue of trees, with the river below on the right. The pink tinge noticeable in the walls bordering the road and in parts of the screes opposite betrays the presence of various ores of iron in the rock. After skirting the grounds of Wasdale Hall, now a youth hostel, the road drops to the lakeside with the view up the valley revealed uninterrupted for the first time.

Ahead is the famous prospect of Great Gable framed by Yewbarrow and Lingmell which has been the subject of many a picture. Sca Fell and Scafell Pike only come into prominence higher up the lake as the screes are passed. The screes, sloping at an angle of about 40° and towering nearly 1,700ft (500 metres) above the lake are an impressive sight. From the way they drop straight down to the water's edge it is not hard to appreciate why Wasdale can claim England's deepest lake as well as her highest mountain.

The journey up the valley is one of magnificent scenery throughout and enjoyed in no better way than from a bicycle. The road twists and turns, but never strays far from the waterside while the ever-changing outline of the mountains holds the interest. At the end of the lake one may be surprised to see a broad and fertile strath rather than the bare upland vale one might have expected, but although hemmed in by hills the dale bottom is still less than 250ft (80 metres) above the sea. A mile beyond the end of the lake is the hotel at Wasdale Head, together with a shop and public toilets.

After looking round Wasdale Head there is not much else for the cyclist to do except to turn round and follow the road back down the lake. The paths over to Ennerdale and Borrowdale, given in Routes 42 and 40, involve a lot of hard work and are not short cuts to anywhere.

Wasdale Head to Strands (5½m) and Gosforth (9½m)

The road back down the lake must be retraced, but this is no imposition even though the finest views are now behind. On nearing the foot of the lake the direct road to Gosforth bears off to the right to climb toward the rocky knoll of Buckbarrow. It saves half a mile over the road through Strands, but this longer road is certainly more attractive. The village is nicely situated on a south-facing hill, over which the Gosforth road runs to rejoin the direct road in a mile. One more hill has to be crossed before the outskirts of the village are reached, strung out for a mile to the main road. On the way the church, with its old Viking cross in the churchyard, is passed. The cross is about 14ft (4 metres) high and estimated to date from about 1000 AD. For the continuation up the coast from Gosforth see Route 17.

Ravenglass to Egremont & Cockermouth

17

Distances from Ravenglass: Holmrook 2½m (Seascale 5¾m), Gosforth 5¼m, Calder Bridge 7½m, Egremont 11½m, Wath Brow 14½m, Frizington 16¼m (Lamplugh Green 21m), Rowrah 18¼m, Cockermouth 28m.

These distances are via the footbridge route out of Ravenglass, described below, which saves half a mile on the main road.

INTRODUCTION

This is the main road round, but outside, the periphery of the Lake District, but the tourist will use very little of it, as the chief places of interest lie off-route; the coast on one side and the magnificent mountainscapes of Wasdale and Ennerdale on the other. Industry also makes its presence felt, with the nuclear power complex of Sellafield (Windscale) and the old iron-producing tract around Egremont and Cleator. Apart from the occasional distant views the scenery is very ordinary.

The road is undulating but contains no taxing hills and the traffic is not high by 'A' road standards. Most industrial traffic is centred on Whitehaven and Workington. Variations worth considering include the road over Cold Fell between Calder Bridge and Ennerdale Bridge (Route 28) and minor roads from Egremont to Ennerdale Bridge and Lamplugh (Route 26).

DESCRIPTION

From Ravenglass the shortest way north is to wheel the cycle over the footbridge alongside the railway bridge to Saltcoats, on the north side of the river Mite. The hillier road out of the village leads up to the main A595, which passes the restored Muncaster Cornmill with its water-powered machinery. The two roads unite and continue on easy gradients through Holmrook to Gosforth. The centre of the village lies to the right of the main road and should be visited for its ninth-century cross in the churchyard, a little way down the Wasdale road.

17

COCKERMOUTH
Great Broughton
Seaton
Brigham
A595
A66
WORKINGTON
Eaglesfield
74m
A596
Branthwaite
153m
Harrington
B5296
Ullock
250m
Mockerkin
99m
Distington
51m
A5086
Loweswater
201m
181m
A595
141m
Lamplugh
Parton
165m
Rowrah
202m
254m
Croasdale
WHITEHAVEN
174m
Kirkland
162m
125m
198m
Frizington
120m
B5295
125m
90m
B5294
Ennerdale Bridge
B5345
CLEATOR MOOR
North Head
83m
77m
Ennerdale Water
Sandwith
126m
A595
A5086
St Bees Head
90m
95m
293m
St Bees
60m
South Head
55m
48m
109m
EGREMONT
B5345
209m
A595
78m
46m
39m
29m
Nethertown
Beckermet
15m
Calder Bridge
Braystones
A595
104m
BNFL Sellafield
Sellafield Station
Gosforth
52m
B5344
A595
Santon Bridge
Seascale
B5344
Holmrook
Drigg
19m
0
5km
0
3m
RAVENGLASS
ROUTE 17

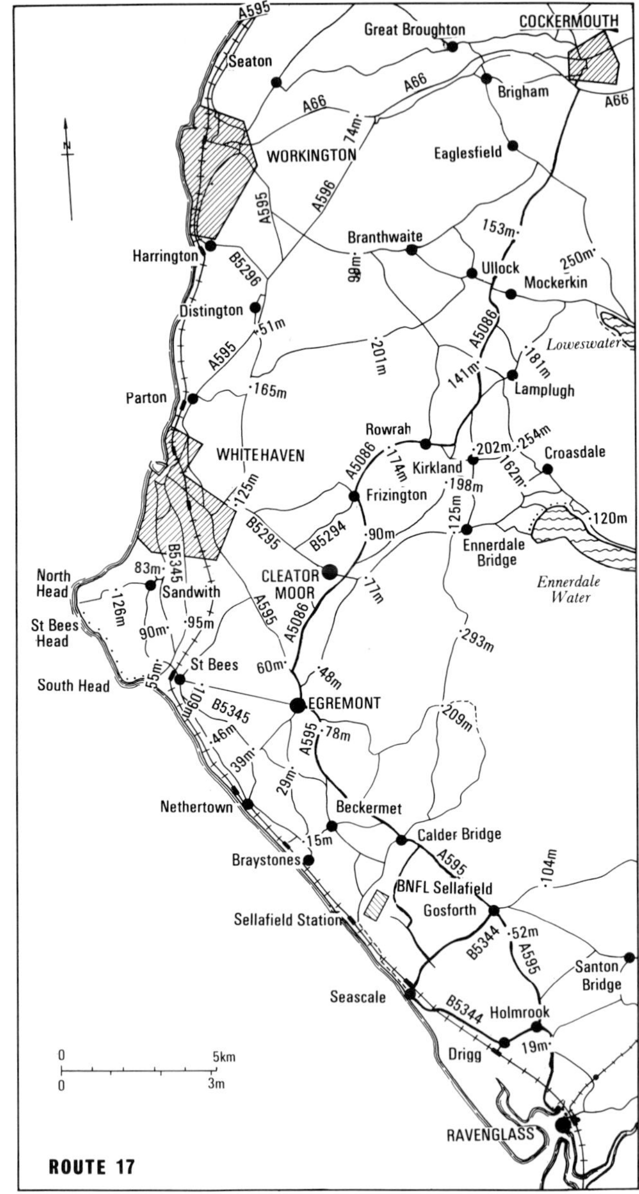

Seascale: This small resort might be conveniently included in any cycle tour of Lakeland. It offers a range of accommodation and acres of sandy beach with good bathing, yet is only an hour's ride from Eskdale or Wasdale. It has a station on the coast railway line and so makes a convenient railhead for these western dales.
Distances from Seascale: Ravenglass 5¾m, Eskdale Green 7½m, Gosforth 2¾m, Wasdale Head 11¾m.

If continuing north from Seascale the best road is via Gosforth. The corner to Calder Bridge may be cut by what must have once been a pleasant country lane through Calder. It is now dominated by the works and in rather poor repair. There is also a path alongside the railway between Seascale and Sellafield stations (1¾m) whence the road skirts the B.N.F.L. complex before turning left for Beckermet and Egremont (7½m). By using this, nearly all of the main road between Ravenglass and Egremont may be avoided.

Beyond Gosforth the road rises to cross some intervening high ground before descending to Calder Bridge. The remains of Calder Abbey (page 135) lie about a mile east but are not currently open to the public. North of the village the road winds up and down on its way to Egremont. To escape briefly from the main road, one can turn off through Beckermet, a pleasant village.

Egremont is entered below the castle, a sandstone ruin of which little now remains. The town centre consists of one broad main street, cheerful enough, but the side streets betray its industrial character. A bypass for the town is proposed.

St Bees Head: The vicinity of St Bees, lying just west of Egremont, boasts the highest cliffs on the north-west coast of England. St Bees village may be approached direct from Beckermet or from Egremont (3¾m by the signposted route, longer but easier than the direct road via Orgill). Unfortunately, the roads in the vicinity seem to have been deliberately planned to provide hard work for the cyclist, defying the lie of the land and natural justice. The route to the village direct from Egremont is a series of ups and downs, as is the road north to Whitehaven (4m), which rises 300ft (90 metres).

The older part of St Bees, quite interesting, is south of the station. Further north, just below the cliffs, is a small promenade and a pebbly beach, with sand at low tide. The cliffs themselves offer a grand ramble as far as the North Head and lighthouse (3m), passing the secluded little bay of Fleswick. The lane from Sandwith to the lighthouse is proclaimed to be private — ie no vehicles.

Between Egremont and Lamplugh, halfway to Cockermouth, there is a choice of roads. The more attractive is via Ennerdale

Ravenglass

Bridge, from which Ennerdale itself might be visited. This is described the reverse way in Route 26. The main road runs through a string of industrial communities, unattractive in themselves but giving the visitor a more balanced picture of Cumbria as a whole. This part of the county prospered in the nineteenth century with the exploitation of iron ore and coal deposits, but since the decline of these industries has always struggled to attract alternative employment.

From Egremont the Cockermouth road turns right in ½m and drops through the old village of Cleator. Rising again to Wath Brow the road is lined with long terraces of cottages, rather reminiscent of the Welsh valleys. Cleator Moor town centre lies just off to the left. Frizington, the next community reached, is another industrial village strung out for a mile along the main road, which rises to over 600ft (174 metres) a little beyond. The views are uninteresting other than towards the distant rift of Ennerdale, too far away to be appreciated. Through Arlecdon and Rowrah the road is accompanied by disused railways and old spoil heaps, but a little further on the mining area is left and there is unspoilt if unspectacular countryside for the remainder of the way. At Lamplugh Cross the road through Lamplugh Green over to Loweswater bears right (Route 26).

The road onwards to Cockermouth is easy going and requires little comment, its most singular feature being that although a number of villages lie just off the road none is actually on it in the ten miles from Rowrah. The western fells occasionally reveal themselves but otherwise there is nothing of note. There is a long gradual fall to the Cockermouth bypass, with a steeper descent thence into the town. For Cockermouth see page 118.

Ravenglass to Wasdale

18

Distances from Ravenglass: Santon Bridge 5m, Nether Wasdale (Strands) $7\frac{1}{4}$m, Wasdale Head 12m.

INTRODUCTION

A link road providing a transition from the sandy shores of the coast through the rich scenery of the lower valleys of the Esk and Mite to the rugged grandeur of Wasdale. Its mountain peaks are visible ahead for much of the way. The road described below is nearly all unclassified, but nevertheless carries a considerable amount of motor traffic. There are various side lanes and bridleways that will appeal to the leisurely explorer.

DESCRIPTION

From Ravenglass cross the river Mite by the footbridge, alongside the railway, which later bears left to pick up the lane through Saltcoats. This soon joins the A595 but this is followed northwards for only about half a mile to the point where the road to Wasdale turns right. This is only signposted for Irton and Eskdale, motor traffic for Wasdale being encouraged to turn off north of Holmrook. A short hill brings one out onto an extensive plain, sloping gently from north to

Wastwater

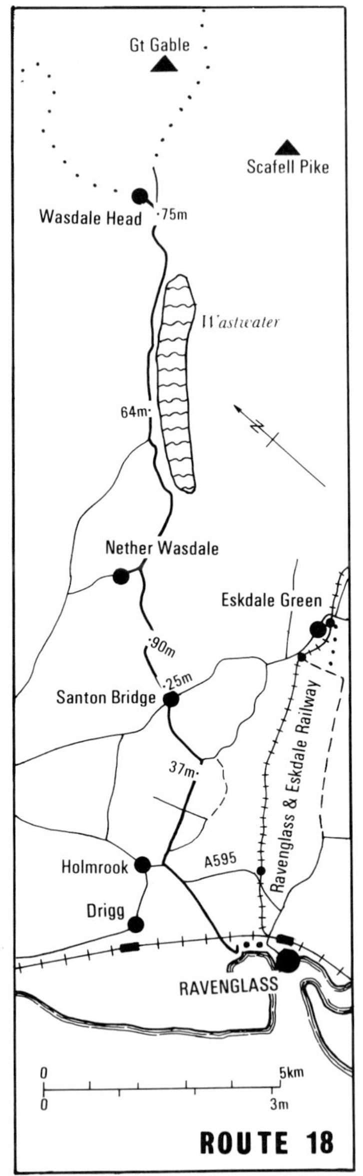

south, across which the road runs straight. Irton Church, seen up on the left, contains an old cross in the graveyard. Passing Irton Hall, the road is hemmed in with richly-wooded slopes as it drops to the river Irt — fine scenery indeed. There is an unexpected and unwelcome hill, before the road drops to the river again at Santon Bridge.

The road on to Wasdale is more fully described in Route 16. After an initial climb the road is an easy one and of ever increasing interest and beauty. The lakeside is joined shortly after passing above the grounds of Wasdale Hall.

Perhaps nowhere in the Lake District is the cyclist at such an advantage over other modes of transport. The walker, anxious to get among the hills, will certainly appreciate the scenery but will find the four miles along the lakeside time-consuming and the views changing too slowly to satisfy his eye. The motorist following the twisting single-track lane will have to concentrate on the road and dodging the hikers and sheep while his passengers will be straining their necks to get the best view. Only the cyclist has the freedom to stop whenever he pleases and to take in the scenery at his own speed.

Kendal to Penrith & Ullswater via Shap

19

Distances from Kendal: High Borrow Bridge 8¾m, Demings Moss (summit, 1,397ft, 426 metres) 10½m, Shap 16½m, Hackthorpe 21¾m, Eamont Bridge 25½m, Penrith 26¾m.

Shap to Bampton 4¼m, Haweswater Dam 6½m, Askham 8m (Penrith 13m), Pooley Bridge 11½m.

NB There are about eight trains a day from Oxenholme station (2m south of Kendal) to Penrith.

INTRODUCTION

The old North Road, now largely superseded by the M6 motorway, was one of the first roads out of Kendal to be turnpiked; the first stagecoach over Shap ran in 1763. The road was extensively rebuilt in the decade to 1825, the date shown on the surviving mileposts. The old road, partly abandoned, runs parallel for most of the way to Shap.

The road is a hilly one taking a direct course across the eastern shoulders of the fells, which the railway and the M6 wisely skirt. The highest point on the road — on top of Demings Moss — is 1,397ft (426 metres), compared with 914ft (279 metres) on the railway. The comparison can be made with later turnpike roads which took a more compromising attitude to the lie of the land. Having said this, however, the road is extremely well graded for the country traversed.

The quality of the scenery is not high, but the road can never be called dull. As all points of interest lie off the direct route, notes are included on the 'Westmorland' Borrowdale and routes north of Shap to Swindale and Haweswater as well as down the Lowther valley to Ullswater and Penrith.

DESCRIPTION

The first few miles are uninteresting, the road climbing steadily through low rounded hills. About four miles from Kendal there is a good retrospective view and, a little further on, the road looks down on the pretty hamlet of Garnett

19

PENRITH
B6412
Culgarth
A66
Eamont Bridge
Temple Sowerby
130m
Clifton
A66
Pooley
Bridge
Cliburn
Bolton
323m
Askham
Hackthorpe
Ullswater
224m
A6
245m
Bampton
B6260
279m
315m
SHAP
Haweswater
Crosby
Ravensworth
Swindale
270m
B6261
A6
Orton
Shap Fells
426m
A685
Longsleddale
Tebay
303m
168m
A6
A591
Staveley
A685
301m
161m
Grayrigg
B5284
52m
KENDAL
Oxenholme
0
5km
0
3m
ROUTE 19

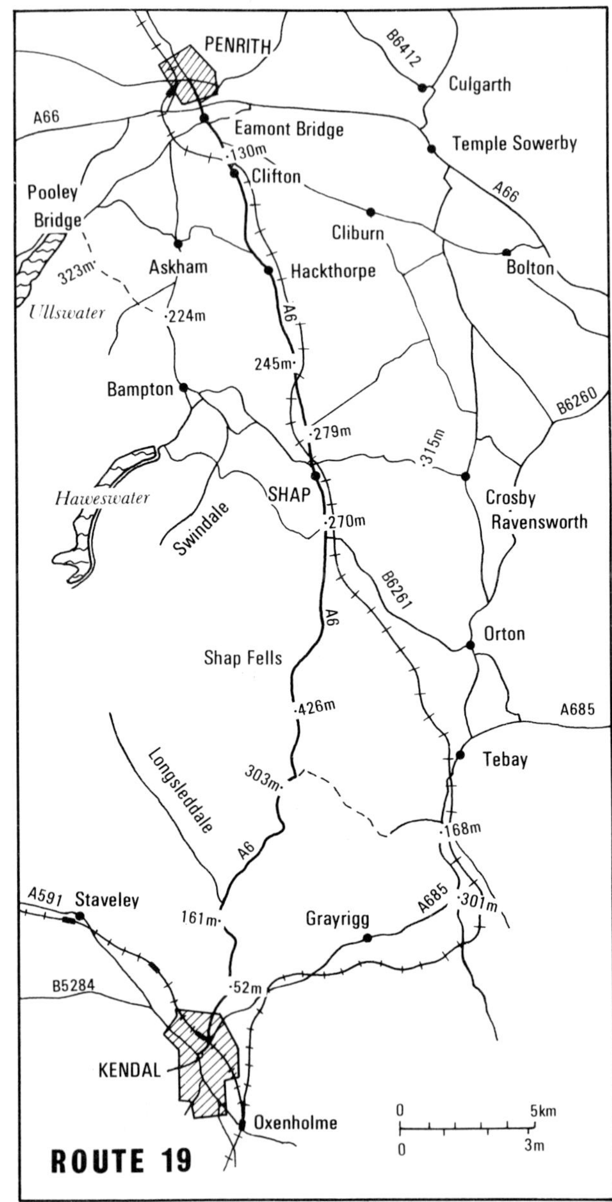

Bridge, standing at the foot of Longsleddale. This charming valley may be followed for about five miles to the road end at Sadgill, but the cyclist who still has to face the assault on Shap will probably resolve to explore it another day. After an undulating stretch, dipping into Bannisdale (nice little loop road on left), a long but not oversteep climb leads to the first major summit — Huck's Brow, 994ft (303 metres) — where the road drops to the Borrow Beck, a tributary of the Lune.

Borrowdale: This quiet valley merits exploration. From Huck's Brow a roughly-metalled track (no signpost) leads down to Low Borrow Bridge (4½m, about ¾-1hr), in the Lune Gorge. It can be used by cyclists all the way, with a little care. The valley, given over to sheep farming, becomes more wooded lower down. From Low Borrow Bridge a return can be made direct to Kendal (9½m) by the A685 or, much more interestingly, by taking the narrow road along the foot of the Howgill Fells to Sedbergh (7½m). This is a most attractively situated little town at the entrance to Dentdale. Sedbergh back to Kendal is 11m, the road rising to 930ft (284 metres).

Main route continued
From High Borrow Bridge there is an unbroken climb for 1¾m to the highest point on the road — Demings Moss (1,397ft, 426 metres). The climb is only relieved by the quiet beauty of Crookdale, the valley eventually deserted by the road. The summit is unappealing, the view extensive but lacking any prominent features other than the various quarries. The immediate surroundings are bleak and windswept.

Askham

The 6m on from the summit to Shap begin with a long descent and then a fast run past the granite works and railway summit. The village, strung out along the once-busy A6, still caters well for the traveller. Its chief claims to fame are its bracing air, which it has in abundance, and the ruins of Shap Abbey. The abbey ruins are situated beside the river Lowther a mile west of the village, reached from the Bampton road. The massive west tower is largely intact, but the remainder of the building has suffered from four centuries of neglect and plunder.

Shap is 11m west of Appleby, by a hilly road through Crosby Ravensworth, in the secluded valley of the river Lyvennet.

(a) Shap to Swindale and Haweswater

From Shap to Haweswater the prettier way is through Bampton Grange, on the road to Ullswater, as described below. An alternative, which permits a visit to Swindale en route, is to take the turning through Keld, beyond which the lane climbs to cross the concrete road built in connection with the Haweswater reservoir scheme. Although not a right of way there can be no objection to its use by pedal cyclists at their own risk. The gate at the A6 end is kept locked, but it may be joined at any of the public road crossings. The reservoir road winds impressively across the moor, meeting after a few miles the road from Bampton to Swindale. This little valley deserves to be visited more often than it is, although this would destroy its air of remoteness and solitude. There is a tarred road as far as Swindale Head, about six miles from Shap. The valley is most attractive and in parts is reminiscent of Great Langdale, though on a smaller scale.

Returning to pick up the reservoir road again, the Haweswater dam is reached in a further 2m. For Haweswater see Route 21.

(b) Shap to Ullswater

From the north end of the village a side road is taken, which after a few miles of high ground makes a splendid descent to Bampton Grange. Continuing down the Lowther valley, one comes through a succession of pretty villages and hamlets to Askham, with its grass-bordered lanes and old cottages. Beyond Askham the signposted way to Ullswater is via Tirril, but the cyclist should take the narrow lane through Celleron, which drops to the foot of the lake at Pooley Bridge.

An alternative route to Pooley Bridge is via the track over Moor Divock (1,061ft, 323 metres), leaving the Lowther valley a little south of Helton. Starting as the road to Widewath Farm, it continues as a metalled lane between splendid examples of dry-stone walling before ending at a gate. A finger post on the horizon marks where the correct path crosses a tarred road up from Helton. The moorland section beyond is rideable throughout, a broad track of turf or fine stone leading unhesitatingly across the rolling acres of bracken. Eventually Ullswater, backed by the Helvellyn range comes into view on the long gradual descent to Pooley Bridge.

(c) Shap to Penrith

Here the alternative is between the quiet lanes down the Lowther valley and keeping to the A6. The latter is much the faster route and nowadays has only light traffic. After the summit, a mile or so north of the village, the trend is downhill to Eamont Bridge: southbound the gradients will be found steady rather than steep. The road is accompanied by the railway and motorway and runs through surprisingly well-wooded country around Hackthorpe, where a branch road leads to Lowther Castle and Askham. The castle is now only a shell, with part of the grounds made into a wildlife park of European fauna. The main road continues through Clifton, with its defensive pele tower, to Eamont Bridge, which marks the former boundary between Westmorland and Cumberland. Some notes on the antiquities of the vicinity are given under Route 22. Penrith is a mile beyond the bridge, a bustling market town mainly built of red Sandstone. The ruins of its castle are just by the railway station.

20 Approaches from Carlisle

Distances: See below.

INTRODUCTION

As the Border City is the focal point for many routes from Scotland and the north-east of England, some brief notes on the various approaches from there to the principal centres in the Lake District may be useful. It should be pointed out that from south of Carlisle to the fringe of Lakeland the scenery is not of a high standard and the roads are rather uninteresting. An exception is the coast route from Carlisle to Maryport, which is described separately (Route 29).

In spite of, or rather because of, its turbulent past as the centre of conflict between Englishman and Scot, Carlisle retains comparatively few historical buildings and dates mainly from the last and present centuries. The principal points of interest in the town are most easily included by a walk north from the station to the castle ($\frac{1}{2}$m). Passing the mainly nineteenth-century Citadel, continue along English Street to the Old Town Hall, now an information centre. Nearby is the fifteenth-century Guildhall, recently restored. Continuing up Castle Street one comes to the red sandstone Cathedral, the Tullie House Museum and finally the castle itself.

(a) Carlisle to Penrith

High Hesket 8$\frac{3}{4}$m, Plumpton Wall 13$\frac{1}{2}$m, Penrith 18m.

The obvious route via the A6 is a good straight road with easy gradients. There are two parallel routes, only slightly longer, traversing the old Inglewood Forest, but, as nearly all traffic now uses the motorway, there is no need to avoid the A6 on this account. The most pleasant ways are along the Eden Valley.

(b) Carlisle to Ullswater via Greystoke

Hutton in the Forest 13$\frac{1}{2}$m (Penrith 19m), Greystoke 17$\frac{1}{2}$m, Dacre 21$\frac{1}{4}$m, Pooley Bridge 24m, Dockray 24$\frac{3}{4}$m (Patterdale 29$\frac{1}{2}$m).

A quiet cross-country route through Inglewood Forest, a royal hunting chase enclosed and cleared at the beginning of the nineteenth century; most of the roads are straight, and the villages few in number. Carlisle is best left by following the A6

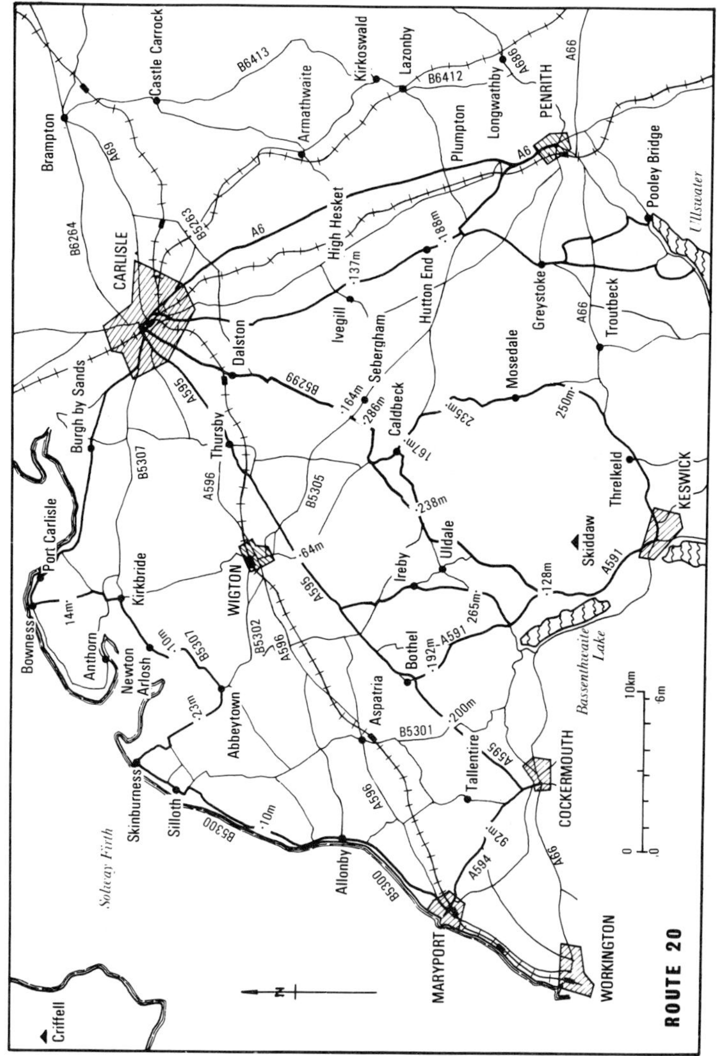

south from the station, turning right in ¼m (signposted Blackwell). This crosses the railway and continues as Blackwell Road, bearing left where joined by Currock Road. After passing the racecourse on the outskirts of the town, there is nothing of note until Hutton in the Forest, the road flat and monotonous.

The house, seventeenth century, and gardens are occasionally open. The road onwards now becomes more varied, the Lakeland peaks beyond Ullswater making a welcome appearance ahead. Blencow village contains many old buildings, none more interesting than Blencow Hall. For Greystoke see page 113.

There are various roads from Greystoke to Ullswater, all traversing high ground. Perhaps the best route, as it enables all of the lake to be followed, is via Dacre (its castle is interesting but private) to Pooley Bridge. The alternative road south from Greystoke to Bennet Head (turn right there) gives a grand terrace-view of Ullswater before the road descends past Watermillock church. The most direct road to Patterdale rises to 1,000ft (300 metres) before Matterdale, with a magnificent descent from there to the shores of Ullswater. For continuation see Route 22.

(c) Carlisle to Keswick & Cockermouth
Thursby 6¼m (Wigton 11½m), Red Dial 11½m, Mealsgate 15½m, Bothel 18¼m, Castle Inn 23¼m, Keswick 30¾m, Cockermouth 25¾m.

NB For coast route between Carlisle & Cockermouth see Route 29.

The old Roman road from Carlisle to Papcastle, near Cockermouth, is good, sufficiently undulating to avoid boredom and has no long hills save a gradual one near Bothel. The small market town of Wigton may be included at the cost of an extra couple of miles. Beyond Bothel the Cockermouth road rises to nearly 700ft (200 metres) and keeps to high ground with a consequently long hill into the town. For Cockermouth see page 118.

The Keswick road beyond Bothel is much quieter, despite extensive improvements. It rises to 631ft (192 metres) just

Keswick Moot Hall

beyond Bothel, gradually losing height before the Castle Inn. An alternative road, shorter but hillier, turns off the A595 14m from Carlisle to run through Boltongate and Ireby, an interesting old village and former market town. From the Castle Inn it is a pleasant run along the east side of Bassenthwaite Lake, though little of the lake itself is seen. For a fuller description, see Route 24.

It is difficult to say which is the better route between Carlisle and Keswick — via Bothel (main road throughout) or via Greystoke and Threlkeld. The distances are the same. The alternative through Caldbeck is rather hilly, rising to 938ft (286 metres). There is also the option of taking the trains as far as Aspatria, from where it is 8½m to Cockermouth, and 17½m to Keswick via Isel (page 117) and Castle Inn.

Maryport Harbour

21 Penrith to Haweswater

Distances from Penrith: Askham 5m, Helton 6m, Bampton 8¾m (Shap 13m), Haweswater Dam 11m, end of lake (Mardale Head) 15m.

From Pooley Bridge, on Ullswater, it is 3½m to Askham. For the track over Moor Divock (quite practicable) from Pooley Bridge to Helton, see Route 19.

INTRODUCTION

Haweswater is probably the least visited of the major lakes, including even the remoter Wastwater. Lying some way east of the main tourist beat and in a blind valley, it is difficult to include it in any itinerary without straying beyond the bounds of true Lakeland scenery. Nevertheless the approach from Penrith up the Lowther valley is, in a quiet way, very pleasant, and even if a first sight of the lake disappoints, the fine mountain setting of its upper reach will surely provide compensation.

The lake, originally 2½m long, was converted by Manchester Corporation into a reservoir in the 1930s and its level raised nearly 100ft (30 metres). Mardale, a name now lingering on only a few old signposts, was flooded and the one building in the valley is the Haweswater Hotel, purpose-built along with the present road.

As at Thirlmere, Haweswater's role as a source of water has hitherto prevented any public access to the shore, and similarly no bathing or boating is permitted. Although these restrictions are likely to be relaxed in the case of Thirlmere, it is proposed that Haweswater should be preserved as a 'quiet' lake.

DESCRIPTION

From Penrith the A6 is followed south to Eamont Bridge, after which the B5320 Pooley Bridge road is taken. Just by the junction is the so-called 'King Arthur's Round Table' (page 107). The next few miles on the branch road to Askham are gently uphill, and followed by a long descent to the village, during which the turrets of Lowther Castle are conspicuous across the valley. Askham presents a trim appear-

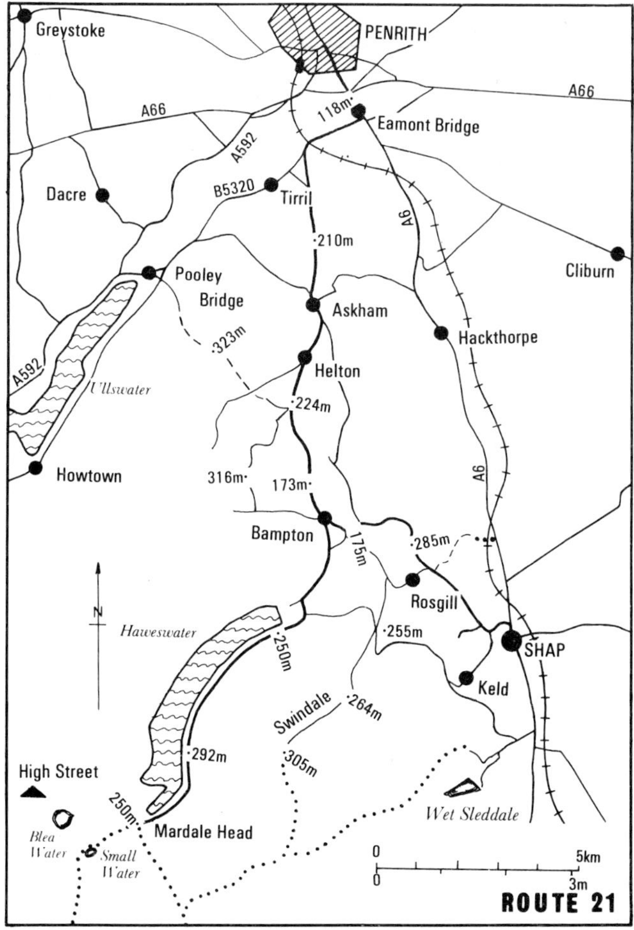

ance and is certainly one of the most attractive villages in Cumbria. It must be admitted that most Lakeland villages are straggling and prosaic in character; Askham corresponds much more with the usual conception of what a village should look like. Just to the east are Lowther Castle and Wildlife Park.

Continuing up the valley, the going is easy and the scenery fine. Bampton is another pleasant village at the junction of the roads to Shap and to Haweswater.

Swindale

Bampton to Shap
Of the two roads the upper (left through Bampton Grange) is preferable for the sake of the better views, over Haweswater to the High Street range, and easier gradients. The first mile is steep — then the road is more or less level. Shap Abbey (page 96) lies just off-route. For Swindale and the reservoir road from Haweswater to Shap, see Route 19.

Turning right in Bampton, the road to Haweswater soon enters a side valley and begins to climb through dense woodlands until the lake is suddenly revealed. The dam is completely concealed from below.

Haweswater reservoir lacks the charm of the other major lakes, its western shoreline is smooth and the surrounding fells are not distinctive. Beyond the Haweswater Hotel, however, the scenery improves considerably — the prominent feature being the long ridge thrown down by High Street which conceals the uppermost reach of the lake. Here the road rises some way above the water, before a corresponding descent to the road terminus and car park at Mardale Head.

The grand scale of the scenery means that there are no short walks of any variety to be recommended, and many will reach the road end, only to turn straight round. If one has a reasonable amount of time, however, the best excursion on foot is to Small Water, reached by the Nan Bield track (about an hour there and back). It is a superb example of a mountain corrie tarn, almost surrounded by seemingly unscalable crags. Nearby Blea Water is perhaps an even more impressive sight, but the path to it is rather wet and monotonous.

Of the pedestrian routes out of Mardale, the Gatesgarth Pass over to Longsleddale is described in Route 38, and the Nan Bield Pass to Kentmere in Route 39. Cycles can be hauled over both, but neither should feature on any touring itinerary.

Penrith to Ullswater & Windermere

Distances from Penrith: Pooley Bridge 5¾m, Aira Beck 11½m, Glenridding 14m, Patterdale 15m, Kirkstone Pass 20¼m (Ambleside 23¼m), Troutbeck 24m (Ambleside 28m), Windermere 27m, Bowness 28m.

The above distances are via Pooley Bridge; the A592 saves ¾m.

INTRODUCTION

One of the main routes through the district offering a high standard of scenery throughout. In crossing between the lakes of Ullswater and Windermere the formidable Kirkstone Pass, nearly 1,500ft (454 metres) high, must be surmounted, yet the bulk of the road is level and so the route need not deter anyone. Scenically, it is much better traversed from north to south, as then Ullswater is seen at its best, with its surrounding amphitheatre of mountains, while the steep climb to Kirkstone is followed by a triumphant descent to Windermere. Northbound the finest views are always over one's shoulder and the full beauty of Ullswater not appreciated.

There are two roads from Penrith to the foot of Ullswater; the A592 along the north of the Eamont, and that on the southern side from Eamont Bridge, B5320. These roads changed numbers and importance on the opening of the M6, and there is little to choose between them from a cycling point of view.

DESCRIPTION

(a) Via A592 This leaves Penrith past the scant remains of the castle, and in front of the station, to descend to the motorway intersection. The A66 is taken for a mile, a busy dual carriageway which can partially be avoided by turning off on the old road through Redhills.

Quitting the A66, the Ullswater road runs through pleasant countryside, accompanied by the Eamont, passing the fine mansion and deerpark of Dalemain, then crosses a low divide to gain the shores of Ullswater. Before continuing, a diversion should be made to the prettily-situated village of Pooley Bridge (see below), half a mile east.

22

PENRITH
B5288
Greystoke
Eamont
Bridge
A66
A592
Tirril
B5320
Dacre
176m
A66
Troutbeck
Pooley
Bridge
Askham
323m
180m
A5091
Ullswater
Howtown
Dockray
A592
147m
5km
3m
Glenridding
147m
Patterdale
Grisedale
Helvellyn
Low Hartsop
163m
0
0
Brothers
Water
Fairfield
454m
Kirkstone Pass
A592
N
169m
AMBLESIDE
Troutbeck
42m
Brockhole
Windermere
WINDERMERE
BOWNESS
ROUTE 22

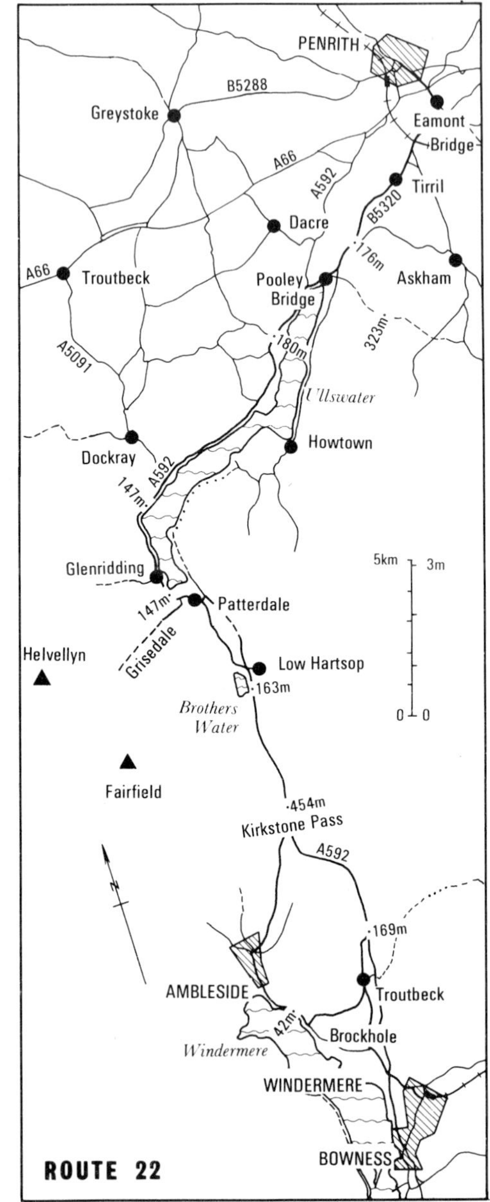

(b) Via B5320

The A6 is followed to and across Eamont Bridge, a fine old structure, dating in part back to 1425. Just across the bridge, a lane on the right leads to Mayburgh, a circular earthwork enclosing an upright stone. There is another smaller earthwork, commonly known as 'King Arthur's Round Table', but like Mayburgh of earlier and uncertain origin, alongside the Pooley Bridge road just where it turns out of the A6 at the southern end of the village.

A little east of Eamont Bridge is Brougham Castle, a picturesque eleventh-century ruin (open to the public). It can be approached direct from Penrith via Carleton and a subway under the A66. If entering the district from the east an interesting stopping-off point is Appleby, the former county town of Westmorland. The town is 13m from Eamont Bridge, by either the busy A66 or the back road through Bolton.

The road on to Pooley Bridge and Ullswater climbs gradually as far as Tirril, to run along the southern flank of the broad valley. A little further on is Barton, now just a hamlet, but formerly a place of some importance, as witnessed by its massive church.

A little before Pooley Bridge a road bears left to Howtown (9m from Penrith, 4m from Pooley Bridge), beautifully situated on a bay of Ullswater. As far as Howtown the road is easy and pleasant, following the edge of the lake, but, beyond the hamlet, it changes in character and climbs to the little Martindale church to lose itself amongst the fells. Patterdale may be reached either by the rather rough path from the road end at Sandwick, or by the steamer from Howtown to Glenridding. Check sailing times at Pooley Bridge pier.

Pooley Bridge is an attractive little village, tucked away at the foot of Ullswater. There are various cafes and hotels to cater for the considerable tourist traffic. In summer a steamer service is run two or three times a day from Pooley Bridge to Glenridding, with an intermediate call at Howtown. Cycles are conveyed (see page 16).

Ullswater is the second largest (after Windermere) of the English lakes and is held by many to be the most beautiful. Certainly the journey up the lake by road or boat is one of ever-growing enchantment as its various charms are unfolded. As the lake is a little over seven miles long and has three distinct reaches, from no single point is all its beauty revealed.

The run along the lower part of the lake from Pooley Bridge is unspectacular, the valley too broad to provide the backcloth which any expanse of water requires to give the best effect. After

Ullswater steamer, Glenridding

Watermillock the road leaves the waterside for a mile or so, but the lake is soon regained as it turns into its middle and longest reach. The character of the lake has now altered, with the view culminating in the towering Helvellyn range, the summit of that mountain partly hidden by its peaked outlier Catstye Cam. Across Ullswater, the Martindale and High Street ranges of fells are glimpsed above Sandwick.

A few miles' run along the lakeside brings one to the bridge over the Aira Beck, where there are some public conveniences and a cafe. A diversion should be made on foot to Aira Force, a fine waterfall reached by a delightful walk starting from the car park. There are various paths and bridges leading up the gorge to the fall and a second smaller fall a few hundred yards further up. The whole area is owned and beautifully maintained by the National Trust.

Continuing up the lake its uppermost and finest reach soon comes into view, as the scenery takes on a new intimacy. At Glencoyne a geological boundary is crossed, the smooth-contoured hills of the Skiddaw Slate group giving way to the volcanic rocks of the Borrowdale series, whose varied hardness and faulted nature produce a more intricate and hence more attractive landscape. The most prominent feature is now Saint Sunday Crag, sweeping down to the head of the lake. Between it and the noble Place Fell is the narrowing valley up to the Kirkstone Pass. The run on to Glenridding is below the truncated spurs of the long ridges thrown down by Helvellyn: one of these, Stybarrow Crag, had to be cut back to enable the present road to squeeze round its foot.

Glenridding is admirably situated, sheltered by enclosing wooded hills and facing Place Fell across the lake. Here are a few hotels and the terminus of the lake steamers from Pooley Bridge. Boat excursions are run, and rowing or motor boats may be hired. The main part of the village lies along a steep road which runs up a side valley to the old Greenside lead mines, an unfortunate blot on the scenery. Glenridding and its near neighbour, Patterdale, are popular hiking centres, being on the interesting (eastern) side of the Helvellyn range. The cyclist is much more restricted in scope, being confined to the main road and such peeps into the mountains as may be obtained from the few side turnings. Really to explore the vicinity one must forsake wheeled transport and take to the hills.

One valley which may be explored awheel is Grisedale. The turning leaves the main road at Grisedale Bridge (no signpost) and soon begins a steep climb which ends as the road emerges from the trees to give a good view up this green and sheltered valley. After ¾m the tarred road ends, but one can continue along the metalled track which finally peters out below Eagle Crag (2½m). Only a rough footpath leads on to Grisedale Hause. The scene is dominated by a spur of Dollywagon Pike, while a stroll up the path will reveal glimpses of the precipitous ridges leading to Helvellyn. On the left of the valley is Cofa Pike, an outlier of Fairfield.

If exploring merely the vicinity of Patterdale, before returning northwards it should be borne in mind that the A592 is fairly level as far as Brothers Water, a few miles on towards Kirkstone. The pretty hamlet of Hartsop deserves a visit, while a return to Patterdale may be made by a rather indifferently-surfaced track along the east side of the valley to Rooking. Part of this is (somewhat surprisingly) defined as only a footpath, so strictly ought to be wheeled. A diversion (with stiles) takes it round the back of Crookabeck.

From Patterdale the road continues up the principal valley, here still level-bottomed and easy. On both sides narrow tributary valleys curve away, with the head of Dovedale particularly impressive. After Brothers Water, the road begins to climb in earnest, the character of the valley changing from U to V. The ascent, 900ft (260 metres) in two miles, is unbroken and tedious, and for most cyclists it will be a matter of getting so far and then pushing. Severe though the assault on the pass may be, it comes after a very easy 18m run from Penrith. Near the top of the climb is the Kirk Stone, a large rock to the right of the road and visible against the skyline.

The Kirkstone Pass Inn lies just beyond the summit (1,489ft, 454 metres) and as its access is difficult from all directions many will feel that a prolonged acquaintance is called for. The inn does cafe meals throughout the day. It is not the highest public house in England — the Tan Hill Inn, an oasis on the Pennine Way, holds that title.

Kirkstone Pass to Ambleside direct (3m)
This is one of the longest and steepest hills in England, with gradients up to 1 in 4. It provides the quickest way to Ambleside but from its twisting and steep nature must be descended with caution, thereby expending in brake friction much of the hard work involved in ascending to Kirkstone. A better way, whether to or from Ambleside, is round via Troutbeck (see below). This adds about five miles, all beautiful. From the steepness of the climb out of Ambleside the direct road was traditionally known as 'The Struggle'.

The descent from the Kirkstone Pass to the shores of Windermere is an excellent one, the initial views over Ambleside and the head of the lake to the Coniston Fells being exchanged for a magnificent prospect across the deep Troutbeck valley to the conical peaks of Froswick and Ill Bell. The road drops steadily for three miles, until, just before the turning off through Troutbeck village, it briefly levels out. Whether bound for Windermere or Ambleside, the route via Troutbeck may be recommended. The village straggles along the foot of Wansfell for over a mile without any particular centre or focus, but exhibiting many quaint nooks and old buildings. Town End, at the bottom of the village, dates from the seventeenth century and is open to the public (National Trust). The direct road to Ambleside bears right just after Town End, to twist and turn down to the shores of Windermere, affording many fine viewpoints. It comes out on the main road about half a mile north of the National Park Centre at Brockhole (page 49). For Windermere town and Bowness, the left fork is taken from Town End, bringing one out on the main road at Troutbeck Bridge. Halfway down the hill is the Windermere Youth Hostel.

The main A592, crossing to the east of the Troutbeck valley, runs some way above the river and loses height only gradually. This part of the run is most attractive, a beautiful mixture of wood and parkland. At the mini-roundabout the Kendal to Ambleside road is crossed for Bowness, while Windermere town and station are reached by the turn up the hill. For Windermere and Bowness see page 47-9.

Penrith to Keswick

23

Distances from Penrith: Greystoke 5m, Sportsman Inn 8½m, Troutbeck 10m (direct via A66 9m), Scales 12¾m, Threlkeld 14½m, Keswick 18½m.

INTRODUCTION

Cyclists setting off from Penrith for a first visit to the Lake District are likely to have their preconceptions of Cumbrian scenery severely dented, at least for about the first ten miles. This part of the journey is an uphill plod across an uninspiring landscape, probably into the prevailing westerly wind, that will have the cyclist thinking that perhaps Norfolk would have been a better choice after all. Only about Threlkeld do the mountains really come into their own and it is not until the final descent into Keswick that the lakes of Derwentwater and Bassenthwaite greet the eye — and then only from the steeper road via Castlerigg.

The improvement of this road was one of the most contentious planning issues to affect the National Park since its establishment. Industrial west Cumbria has, for generations, been a depressed area, following the decline of its basic industries. To assist its rejuvenation, a high-standard trunk road link from Workington across to the M6 was proposed to replace the former A594 through Cockermouth and Keswick. Opposition to this proposal was immense, mainly centring on the contradiction of creating a new route through an area where one of the main planning objectives was the removal of non-essential traffic. In the end, after prolonged debate, the opposition was rejected, and the present scheme approved in 1973.

Now, with the road completed, it is still too early to judge what its effects have been or will be. The greatest impact on the landscape is between the previously-completed Threlkeld bypass and the foot of Bassenthwaite Lake, including the gorge of the river Greta near Keswick. But it is only at the latter that the road can be said to encroach aggressively: the Greta Viaduct, although graceful in its own way, cannot be anything but an intrusion and unhappily the road severs Keswick from one of its favourite viewpoints, Latrigg. However, when seen from Latrigg or any of the neighbouring heights, the road sinks into

23

Derwentwater
Skiddaw
KESWICK
B5322
140m
Threlkeld
Blencathra
225m
180m
Mungrisdale
260m
Dockray
A5091
Troutbeck
A66
285m
Motherby
Ullswater
Dacre
Greystoke
Pooley Bridge
B5288
A66
Askham
159m
Eamont Bridge
PENRITH
0
5km
0
3m
ROUTE 23

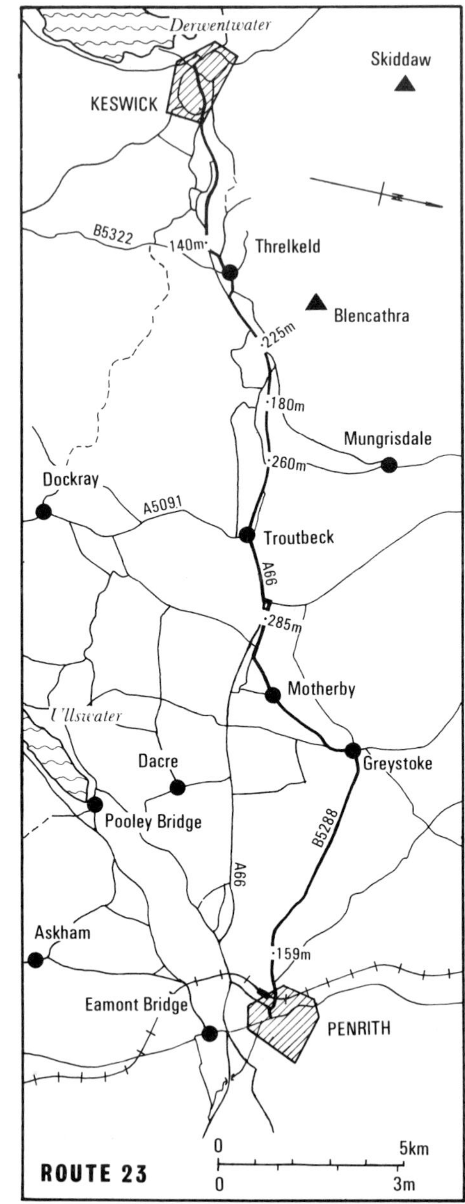

relative insignificance, along with the other visible handiworks of Man. It is also true that, of all the new sections between Workington and Penrith, the section bypassing Keswick was the most necessary and inevitable. While the road may have generated additional traffic, it has relieved the A591 through Windermere and Ambleside to Keswick. Whether the road will achieve much for west Cumbria is debatable — the benefit is probably as much psychological as practical.

Whatever the wider issues, the road does assist the cyclist, who is now able to choose between the fast, easily-graded new road and the much quieter old road for much of the way. The former, where single carriageway, includes a well-surfaced and rideable shoulder which helps to compensate for the speed and volume of motor traffic. Whilst it is possible to divert off the improved sections through Redhills, Stainton and Penruddock, the slightly longer route via Greystoke is much to be preferred and this is the way described below. This, incidentally, used to be the A594, while the direct road, with its steeper gradients, was the 'B' road.

DESCRIPTION

Turn out of the main street in Penrith at the clock-tower, bearing right at the top of the hill to cross the railway north of the station. The road from there to Greystoke is a good one, with gentle gradients, passing through rather plain countryside. Nearing Greystoke, two farmhouses, thinly disguised as eighteenth-century forts, are passed on the left. These were built as follies to enhance the view from Greystoke Castle.

Greystoke village presents a well-kept appearance, with a fine cross in the middle of the green. The castle (not open to the public) is concealed amongst its wooded grounds. Beyond Greystoke the road continues much as before, though rising more steadily to Motherby, another trim village. A little further on the former main road from Penrith through Penruddock is joined, just before this turns left to meet the new A66. By carrying straight on, the main road can be avoided a little longer, until just past the Sportsman Inn. The scenery here is somewhat dreary — bleak moorland stretching in all directions.

The road for the next few miles, on either side of Troutbeck, was the last stage of the Penrith to Workington improvement to be completed. The section of road it replaced, above on the right, was a most hazardous one for the cyclist with a number of blind dips. Troutbeck, a few buildings and an inn clustered round the old station, is about the halfway point between Penrith and

23

Keswick and it is from here that the scenery begins to improve. The road drops to cross the river Glenderamackin, which is to be followed all the way to Keswick, but there first comes a steady slog up to Scales. The old road loops round to the south. From Scales it is all plain sailing down the A66 to Keswick. The precipitous southern aspect of Blencathra (Saddleback) is prominent on the descent to Threlkeld, a village much improved since being bypassed. A little further on the old and new roads diverge, the latter follows the gorge of the Greta but the old road climbs up the hillside and offers the better views, as well as being almost traffic-free. A slight diversion from it takes one past the Castlerigg Stone Circle (page 150), one of the most dramatically situated of our prehistoric monuments. The descent into Keswick offers a fine panorama, missed from the lower roads. For Keswick see page 71.

Threlkeld and Blencathra

Keswick to Cockermouth

Distances: 12-15m. See below.

INTRODUCTION

The student interested in the development of our roads would do well to study what might be termed the 'A66 Corridor' east and west of Keswick.

The original turnpike road trusts took the old packhorse tracks — direct but hilly — and greatly improved them. Increased traffic and the desire for speed resulted in new lengths of road being constructed, taking a more concilitory course, with successive improvements made. The Railway Age brought nearly a century of stagnation, but with the rise of motor traffic improvements were resumed, culminating in this particular case in the present A66, ironically much of it built on the line of the former railway. This should be adequate until the world's oil runs out.

The earliest turnpike from Keswick to Cockermouth was over the Whinlatter Pass, a beautifully-engineered road, winding up the hillside on steep but steady gradients. Next to be turnpiked was the road along the east side of Bassenthwaite Lake to Castle Inn, then taking a direct course to Cockermouth. This western section was replaced by a more level alignment through Embleton, which was later linked to Keswick by a new road along the west of the lake. No major improvements were made until the 1970s, when the present A66 was constructed.

The cyclist thus has an inheritance of a wide choice of routes; via Whinlatter, via the eastern side of Bassenthwaite, or along the western shore of the lake. Each will be described in turn. From Keswick the circuit of Bassenthwaite Lake makes a pleasant and very easy run of about eighteen miles.

DESCRIPTION

(a) Via Whinlatter Braithwaite 2½m, Whinlatter Pass 4½, Cockermouth 12m.

This is by far the hilliest of the available routes, but is nevertheless well worthwhile. As it forms the best route from

Keswick to the west coast it is fully described as far as Lorton under Route 26. North of that village (which lies just off the direct road but worth a detour) the road runs through pleasant wooded countryside for a few miles, rising to a low ridge, then providing an easy descent into Cockermouth.

(b) Via east side of Bassenthwaite Lake
Castle Inn $7\frac{1}{2}$m, Ouse Bridge $8\frac{1}{2}$m, Embleton 11m, Cockermouth $14\frac{1}{4}$m.
From Keswick the Carlisle road is taken. Just after the bypass is crossed, a hilly but rewarding diversion may be made by turning up to Applethwaite. From the terrace-like road there is an excellent view over Derwentwater to the fells enclosing Borrowdale. Amongst them may be spotted an 'intruder' — the conical Pike o' Stickle, one of the Langdale Pikes. The A591 is rejoined about $2\frac{1}{2}$m out of Keswick, a shady, winding road, tucked under the foot of Skiddaw. It rises gradually for a few miles, after which a loop road down to Scarness may be taken if the main road seems rather busy. Bassenthwaite village can be included by a subsequent detour but contains nothing of particular note. A little further on is the Castle Inn, an old coaching inn at a once-important crossroads.

Turning left at the inn an easy run of a mile takes one past Armathwaite Hall to Ouse Bridge, where the river Derwent, after flowing through Bassenthwaite Lake, resumes its beautiful journey to the sea.

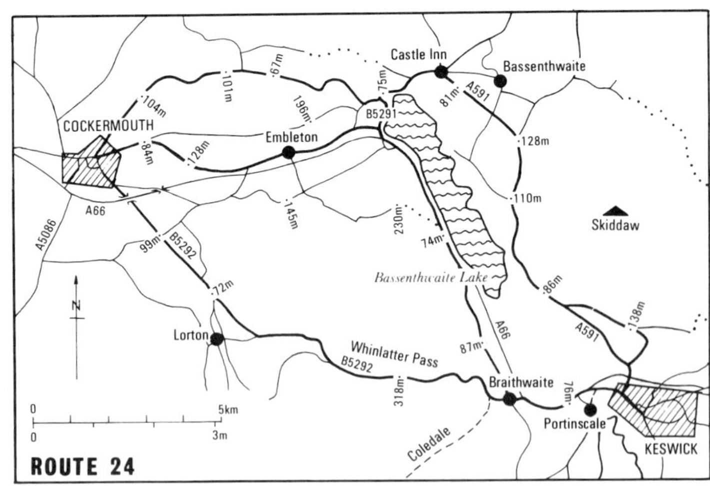

ROUTE 24

From Ouse Bridge, Cockermouth can be reached by various roads, the shortest, rising over Setmurthy Common, being the least interesting as well as the hilliest. Perhaps the pleasantest way is by the winding lane following the Derwent, passing Kirkhouse. Isel Church, just north of the fine old bridge, is partly Norman. The bridle-road along the north side of the river between Armathwaite and Isel Bridge is now so overgrown and muddy as to be barely passable even on foot.

For Cockermouth, via Embleton or the A66, it is preferable to turn left, not right, on crossing Ouse Bridge, the road running along the foot of the lake. Steps lead down from the roadside to the stony water's edge. Just before reaching the A66 the old road, recommended, curves away to the right. For continuation to Cockermouth see below.

(c) Via the west side of Bassenthwaite Lake
Thornthwaite 3½m, Embleton 9½m (Lorton 13¾m), Cockermouth 12¾m (13¾m via A66/A5086).
The new road, as opposed to the old, which looped through Portinscale and Thornthwaite, certainly has the merit of speed and, being less enclosed, the finer views. Most cyclists will, I am sure, prefer to keep to the earlier road, winding a quiet course below the fellside. Between the trees are glimpses of the massive Skiddaw range, rising beyond the broad and level vale partly occupied by the lake. The hills on the south side of the valley are too close to be appreciated properly, but one distinct feature is the Bishop of Barf, a white-painted rock a little way up the mountain. The new road is rejoined at a picnic area enclosing a solitary oak tree, though the gated road onwards allows a further half-mile of freedom from traffic. Beyond Beck Wythop the old road forms the northbound carriageway, concealed among the woods, while southbound the new section of road built along the railway provides good views of Bassenthwaite and Skiddaw.

At the end of the lake the old road, after looping past the Pheasant Inn, crosses the new, and here a link (B5291) runs across to the Castle Inn (see above). The two roads run parallel, but independently, for a few miles, the former undulating, the latter pursuing a level and relentless course.

Beyond Embleton one should cut up to the old road, if not on it already, as by keeping to the A66 Cockermouth is entered from the south on the A5086, and this adds a mile. The old road climbs a little to give a good view south to the Buttermere fells, and then drops gradually into the town.

NB If travelling from Bassenthwaite to Lorton and Buttermere one must turn off beyond Embleton. A hilly lane leads across to the B5292

2m south of Cockermouth. There is no link between this road and the A66 where they cross.

24

Cockermouth is a pleasant country town, away from the hurly-burly of the Lake District, yet within easy reach of it. This fact makes it appealing as a halting place in summer, when neighbouring Keswick is overrun. The broad tree-lined main street is its principal feature, setting off a number of old buildings. It also links the town's main attractions, Wordsworth's house at the western end and the castle on its hill at the other. The house where Wordsworth was born in 1770 and spent his childhood, is a large residence in severe Georgian style, somewhat difficult to associate with nature's poet. It is administered by the National Trust. The castle is a private residence, but the grounds are occasionally open.

From Cockermouth on to Workington is 8m, to Whitehaven 13½m. Neither road offers any interest to the tourist. For Maryport (7½m) see Route 29.

Skiddaw from near Ouse Bridge

Keswick to Ullswater

Distances from Keswick: Threlkeld 4m, Troutbeck 8½m, Dockray 12½m, Ullswater (Aira Beck) 14m, Glenridding 16½m, Patterdale 17½m.

INTRODUCTION

Derwentwater and Ullswater are two of the major attractions of the Lake District and neither should be omitted by the visitor. The road route between them, however, is scenically uninteresting, traversing a bare upland that contrasts strongly with the surroundings of the rival claimants for the title of England's loveliest lake. A fair amount of hillclimbing is also involved in crossing the watershed, without the compensation of fine views.

The quickest route is to follow the Penrith road to the hamlet of Troutbeck and there take the A5091 south through Dockray, descending to the shores of Ullswater near Aira Force. If the main A66 can be tolerated for another four miles, the cyclist can turn off through Dacre to the foot of Ullswater at Pooley Bridge (16m from Keswick), and thereby enjoy a ride up the full length of the lake (Route 22). An alternative way to Dockray which may interest the more adventurous is described below. This is via the so-called Old Coach Road, running from Wanthwaite in the Vale of St John.

DESCRIPTION

(a) Via Troutbeck As far as Threlkeld, the main A66 is unbeatable for ease of gradient and speed, but there are alternatives, either via the old road or the back way through Brundholme, as described in Route 31. Beyond Threlkeld there is a steady climb to Scales, before the road sweeps down to cross the river Glenderamackin and a long ascent to Troutbeck. The old road, forming a loop southwards, may be taken to escape from the traffic for a while, or the slightly longer diversion via Wallthwaite. For the latter, avoid the mistake of turning right again before the river has been crossed.

Troutbeck consists of a hotel and a few cottages in bleak moorland surroundings, about as unlike the other Troutbeck,

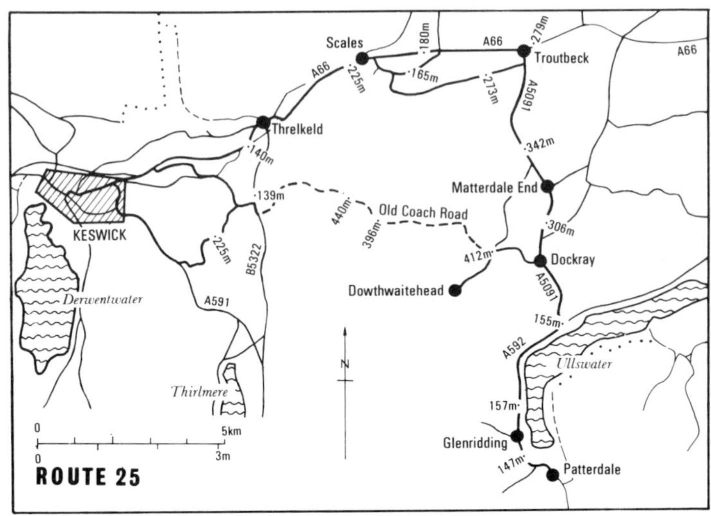

near Windermere, as could be imagined. It was once an important changing-point, for here the horse-drawn coaches for Ullswater would connect with the trains from Keswick and Penrith. Now both services are just memories.

The main road south from Troutbeck is generally quiet, carrying little other than tourist traffic: it consists initially of long tedious straights working up the extensive moor, and is only relieved by some conifer plantations. Once Great Mell Fell on the left has been passed, the scenery picks up as the road, now twisting, descends to the hamlets of Matterdale and Dockray.

Gradually, the more interesting fells that lie beyond Ullswater come into view, but the lake itself is not seen until the long final descent. A car park denotes the point where a footpath leads down to the upper fall of Aira Force (page 108), below on the left. The road from Penrith to Patterdale is joined near the main entrance to the falls, and this forms the better approach.

From the shore of Ullswater at Aira Beck to the village of Patterdale is a level and beautiful run of about three miles, fully described in Route 22. It is one of the most scenic roads in the Lake District, with Place Fell rising majestically across the head of Ullswater.

(b) Via the Old Coach Road

This runs from Wanthwaite, just south of Threlkeld, to Dockray. About $1\frac{1}{2}$hr should be allowed for the 6m. The name

Matterdale Common and Blencathra

given to it on the OS map is something of a misnomer as it never has been a through route for wheeled traffic. Some improvements were made about 1890, prior to which contemporary sources describe it as a bridle road or cart track.

Wanthwaite Bridge, in the Vale of St John, may be reached in about four or five miles from Keswick, by the old or new Penrith roads. A more hilly way, in keeping with what is to come, is to take the Ambleside road to Dale Bottom ($2\frac{1}{2}$m from Keswick) and then cross the ridge via St John's Church (see Route 31).

The track to Matterdale is signposted out of the valley road $1\frac{1}{4}$m south of Threlkeld. It climbs the hillside, crossing first the former railway and then the road serving the quarries higher up the vale. The track is metalled but generally too steep to permit cycling, at least in this direction. The summits directly behind are Grisedale Pike and Crag Hill, separated by Coledale Hause. Across the valley is the rugged southern aspect of Blencathra with the village of Threlkeld strung out along its foot. The immediate surroundings are uninspiring, a smooth rolling tract of sheepgrazing moor, while the distant Pennines and Scottish Lowlands are too far off to show more than a dull outline.

The initial 2m are mainly uphill and slow going, but eventually the track drops to the bridge over the Mosedale Beck, first crossing a rather soft stretch over peat. Another dip follows, after which the track improves and is cyclable for the remainder

25

Ullswater from Dockray Road

of the way with a smoother surface and gentler gradients. The care with which the track picks its way across the driest parts of the moor will be appreciated. Eventually, after passing a plantation, the fells south of Ullswater provide a welcome change in the scenery, and the track drops to a crossroads, where a good tarred road commences. Before descending to Dockray a pleasant diversion may be made to Dowthwaitehead, a sequestered hamlet lying in the fertile upper valley of the Aira Beck. At Dockray the main road is regained, the descent continuing for a mile or so to the shores of Ullswater. For continuation see Route 22.

Derwentwater Youth Hostel

Keswick to Loweswater, Ennerdale & Wasdale

Distances from Keswick: Braithwaite 2½m, Whinlatter Pass 4½m, Hopebeck 8m (Buttermere 13¼m), Loweswater village 10½m, Lamplugh Green 15m, Ennerdale Bridge (direct) 19m, Egremont 24¾m, Calder Bridge 28¾m, Gosforth 31m, Ravenglass 36¼m, Nether Wasdale 35m, Wasdale Head 40½m.

The circular trip from Keswick to Buttermere, outward via Whinlatter and returning via Newlands, is about twenty-five miles, thirty if Loweswater and Buttermere lakes are to be explored properly.

INTRODUCTION

Despite its rather intricate appearance on the map, this is one of the main routes to the coast and western dales for both cyclist and motorist. There are a number of variations, depending on whether Buttermere and Ennerdale are to be included and one's ultimate destination. The route to be described is from Keswick to Ennerdale Bridge and Egremont and from there round via Gosforth to Wasdale, with notes or references to the other places of interest; it will be found a very full day! Note that there are no shops at Loweswater, Lamplugh Green or Croasdale.

There are three ways (short of going round via Cockermouth) of reaching Loweswater from Keswick:

Whinlatter Pass	1,043ft (318 metres)
Newlands Pass	1,096ft (334 metres)
Honister Pass	1,176ft (356 metres)

Thus there is little difference in the amount of hillclimbing involved, although via Newlands there is also a low hill beyond Portinscale. Scenically the most attractive route must be Borrowdale and over Honister Hause, but Derwentwater and Borrowdale require, and deserve, a day to themselves. Via Newlands, the attractions of the ride up from Lorton to Buttermere are missed, but this route is suggested to those travelling from west to east or as the return leg of a round trip from Keswick. The recommended outward route, therefore, is over the Whinlatter Pass.

26

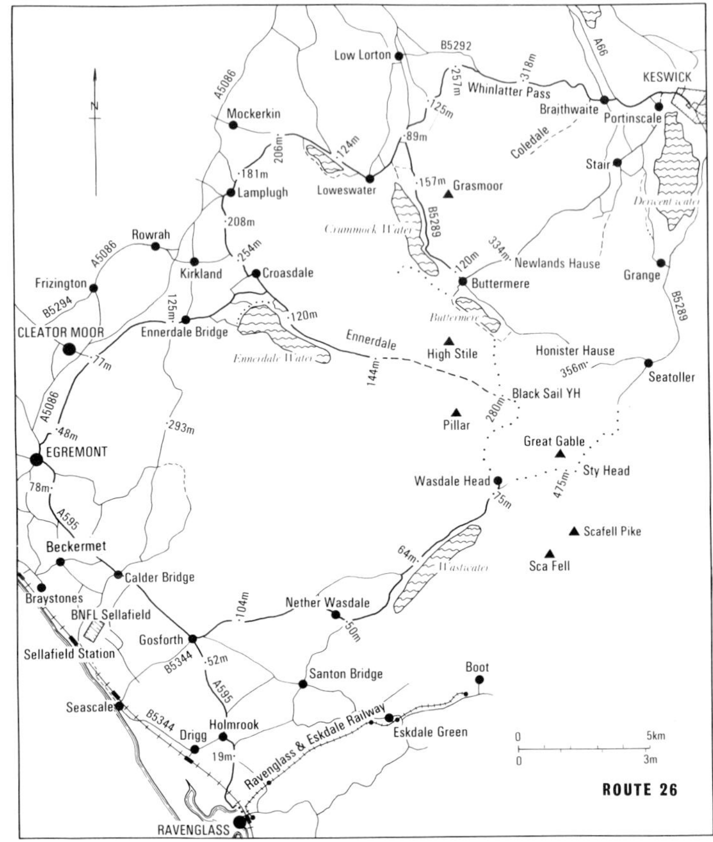

DESCRIPTION

From Keswick the Cockermouth road is taken out of the town which, after joining the bypass, continues as a fast level road. The Whinlatter road B5292 turns off a mile further on, and winds through the narrow village streets of Braithwaite, before starting the long climb up the hillside.

Coledale: At the small car park a little way up the hill a side track doubles back left into Coledale. It is rideable by cyclists for about two miles, mostly uphill, to the old mines at the foot of Force Crag.

The Whinlatter road continues to climb on a well-engineered gradient through dense Forestry Commission plantations.

There are occasional views over Bassenthwaite Lake to Skiddaw before the road disappears into the trees. After a total of about 1½m of climbing steeply, the gradient eases for the last stretch to the summit. Just above the road here is the Forestry Commission Visitor Centre which has some interesting displays and information on afforestation in the Lake District, including the early and much-criticised plantations along the pass.

The descent from the pass is good, and the road may be followed down to Lorton, there cutting across to the Cockermouth to Buttermere road. A shorter way, perfectly suitable for cyclists, is via a minor road bearing left 1½m west of the summit (signposted Hope Beck). This rises a little to a fork where it bears left (straight on is the old road to Lorton). This road gradually descends into the fertile vale, offering a distant view northward to the Solway Firth and Scotland. The road, though narrow and gated, is tarred throughout (information not to be given to motorists!).

At Hopebeck a minor road up the valley is gained, which in a mile meets the main road from Cockermouth. A little further on this road forks — the left turn leading to Buttermere, the right to Loweswater and the west.

There is so much fine scenery in the vicinity of Loweswater, Crummock Water and Buttermere that everyone should spend a little time here before moving on. If continuing to Loweswater the valley up to Buttermere should first be explored: similarly if returning to Keswick via Buttermere a run up to Loweswater ought to be made. The district round the three lakes is more fully described under Route 27, as is the return route from Buttermere to Keswick via Newlands.

Keswick to Buttermere via Newlands 8½m

Follow the Cockermouth road for about a mile, bearing left to enter Portinscale by the footbridge. Turning left in the village the road rises through woods before descending past Swinside to Stair. Causey Pike is conspicuous ahead. A steep climb leads up to the road from Braithwaite, which continues to ascend out of the Newlands valley into Keskadale. The road can be seen snaking ahead to the very top of the pass. The climb is not oversteep, until the final pull to Newlands Hause (1,096ft, 334 metres). There is a good view of Moss Force while approaching the summit. The descent to Buttermere is precipitous — 1 in 4 in places. For Buttermere and district see Route 27. Loweswater village is 5½m further by road along the shore of Crummock Water to the fork mentioned below.

The Loweswater road rises from the fork to the Scale Hill Hotel and then drops to cross the river Cocker near its exit from

26

Crummock Water. Ahead is the graceful broken-backed ridge of Mellbreak and a fine view of the High Stile range above Buttermere. Turning west, the road winds up to the small village of Loweswater and a little further on the lake itself is reached. Although not on the same scale as the larger lakes, the scene presented is nevertheless very beautiful.

Beyond the lake the road rises 300ft (90 metres) to a little beyond Fangs Brow, where the Lamplugh road bears left. On the ascent one should take a good last view back over Loweswater to Grasmoor and the neighbouring fells, as no comparable scenery will be experienced for some time. Westwards the view extends over undistinguished rolling countryside to the Solway Firth. The conspicuous chimneys are just south of Whitehaven. Fangs Brow is on the geological boundary between the Skiddaw Slates, of which most of the northern fells consist, and the coal and iron measures of the coastal belt. The change in the landscape is equally abrupt.

There is a gradual descent to the hamlet of Lamplugh, or Lamplugh Green, as it is now referred to. The hall, opposite the church, retains some old features. The village is 7¼m south of Cockermouth by a good road, the only hills of note being out of the town and from the main road up to Lamplugh. From Cockermouth to Ennerdale the road round via Kirkland to Ennerdale Bridge (11m) is a little easier than that given below.

Some distances from the coastal towns and railheads:

Workington: Branthwaite 5m, Loweswater village 11m, Lamplugh Green 8½m, Ennerdale Bridge 11m.

Workington station is ½m further at the west end of the town.

Whitehaven: Frizington 5m, Lamplugh Green 9¾m, Loweswater village 14¼m, Ennerdale Bridge 7½m.

All these roads are uninteresting and involve long climbs from the coast. For map see Route 17.

Lamplugh Green is the junction of the routes to Ennerdale via Croasdale and the various roads down the coast. The way forward via Ennerdale Bridge is to be described, but as most visitors will be keen to explore Ennerdale, the diversion to the valley and lake will first be included.

Lamplugh Green to Ennerdale

The road down from the village bears left in half a mile and soon begins to climb again, steeply in parts, to 850ft (254 metres). In the dip before the final summit some old mine workings show the distinctive red of the iron ore. There are also the remains of the old railway to the workings on Kelton Fell. Looking back one can see the Galloway hills, across the Solway Firth. A little further on, a magnificent panorama of Ennerdale is revealed, weather permitting. The low hill jutting out into the lake is Bowness Knott, overlooking the terminus of the motor road which can be seen winding down the intervening slopes. Beyond Bowness Knott is Scoat Fell, better known for its prominent northern rampart — Steeple. The mountain to its left is Pillar, that to its right Haycock.

The descent to Croasdale is inviting, but caution is advised on some of the sharp bends. Turning left at the foot of the hill the road winds through Croasdale and over an intervening ridge to emerge overlooking the lake to which it eventually descends. The public motor road terminates at a car park below Bowness Knott, $4\frac{3}{4}$m from Lamplugh Green and $3\frac{1}{4}$m from Ennerdale Bridge via Croftfoot.

There are three access points to the lakeside — at the river Ehen outlet, below How Hall (the site of the old Anglers' Hotel) and the road to the car park at Bowness Knott. The three are linked by the shore path, along which cycles can be wheeled without difficulty. The Bowness Knott car park is the start of various waymarked footpaths (leaflets are available from the dispenser near the road gate). There are also toilets and a footpath map of Ennerdale.

Ennerdale is not typical of the major Lakeland valleys in that it has been densely afforested and there is no motor road along it. The Forestry Commission road has replaced the old bridle path up the dale and cyclists may thus continue a further $5\frac{1}{2}$m to Black Sail. The road is mainly tarred as far as the farms and Youth Hostel at Gillerthwaite (2m), and then has a good stone surface. The section along the lake is very attractive, the road running just above the water level, and every visitor should come at least this far. The lake was raised when adapted to supply water for west Cumbria.

The valley's main interest, other than Ennerdale Water, lies in the grand fells that border it. Of these the finest is Pillar which projects a most impressive array of crag and boulder along the southern side of the valley. It takes its name from the Pillar Rock, a prominent spur on its north face. Another fine profile is presented by Steeple. The fells to the north of the valley which present such a spectacular front when seen from the Buttermere side cannot be appreciated from Ennerdale and their lower flanks are unbroken and featureless. The views are much hindered by the dense plantings, but recent clearings have produced a great improvement. There is a typical Forestry

Commission road, though it has a better surface than most.

The only habitation after Gillerthwaite is the tiny Youth Hostel of Black Sail, ¼m beyond the forest limits and at an elevation of 950ft (290 metres). Notwithstanding its remote situation the hostel is popular and accommodation cannot be relied upon, unless pre-booked. Only bridleways lead out of the valley — over Scarth Gap to Buttermere (Route 41) and the Black Sail Pass into Wasdale (Route 42).

Lamplugh Green to Ennerdale Bridge, Egremont etc

NB The main road from Lamplugh Green to Egremont (A5086) is described in the reverse direction in Route 17. The direct road south from Ennerdale Bridge over Cold Fell to Calder Bridge is given in Route 28.

The road descends to Lamplugh Cross where the main road from Cockermouth is joined, only to be left half a mile later. The road rises to the village of Kirkland and offers good views before commencing a long descent, dropping 300ft (90 metres), to Ennerdale Bridge, a nicely situated spot. The Egremont road (signposted Cleator Moor and Whitehaven) runs alongside the Ehen through pastoral country whereas the built-up areas across the river testify to the proximity of industry past and present. The fine bridge at Wath Brow may be crossed, or the unclassified road on the south side of the river used. This finally crosses the Ehen by a graceful single span and enters Egremont by East Road.

Egremont and the coastal belt south to Gosforth and Ravenglass are fully described in the reverse direction in Route 17. The main road is reasonable, rising to no great heights scenically or physically. On the descent to Gosforth the turning to Wasdale leads through the village centre passing the church with its old cross (page 86). A steep hill leads to a pleasantly wooded stretch of undulating road along the winding valley of the Irt.

About three miles from Gosforth a fork is reached, the road climbing to the left saving half a mile to Wasdale Head. The right turn, leading through Nether Wasdale (Strands) is the more attractive, passing through particularly rich scenery. When revealed, the stern grandeur of the lake and the famous Wasdale Screes provide a sudden contrast. The run along the lake to the road end at Wasdale Head is one of ever-changing interest and beauty, described more fully in Route 16.

Cockermouth to Loweswater, Buttermere & Borrowdale

27

Distances from Cockermouth: Lorton 4m, Loweswater village 7½m, Buttermere (direct) 10¼m, Seatoller 15¾m, (Keswick 23¼m).
Loweswater village to Buttermere 5½m.

INTRODUCTION

This is an excellent run of ever-increasing interest and — until the long final climb to Honister Hause — easy cycling. By returning via Keswick and Bassenthwaite, a round trip of about forty miles may be enjoyed, with the various attractions on route, occupying a full day. Alternatively, Keswick may be reached via Newlands Hause and the delights of Borrowdale saved for another day.

The run from Cockermouth out to Loweswater and Buttermere makes a grand afternoon or evening excursion which can be varied by returning along the lanes on the west side of the river Cocker. Loweswater can also be reached by taking the Egremont road, turning off via Akebank Mill and Mosser but the road thence to Loweswater rises to 820ft (250 metres). Apart from the descent to the lake this is a scenically inferior route to that described below and care needs to be taken on the steeper sections.

DESCRIPTION

The Buttermere road B5289 twists and turns out of Cockermouth and gradually climbs to pass under the A66 bypass to meet the link road from Bassenthwaite and Embleton at the hilltop 2m out of the town. The next 2m to Lorton are pleasant enough, though without being particularly scenic. Approaching Lorton the B5289 to Keswick via the Whinlatter Pass bears off to the left and the B5292 valley road taken, although a little further on this may be forsaken for the unclassified road passing Lorton church to Hopebeck, which provides a quiet alternative to the main road for these few miles (if aiming for Loweswater there is also a narrow and somewhat

27

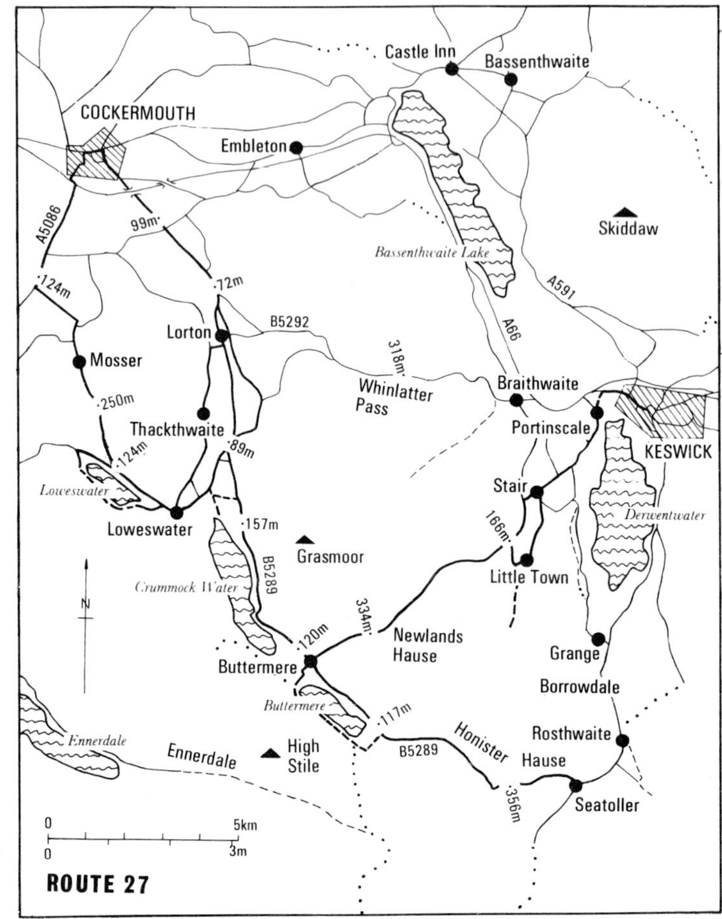

more hilly lane up the west side of the valley from Lorton, through Thackthwaite).

Lorton is nicely placed, a scattered village strung out along the web of lanes that here span the valley. About two miles further (ie 6m from Cockermouth) the roads to Buttermere and Loweswater go their separate ways round Lanthwaite Hill. Even if proceeding to Buttermere the right fork should first be taken for a mile, to the bridge over the Cocker just below the Scale Hill Hotel. From the car park here, a number of passable tracks lead through Lanthwaite Woods (National Trust).

By bearing successively to the right, the foot of Crummock Water is reached in half a mile, with the view up the Buttermere valley revealed effectively for the first time. The first fork to the left from the car park is a bridleway that leads to the Buttermere road. After crossing another track coming down from the hotel, it rises more steeply to a gate, from where a path may be taken to the summit of Lanthwaite Hill (674ft, 208 metres, not named on OS map). The view is similar to that from the lake foot, but obviously gains from its higher situation. The track onwards from the gate is partly rideable, concluding as a grassy (sometimes muddy) lane coming out on the Buttermere road a little north of Lanthwaite Gate. This bridleway avoids the return up the Cockermouth road to the junction mentioned above.

From the river Cocker bridge it is only ¾m, though uphill, to Loweswater village, and by continuing a little further, one is rewarded with a view of the lake of the same name. The environs possess a quieter beauty than those of neighbouring Crummock Water and Buttermere but are very appealing to the eye. There is access to the waterside from the road, while a circuit of the lake can be made by returning along a bridleway through the woods on the south shore. This links two farm access roads and is mainly rideable, although wet in places.

After a long gradual climb to skirt Lanthwaite Hill the Buttermere road emerges to reveal a magnificent view over Crummock Water which unfolds on the descent. The long peaked ridge that separates this valley from Ennerdale presents a particularly fine outline. Rounding Hause Point the upper part of the valley appears, culminating in the symmetrical Fleetwith Pike, and after crossing a low intervening hill, Buttermere village is soon reached.

The situation of the little village is delightful, nestling in a fold of the hills below the Newlands Pass. Its namesake lake and Crummock Water are both about half a mile distant. There is only a small difference in level between the two lakes and it is considered that they once formed a single expanse of water, until separated by the detritus washed down from the encircling hills. Directly across the valley from the village, but only prominent after rain, is Sourmilk Gill, a cascade tumbling down from the unseen Bleaberry Tarn below Red Pike.

Buttermere is ideally placed for a number of mountain ascents, but opportunities for more leisurely strolls are rather limited. Paths leading down to the margins of Crummock Water and Buttermere provide the obvious attractions, while a longer walk (2m each way) is to Scale Force, one of the highest falls in the Lake District. Unfortunately, it is at its most impressive

27

when least accessible, the path along the western side of the valley from Scale Bridge being extremely rough and wet. The lane to the left of the Fish Inn is taken; that to the right leads only to the lake. The force lies in a little side valley some way above Crummock Water, and has worn itself a deep gorge into which the water plunges in a single drop of 100ft (30 metres).

The tracks through Birtness Woods on the west side of Buttermere are, by contrast, much easier, and cycles may be taken round the lake. From the foot of Sourmilk Gill two paths diverge — the lower ('permissive') path, well surfaced, and the old bridle-road starting a little higher up. Access to both is difficult after wet weather. The lower path offers the only worthwhile views, but these cannot match those from the road opposite. The upper path, chiefly of interest for the fungi to be seen, meets the lower at the stream crossing beyond the woods. The shore path on to the foot of Scarth Gap is partly rideable with care and due respect for the numerous walkers. The track across the valley to Gatesgarth is level and flood-prone.

Buttermere to Keswick via Newlands Hause, 8½m

This forms the best route from Loweswater and beyond to Keswick, assuming Borrowdale is to be visited separately. There is a steep ascent from Buttermere, the road rising 700ft (213 metres) in little over a mile to Newlands Hause (also, and more logically, known as Buttermere

The road to Buttermere, Crummock Water

Hause). Once the top is reached, it is downhill most of the way, the road dropping steeply at first and then levelling out as it contours down Keskadale. Below are the rich pastures of the Newlands valley.

For a more leisurely exploration, take the narrow road down to the right which drops to the whitewashed church. Keskadale has vanished without trace, the views now extending up the Newlands valley proper past the steep-sided Scope End, a miniature Fleetwith Pike. On nearing Little Town a track doubles back up the valley to some old mines (1½m, rideable each way). The valley is bleak but its head majestic, the perfect spot for those who prefer looking at mountains to climbing them. Little Town itself is idyllically situated amidst some shapely hills.

The direct road crosses the valley lower down, through the hamlet of Stair, after which there is a slight rise before the road descends through woods to Portinscale. Here, turn right (not left) for Keswick, crossing the Derwent by the suspension footbridge.

Main route continued

From Buttermere the Honister road continues up the valley some way above the lake which is partly screened by trees. The fell scenery is very grand, Fleetwith Pike presenting an apparently unscalable front, although a narrow path will be made out up the ridge. Across the valley can be seen the steep and rough track over Scarth Gap and down into Ennerdale (Route 41). At Gatesgarth, the last farm in the valley, the road and river bend round to the left and for a mile or so the gradient is not too severe. After crossing the bridge, the climb begins in earnest, with the last half mile very steep, up to 1 in 4 in places. To the right, towers the rugged flanks of Honister Crag, marked with slate workings. At the top of the pass (1,176ft, 356 metres) are the Honister Hause Youth Hostel and the quarry buildings. Honister is a popular walking centre, being well-placed for the Derwent Fells and the ridge south to Great Gable.

The road over the hause was long regarded as one of the worst in the district and not advised for motorists until it was completely rebuilt in 1935-6. About twenty-five years earlier the slate company had a toll road built down to Seatoller on an easier gradient mainly to the north of the public road which drops steeply alongside Hause Gill. The slope is again 1 in 4 in places.

From Seatoller it is 7½m along a level road to Keswick, but Borrowdale has much to offer the leisurely tourist. It is described fully in Route 32.

28 Ennerdale Bridge to Calder Bridge via the Fell Road

INTRODUCTION

The direct road from Ennerdale Bridge to Calder Bridge across the fells will be a disappointment to anyone expecting grand vistas of the Lakeland mountains and across the Solway Firth to Galloway. As the road is enclosed by smooth rounded hills, many of them afforested, the principal features are manmade; the tall chimney south of Whitehaven and the futuristic architecture of the Windscale (Sellafield) nuclear power installations. Nevertheless, the road is a good one for the cyclist, the gradients though long are gradual and he may sail down what he has toiled up — a comparative rarity in this part of the world. There is no principal summit. For those who are not in a hurry and enjoy the solitude of the fells the diversion via Thornholme and the east side of the Calder has been included.

This road forms the shortest route from Ennerdale Bridge to Wasdale, Ravenglass etc, being about 2½m less than the alternative down the Ehen valley to Egremont and then along the main A595. This latter road, preferable on a wet or windy day, is described in Route 26, together with the approaches to Ennerdale Bridge from Keswick and Cockermouth.

DESCRIPTION

From Ennerdale Bridge there is a long but not oversteep ascent until the open fell is reached. The wording on the cattle-grid sign suggests that it was erected in an age of more cautious cyclists. The road continues gently upwards across the moor, passing a small stone circle on the left, a reconstruction of no antiquity. After reaching its highest point, 950ft (293 metres), the road winds between the hills with the Windscale and Calder Hall works appearing ahead. The road then drops to a crossroads in the dip between Wilton Fell and Cold Fell, 4m from Ennerdale Bridge.

Diversion via Thornholme

This will add about ½ an hour to the journey time. At the above-

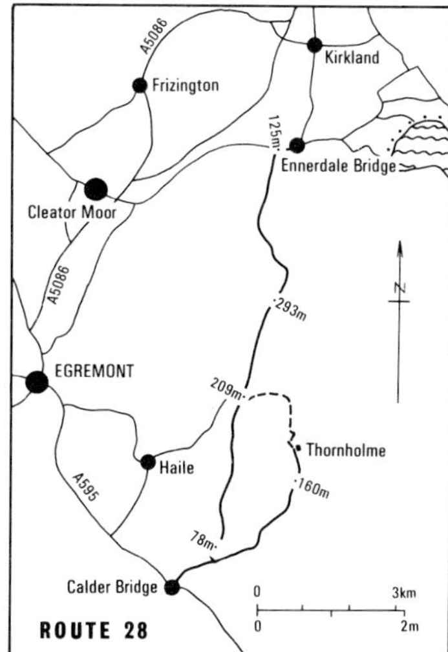

mentioned crossroads take a bumpy track down to the left, bearing right in ¼m. The track is not signposted and there is no indication that it is a right of way, although it is a bridleway throughout. At the foot of the hill, the river Calder is crossed by a new footbridge, superseding the rather tricky ford alongside. There is an old packhorse bridge, generally known as Monks Bridge, about 150 yards upstream, reached from the far bank. It is a delightfully primitive structure, without any parapets.

On the far side of the new footbridge the track is followed as it slopes up the hillside. This track gradually peters out, but by continuing in the same direction, ie parallel to but well above, the river, it is picked up again as the farm of Thornholme comes into view ahead. The track then winds down the hillside to Worm Gill, which is crossed by a footbridge just upstream of the old ford. From this it climbs up a steep bank to join a tarred road at the side of the farm. From here, it is 3m along a gated road down the valley to Calder Bridge, with Calder Abbey (see below) passed on the way.

Main route continued

After a short descent across the northern extremity of Cold Fell there follows a long, more gradual, drop down the hill's western flank with views over the sea to the Isle of Man. At the junction at the foot of the hill, turn left for a few hundred yards for a view of Calder Abbey. This was commenced in 1134 and was affiliated to Furness Abbey. The abbey itself is in private grounds but it can be seen from the road. The last mile into Calder Bridge is level.

29 Along the Solway Firth to Carlisle

Distances from Cockermouth: Maryport 7½m, Allonby 12½m, Silloth 20¼m, Skinburness 22m, Abbey Town 27¼m, Newton Arlosh 31¼m, Kirkbride 33¾m, Bowness (direct 38m, Burgh by Sands 45½m, Carlisle 51¼m.

Direct distances to Carlisle: Cockermouth 25¾m (Route 20), Wigton 11½m, Maryport 27½m, Allonby 23¼m, Abbey Town (via Wigton) 17½m, Kirkbride 11½m.

INTRODUCTION

The complete antithesis to the Lake District, but an area which will appeal to cyclists who perhaps are tiring of steep winding byways and long for the open road. The route described here, more or less hugging the coast from Maryport, provides an easy day with which to finish a holiday for those returning to or via Carlisle. For those who run short of time, the direct distances to Carlisle are also given above.

The countryside traversed is flat and uninteresting, but all the towns and villages passed through have some note of individuality, and the views of the sea and distant hills on both sides of the Solway are excellent. The best map is Bartholomew's 1:100,000 sheet 38 'Carlisle and the Solway', but otherwise the text and key map will suffice. There is no high ground to speak of between the Maryport to Carlisle railway and the coast. A useful book recently published is *Exploring the Solway* by M.A. Wood (Dalesman Publications).

DESCRIPTION

Leave Cockermouth by the bridge across the Derwent at the west end of the town. Papcastle, a pretty village on a loop road, is the site of the Roman fort of *Derventio* though few traces of it remain. Remember to turn right in the village. The road on to Maryport is undulating, without any severe hills, and offers a first view over the Solway to Scotland. There is a long descent into Maryport.

The coast road, B5300, may be taken without going into the

A7
A74
CARLISLE
N
Burgh by Sands
Moorhouse
Dalston
Annan
Port Carlisle
Glasson
Kirkbampton
Thursby
Bowness on
Solway
·14m
B5307
A596
Kirkbride
Anthorn
B5307
WIGTON
Newton Arlosh
10m·
B5302
A595
Blencogo
Skinburness
B5302
Abbey Town
23m
SILLOTH
B5300
B5301
Bothel
W. Newton
Solway Firth
ASPATRIA
·10m
A596
A595
Allonby
B5300
Tallentire
0
10km
0
6m
·92m
A594
COCKERMOUTH
ROUTE 29
MARYPORT
Great Broughton

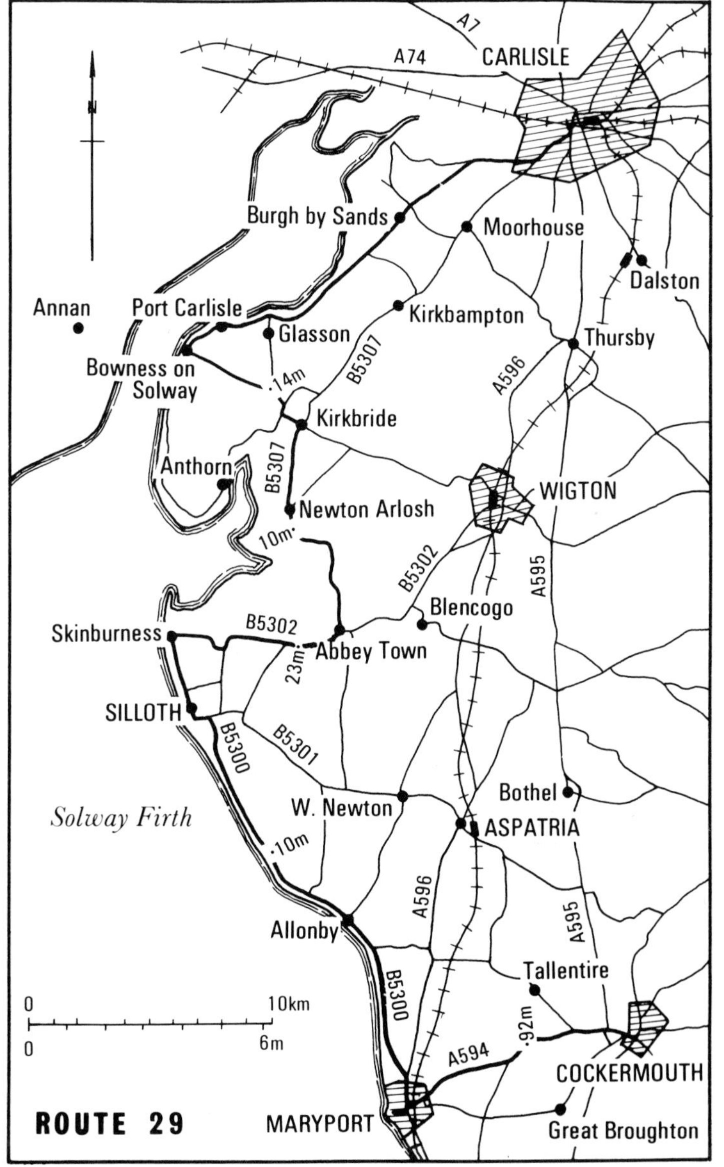

29

town, but this would be to miss one of the most interesting of our
old industrial centres. Its various stages of development are all
laid out like the pages of a book. The old town, to the north of the
29 harbour (with its small maritime museum) dates from the middle
of the eighteenth century.

From Maryport, the road runs inland at first, reaching the coast about a mile north of the town. Alternatively, the promenade cum seawall may be followed, but this expires just before the road is reached, involving an awkward stretch of path. There then follows an easy run along the bay to Allonby. Although now just a sleepy village, this was a 'watering place' of some note in its eighteenth-century heyday. The original turnpike road from Wigton to Maryport looped round to serve it, and the name of the former still remains on the milestones. Allonby still retains many old cottages in its quiet cobbled backstreets, and has an extensive greensward fronting the sea. The prominent hill seen across the Solway is Criffell, near Dumfries, which, from its southerly position, elbows out its higher compatriots in much the same way that Black Combe, near Millom, dominates that part of the coast.

The next few miles towards Silloth are close to the sea, before the road turns inland through Blitterlees. The approach to Silloth is unprepossessing, but the town itself is a pleasant surprise. Its broad sett-paved streets and trim Victorian terraces face a well-kept lawn, beyond which is the promenade and beach. The town dates from the middle of the last century when it was developed as a leisure resort and commercial port, (a surprising number of our coastal towns once had these dual aspirations though invariably one purpose defeated the other). In its prime it could boast passenger steamers to Liverpool, the Isle of Man and Dublin, but now the place is little known outside Cumbria. There is swimming, and the usual other amenities of a modest seaside resort.

From Silloth one may turn inland or continue northwards to Skinburness, the site of a medieval town destroyed by flood in 1301, but which now is only a straggling suburb of Silloth. Turn right at the hotel. The main road, now B5302, is regained in a few miles, crossing a pancake-flat land criss-crossed by drainage ditches. Across the mouth of Moricambe Bay rise the masts of Anthorn radio station.

Abbey Town, a sizeable village at the junction of the roads to Carlisle via Wigton and via Kirkbride, has a number of old cottages, many of which incorporate material from Holme Cultram Abbey. The only surviving part of the abbey is the nave, which serves as the parish church.

The Kirkbride road, B5307, bears left at the abbey and continues on a winding but level course. 4m from Abbey Town is Newton Arlosh, also appropriately known as Long Newton, built as a replacement for the abandoned Skinburness. The only point of interest is the church, which, like so many in the Borders, also served as a refuge from raiders from the opposite side of the Solway. The tower is purely defensive in character, squat and strongly built.

A few miles further on is Kirkbride, mainly strung out along the road to Wigton, 6m south. Turning left, the lazy waters of the river Wampool are crossed by a narrow metal bridge, after which the direct and coastal roads to Bowness go their separate ways. To keep in spirit with this circuit of the Solway, one should follow the latter, doubling round through Anthorn and Cardurnock, but the views will by now be familiar, and the radio station hardly improves the scenery. This road also adds another 6m. Unless following the Cumbria Cycle Way, most cyclists will, I suspect, opt for the direct road to Bowness cutting across the headland.

The village of Bowness lies at the western end of Hadrian's Wall, at the lowest point where the Solway could be forded. The fort that once stood here was long ago plundered for building stone. Of the wall itself, hardly anything is distinguishable west of Carlisle and it can only be traced from a large-scale map. A more recent earthwork, just west of Bowness, is the embankment of the long-abandoned railway that ran across the estuary to Annan. The houses of that town, only 3m away, can be seen across the water, together with the cooling towers of Chapelcross power station.

Continuing eastwards a short run brings one to Port Carlisle, built, as its name suggests, as a sea outlet for that town, to which it was connected by canal. The venture proved a commercial failure and the canal was soon converted to a railway and extended to Silloth. Now the remnants of the old harbour are gradually crumbling away.

Beyond Port Carlisle, another short run leads to the hilltop hamlet of Drumburgh, where the line of the Roman road is crossed; a dead-straight and monotonous ride then follows across the Solway marshes to Dykesfield. Here there is a welcome return to trees and greenery on the approach to the attractive old village of Burgh by Sands. The church is another example of the fortified style found in the Borders.

Edward I Memorial: This marks the spot where, in 1307, the Hammer of the Scots died, while on his way north to do battle once more. The monument stands alone (except for a picket of cows) on the marshes about a mile north of the village, from which it is signposted.

29 The road on to Carlisle winds its way across the coastland, through leafy Kirkandrews upon Eden, until the rather ordinary suburbs of the city are met. It is then an easy run of 2m to the city centre.

Like most sizeable towns, Carlisle has tackled its traffic problems with the construction of a ring road, the creation of a central precinct and a warren of one-way streets. As a consequence, the cyclist who does not know his way around is likely to be misled. The best way to the city centre is to take the slip road off the dual carriageway immediately after passing in front of the castle, followed by a right turn into Scotch Street.

For those in a hurry to catch trains, the following short cut to the station may be recommended. On the river Caldew bridge on the main western approach, push across the dual carriageway and turn down a narrow road alongside the railway. Passing through a viaduct arch, one comes out on a parallel road east of the line which leads into the station forecourt. For a brief description of Carlisle see page 98.

A circular tour from Ambleside

Distances from Ambleside: Hawkshead 5¼m, Tarn Hows 7¾m, Coniston 10m, Little Langdale (3 Shires Inn, via Tilberthwaite) 14½m, Dungeon Ghyll (Gt Langdale) 18½m, Grasmere 23½m, Ambleside 27½m.

INTRODUCTION

This provides an extremely enjoyable circular tour covering the many places of scenic interest in the vicinity of Ambleside. It can, of course, be started and finished at any intermediate point. Although it covers less than thirty miles, it is crammed full of sufficient 'lollipops' for it to occupy a whole day; yet the rider is never more than eight miles from Ambleside. The road involves a fair number of hills in crossing from valley to valley. Because of the one-way system in operation at Tarn Hows, the route is best taken in the direction described, ie from Hawkshead to Coniston.

DESCRIPTION

The Coniston road is followed to Clappersgate, a mile from Ambleside, where the bridge over the Brathay is crossed for Hawkshead. The road winds between woods and hummocky hills, very typical of this corner of Lakeland, with few long views.

Ambleside to Tarn Hows direct (6m)
This turns off the B5286 2m from Ambleside, to climb via the 'Drunken Duck' Inn to Hawkshead Hill. Perhaps the best route, if Hawkshead is not to be included, is via Skelwith Fold (page 27), and then the 'Drunken Duck'.

The road forward to Hawkshead continues its hilly course, eventually dropping into the village. Hawkshead is fully described on page 44. While in the vicinity, half an hour or so might be devoted to a spin round Esthwaite Water (5m).

The road on to Coniston involves retracing one's steps northwards for half a mile, to near the old courthouse, for the climb over the ridge separating Esthwaite Water and Coniston Water. This necessitates an ascent of 550ft (165 metres) in this

30

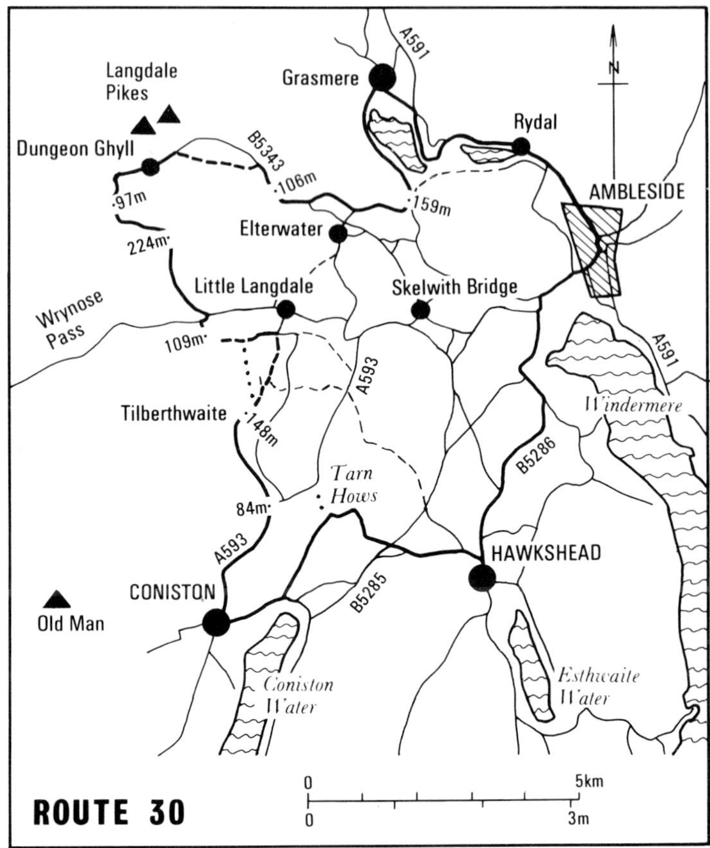

direction, or 400ft (122 metres) if proceeding direct to Coniston on the B5285. Such are the attractions of Tarn Hows that no one begrudges the extra climb and distance. Also, because of the one-way system in operation, it is necessary to approach the place from the east, even if coming from Coniston.

From Hawkshead, there is a mile of almost unbroken ascent, with a brief respite where the right fork for Tarn Hows is taken. This lane steepens, the worst bit coming just before the summit, shortly after which the lake is revealed.

Tarn Hows, alias The Tarns, is one of the best known and photographed Lakeland beauty spots, but no single picture can encompass the attractiveness of the indented lakelet and the panoramic backcloth provided by the distant fells. By rambling over the grassy tumps that cradle the tarn, a variety of enchanting scenes are revealed, with the Langdale Pikes, Coniston Water, the Old Man, Fairfield etc presenting themselves in turn. 30

The attractiveness of the lake is largely man-made, an inconspicuous dam converting two small and marshy tarns into the present sheet of water. Some judicious tree-planting completes the picture. The area is owned and maintained by the National Trust.

The road on to Coniston is one-way after the last car park is passed, an unfortunate but very necessary measure in response to the pressure of motor traffic to this beauty spot. (Tarn Hows on a summer's day, and Tarn Hows at sunset, after the crowds have gone, are two completely different places.) The single-lane road drops, not too steeply at first, with glorious views over to the Coniston Fells, and then plunges into woods, eventually to emerge on the direct road from Hawkshead ½m north of the lake and 1½m short of Coniston. The rest is easy cycling, but the road apt to be busy. The northern end of Coniston Water is fringed with shingle, and, being shallow, is a popular bathing and paddling spot, resembling a seaside beach at times. Coniston and its surroundings are described on page 55.

From Coniston, the Ambleside road is taken, running through beautiful scenery below the precipitous Yewdale Fell. The blend of greens and greys, especially in autumn when enhanced with the browns of the dying bracken, is gorgeous. It is one of the prettiest sections of 'A' road in the country, but also one of the most twisting — long may it remain so!

About 1½m north of the village, turn up a branch road, which

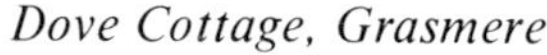

Dove Cottage, Grasmere

bears left, signposted to Tilberthwaite Ghyll. A mile up this side valley, a car park and old mine spoil heap mark the start of the path.

The first few hundred yards of the path, a steep climb alongside the old coppermines, are unpromising. Then a fork right leads down into the ghyll, a steep-sided cleft enclosing the stream. A bridge crosses its rocky bed to the northern side and the path seems to disappear, but the nimble-footed can follow the ghyll up to a second bridge, a dead-end, situated at the foot of some little cascades. By retracing one's steps a little, and then climbing to the left, the well-defined track coming down from Wetherlam is met.

The tarred road ends at High Tilberthwaite, but it continues as a metalled lane through the farmyard (pass through two gates and keep right). It winds through secluded glades of birch, but, even in this out-of-the-way spot, evidence of man is revealed in the remains of old slate workings. Half a mile from the farm, take a right fork (the path straight on, through the gate, leads only to a slate quarry). This turning drops down a rough pitch to a small clearing by the stream. Here a track leads sharp right to Hodge Close and the Coniston to Ambleside main road. For Little Langdale continue straight on, the track now rideable again, though bumpy, to reach the footbridge across the Brathay in ½m. A pull up the lane brings one out at the inn and hamlet of Little Langdale.

NB The road route from Coniston to Little Langdale, round via Colwith Bridge, adds about a mile but saves a little time.

If going up the valley, a more interesting alternative is not to cross the footbridge, but to take the minor road along the south side of the river. In about a quarter of a mile, a footpath leads from this to Slaters' Bridge, near the outfall from Little Langdale Tarn. It is a most primitive structure, evidently designed on a Monday and built on a Friday, thrown across the river in a most irregular fashion. Beyond Low Hall Garth, the lane peters out into a cart track of variable quality but mainly rideable. It makes an excellent cycling route, free from traffic and epitomising all that is best about 'off the road' cycling, without troubling the most cautious rider. The views are excellent, including the Langdale Pikes and, a little further on, the majestic sweep of the northern flanks of Wetherlam and Swirl How. Ahead, cars can be seen climbing like snails up the long drag to Wrynose Pass.

After crossing the river, the road up the valley is gained a little short of Fellfoot. The road across to Great Langdale is reached by turning first right and then left at the cattle grid. From there the road climbs immediately, steepening under the brow concealing Blea Tarn. There is a good rear view of the Wetherlam and Birk Fell ridge, but Blea Tarn and its surroundings are rather desolate. Contouring around the lake basin, the second (and higher) summit is reached, with the familiar Langdale Pikes seen in full splendour at last. This summit (722ft, 224 metres) reveals the green valley far below and the array of mountains that guards its head. On the left is the deep Oxendale leading up to the aptly-named Crinkle Crags. These continue round to the majestic Bow Fell, with the long ridge known as the Band stretching down almost to one's feet. To the right is the level strath of Mickleden, from the head of which steep paths lead over into the inner recesses of the mountains. Directly opposite one's viewpoint tower the Langdale Pikes, all their well-known features readily identifiable.

A much superior viewpoint, easily reached from the road summit, is Side Pike (1,187ft, 362 metres). As well as showing Langdale and the Pikes to greater effect, Helvellyn, Fairfield and the Coniston Fells come into view. The climb takes about fifteen minutes.

The descent into Langdale is extremely steep (up to 1 in 4) and made worse by the many twists and turns. One must not expect much consideration from motorists coming up the hill, and care should be taken especially in wet weather. Across the valley is the Dungeon Ghyll Old Hotel and a little further on the New Hotel, both well patronised by the walking and climbing fraternity on days both wet and dry. There is a cafe near the New Hotel, which is the starting point for the paths up to Dungeon Ghyll and the Langdale Pikes (see Route 11).

Old road through Langdale
This leaves the modern road through the car park opposite the turning to Stickle Barn. Running down the centre of the valley, it offers the better views, especially in retrospect, and rejoins the present road after a mile.

The road from Dungeon Ghyll down the vale to Chapel Stile is very scenic, though the best sights now lie behind. At Chapel Stile, a slate quarrying village, the roads to Ambleside and Grasmere diverge, the latter — very narrow — climbing up the hillside to a terrace-like stretch before rising again across the open fell. Below, half hidden amongst the trees, is Elterwater. Further up the hill, the views open up, before the road dodges behind the high walls of High Close Youth Hostel.

Near the road top, opposite the NT plaque, a broad footpath branches left. In a quarter of a mile it reaches a rocky pinnacle, affording an exquisite prospect over Grasmere much superior to that from the road below. Return to High Close the same way.

Rounding the hostel wall the road meets that coming up from Skelwith Bridge in a dip, before descending to the top of a steep pitch, Red Bank, and dropping down to Grasmere.

Loughrigg Terrace
This is one of the most popular walks in the neighbourhood. The path turns out of the road just below the top of Red Bank to fall gently along the northern flank of Loughrigg Fell. The views, first over Grasmere, and then over Rydal Water to the long ridges thrown out by Fairfield, are magnificent. The path is classified as a bridleway and is mainly rideable, but is so much used by walkers that it would be somewhat churlish to traverse it other than on foot.

On the descent of Red Bank the characteristic situation of Grasmere is revealed; the lake in the foreground, the village with its squat church lying beyond, the distinctive Helm Crag rising steeply out of the vale and to its right the severe line of the road climbing to Dunmail Raise. The top of Red Bank is very steep, but lower down the gradient eases and permits a more leisurely appreciation of the view. For a description of Grasmere and vicinity see page 69.

The circuit of Thirlmere (Route 31) can be included by an extension of 17m from Grasmere. The lake lies just over the watershed of Dunmail Raise.

The final stage of the journey, back to Ambleside, is via the invariably-busy A591, but the road is no anticlimax. The run, a welcome gentle downgrade, first skirts Grasmere and then follows the sparkling Rothay to Rydal Water, beautifully backed by Loughrigg Fell. Ambleside is reached through scenery of a park-like richness. As a final flourish, one should sample the little lane below Loughrigg Fell, passing to the west of Ambleside.

Bridleway lovers may be interested in the original packhorse road from Grasmere to Rydal, reached by crossing the A591, ascending the hill and ignoring all turnings to left or right. It eventually peters out into a rather rough footpath, before improving again on nearing Rydal. Here one must cut down to the main road. Like Loughrigg Terrace, across the valley, this bridleway is a well-used pedestrian route, linking two of Wordsworth's homes as well as offering excellent views.

Keswick to Threlkeld, St John's Vale & Thirlmere

Distances from Keswick: Threlkeld 4½m, Thirlspot 9¾m, Wythburn Church 12½m, Thirlmere Dam 17¾m (Threlkeld 27½m), Keswick (direct) 22¾m.

INTRODUCTION

This makes an extremely pleasant half-day's tour from Keswick; it includes the circuit of Thirlmere and largely avoids the main roads. The outward route to Threlkeld also forms an attractive and almost traffic-free (albeit much slower) alternative to the A66 or the old main road. As Thirlmere is at a higher elevation than Keswick and the direct road between them crosses an intervening hill, it is preferable to save this road (A591) for the return journey.

DESCRIPTION

From Keswick take Station Road which leads up the side of the park, passing the Youth Hostel entrance and the museum. The road bears right, to pass under the old railway, and joins a lane running round the north of the town from Crosthwaite. Here turn right again, following the signpost for Windebrowe and Brundholme. The road is tarred for 2m, though shown 'uncoloured' on the OS map.

The road gradually ascends to cross the bypass. From the bridge there is a fine view over Keswick to the circle of fells enclosing Derwentwater, although only a small part of the lake is seen.

From the top of the hill on the road the same view reappears, but with Derwentwater more prominent. Ahead is the long Helvellyn range, but that mountain is not seen to any advantage from the west. The next mile or so is a gorgeous run along a terrace road, with the river Greta glimpsed far below through the tall woods that clothe the hillside. Eventually a gate is reached, at which a lane dropping down sharply to the right is taken, passing Brundholme. (Care should be taken, as the road surface is very loose in places.) The meeting of the rivers near the bridge at the bottom is a lovely spot. After passing through another gate,

31

Skiddaw
Blencathra
A66
Threlkeld
192m
165m
KESWICK
150m
B5322
214m
225m
A591
St John's Vale
156m
N
191m
169m
Thirlspot
189m
215m
Thirlmere
A591
0
5km
0
3m
Helvellyn
Wythburn
179m
ROUTE 31
Dunmail Raise

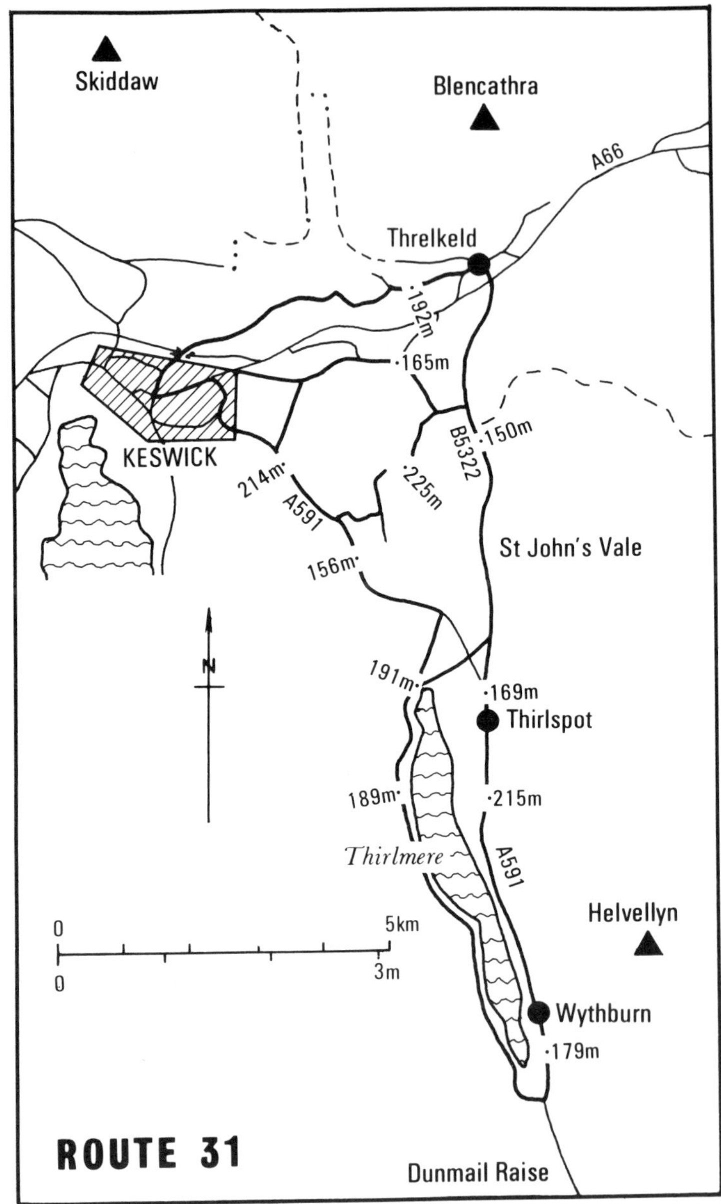

there is a climb up to the hamlet of Wescoe. On the way one can see the erosion caused by the streamlet on the left of the road.

From the hilltop, there is one last view back over to the Derwent Fells, before one gently descends to Threlkeld. Ahead are the large Threlkeld granite quarries and, on the horizon Cross Fell, the highest summit on the Pennine Chain, may be discernible. As one enters the village, the enormous ravines of Blencathra (Saddleback) come into view, together with that mountain's fine summit. Threlkeld, much improved by having its through traffic removed, is now very quiet.

For St John's Vale and Thirlmere, turn out of the main village street by the shop (signposted 'no through road'). A gate at the bottom brings one out onto the bypass opposite the road up the vale, B5322. The road is easy going and there is no better way to sample the scenery than from a bicycle. At Wanthwaite, two alternative roads from Keswick join, but as they involve a considerable climb out of the town, they will be described below as options for the return journey.

The road beyond Wanthwaite is one of growing interest, the valley gradually narrowing and the hillsides becoming more craggy and wooded. Amidst the finest parts of the scenery is the 'Castle Rock of Tremain', an impressive outcrop on the east side of the valley. Here a road (now gated) strikes off right to the Thirlmere dam.

If one intends to circle the lake in a clockwise direction, continue southwards until the A591, the direct road from Keswick, is reached, ¾m short of the King's Head Inn at Thirlspot. The lake is not seen until the rise beyond the inn is breasted, where there is a fine viewpoint (the best from the main road), especially if the adjacent little knoll is ascended. This reveals more of the lake and the massive flanks of Helvellyn. The road gradually drops to the lakeside and the little church at Wythburn, the roadside wooded but not so densely as to obstruct the view of the water. The mock castle passed on the right is the start of the aqueduct to Manchester, 96m away.

For the west-side road, turn right shortly after Wythburn church. The well engineered road back up the lake provides an even gradient, but the view of the lake is obstructed by the dense woods that are such a fine feature from the far side. The walls are rather too well constructed and regimented to blend in fully with their surroundings. Gradually, however, the curtain of trees thins out and where the road runs in a rocky cutting some steps on the right lead to the best viewpoint on this side of the lake, Hause Point. This is the only spot on the roadside offering a prospect of the full lenght of the lake. Launchy Gill, a little further on, contains some fine falls.

The road leads on to Armboth, now only a name on the map but once a hamlet until cleared on the raising of the lake. The
31 hillside is heavily wooded, but the view across Thirlmere is largely open. At the end of the lake the road onward leads to Keswick direct, joining the A591 in about a mile. Note that coming from Keswick this road is not signposted, as it is halfway along the dual carriageway section.

A more leisurely return might be made back down St John's Vale, the course taken by the stream emanating from Thirlmere. Take the road across the dam (good view down the lake) to the A591, where the gated road opposite leads across to the foot of the Castle Rock and to the road back to Wanthwaite. The first few miles involve going back over earlier ground but this is the sweetest part of the vale. Reaching Wanthwaite, one of the ways back to Keswick is to continue down the valley to pick up the A66, an effortless 5m. Alternatively, cross Wanthwaite Bridge and then turn right, climbing up to the old main road to Keswick (to gain this road if coming from that town, turn off the A66 where it is signposted Burns, shortly after joining the bypass). One must be careful about describing this as the 'old' road as it in turn replaced the original road, with its steeper gradients, which runs past the Castlerigg Stone Circle. The location of the circle, 700ft (213 metres) up but surrounded by some of the highest fells in Lakeland, is unforgettable. The circle is thought to date from around three or four thousand years ago and, though its exact purpose is unknown, it would form an obvious meeting place. There is a steep drop into Keswick.

Another interesting way back to Keswick is via St John's Church, reached by turning left after crossing Wanthwaite Bridge. The church, mainly nineteenth century, retains a few older features. Its situation, almost on the watershed between two valleys, is very dramatic with steep southern aspect of Blencathra being seen to full advantage. Across St John's Vale, the Old Coach Road over to Ullswater (Route 25) can be seen snaking up the hillside.

Continuing from the church along the lane, another gate is passed through beyond which there is a steep descent into the vale of the Naddle. This is the only part of the crossing not tarred and the loose surface requires a little care. At the bottom, bear left along a lane which, after a twisty mile, comes out on the main A591 road at Dale Bottom, about 2½m from Keswick. There is a fair sized hill to be surmounted first, from the top of which a diversion can be made to Castlerigg Stone Circle (see above). All ways down into Keswick are steep.

Keswick to Borrowdale

About 20-25 miles.
Direct distances from Keswick: Watendlath 5m, Grange $4\frac{1}{4}$m, Rosthwaite 6m, Seatoller $7\frac{1}{2}$m, Seathwaite $8\frac{1}{2}$m, Watendlath-Grange $5\frac{1}{4}$m.

INTRODUCTION

This is perhaps the best (and, except for the diversion to Watendlath, probably the easiest) cycling excursion to be made in the Lake District. The scenery is of the highest standard throughout; but it is so popular with motor traffic that it should definitely be avoided on summer weekends.

The route described below includes all the cycling roads in the valley, together with the digression up to Watendlath. My personal recommendation, however, would be to make this delightful hamlet the subject of a separate visit — perhaps an evening's run after lodgings have been sorted out, and the crowds have gone, but while there is still some gentle evening light to savour. Watendlath is best 'discovered' by the path up from Rosthwaite, and this can be included to extend the exploration of Borrowdale into a leisurely day.

Although the route is described below in a clockwise direction, it is equally scenic taken in the reverse direction, much will depend on whether the cyclist is interested in getting the clearest views or the most sun.

DESCRIPTION

From Keswick, the road ascends gradually out of the town before Derwentwater comes into view, the road running near the margin of the lake below steep, wooded, hillsides. Across the lake is the graceful and distinctive ridge of Catbells and Maiden Moor, with the massed Derwent Fells beyond. 2m from Keswick the side road to Watendlath climbs away sharply on the left.

Watendlath by road
The secluded hamlet of Watendlath lies 5m south of Keswick, at the head of a side valley about 600ft (180 metres) above Derwentwater. From the lakeside there is a steep climb for over a mile. Ashness Bridge,

32

Braithwaite
Portinscale
KESWICK
Nichol End
96m
122m
90m
Stair
Derwentwater
Old Road
154m
80m
Ashness Bridge
Little Town
3km
2m
0
0
88m
85m
249m
B5289
Grange
175m
Watendlath
260m
Bowder Stone
Borrowdale
83m
325m
N
Rosthwaite
Honister Hause
B5289
Seatoller
102m
Stonethwaite
356m
125m
Seathwaite
Langstrath
Stockley Bridge
ROUTE 32

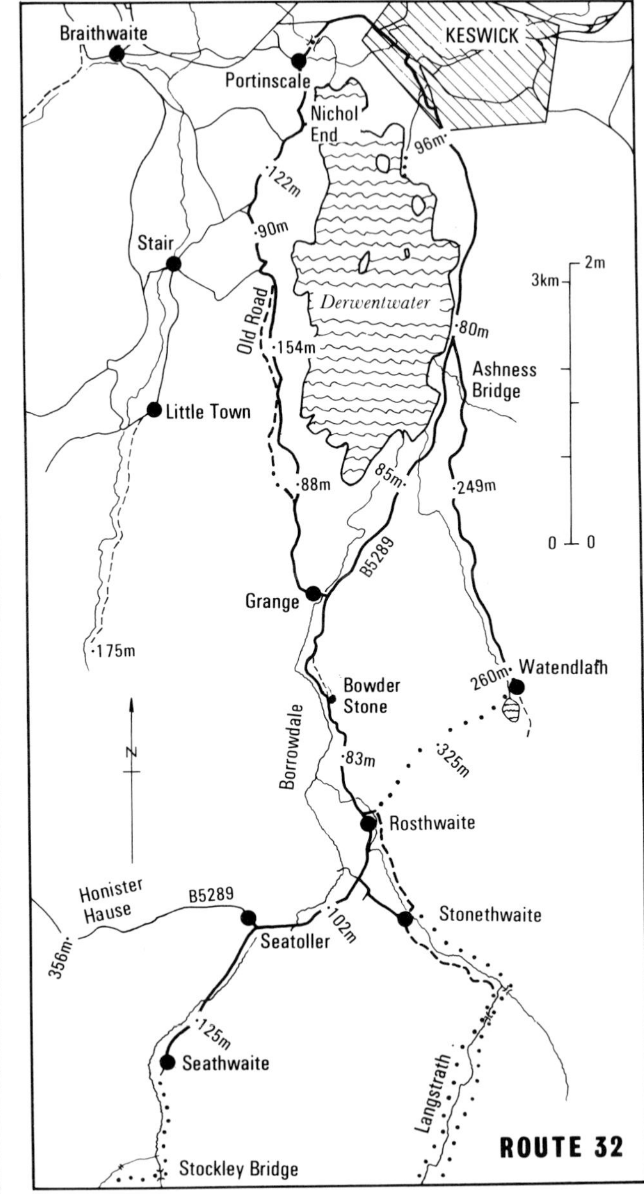

about halfway up, is a well-loved beauty spot; it has a magnificent view of Derwentwater backed by Skiddaw, and the charm of rustic simplicity of the bridge itself. It is one of the most photographed scenes in Lakeland, probably only Tarn Hows gracing more biscuit tins, There is a brief level stretch before the gradient resumes and the woods are re-entered. At one point, unmistakable, a walk of a few yards to the right of the road brings one to a most dramatic viewpoint, with the wooded cliffs falling away apparently vertically to the lakeside below. The summit of the road is a little further on, shortly before it emerges from the woods with the Watendlath Beck on the right. A footpath at this point leads down to some cascades. The remaining mile or so to Watendlath is along the 'hanging' valley and comparatively level. Just below the hamlet there is a pretty bit of rock scenery along the stream.

Watendlath, consisting of a few cottages, farm buildings and a tarn surrounded by bare fells, presents a most tranquil picture. The large car park comes as an unpleasant surprise, but it is necessary; Watendlath is a popular starting point for several mountain walks as well as being visited for its own sake. If the only access for tourists was the steep path up from Rosthwaite, there would be many fewer of them, and the place would be all the better for it. Refreshments are available at a couple of the cottages.

There is no alternative return route from Watendlath other than the Rosthwaite path (see below) over which it is possible to heave a cycle, but the views cannot be appreciated if travelling in this way. It is preferable to retreat down the road to regain the lakeside.

From the Watenlath turn, the road runs below high crags, down which tumble the Lodore Falls. The falls require a large amount of rain to be more than a rather disappointing trickle. A little further on the bridge at Grange is reached, but is not crossed on this outward journey. The little village lying across the bridge presents an attractive appearance and the wide river bed testifies to the power and volume of the water after rain. Ahead, the valley is at its most beautiful — the rugged mountains a backcloth to the lower outcrops which are resplendent in a rich and varied clothing of trees. The most prominent feature is Castle Crag, seemingly unscalable and dividing the valley in two.

Continuing, the road runs through a narrow tree-clad gorge, accompanied by the river. Soon a large car park indicates the proximity of the Bowder Stone, a gigantic piece of rock, weighing nearly 2000 tons, that long ago was left behind by the retreating glaciers. From its size and position, it has become a tourist attraction and a ladder erected to take the steady-headed to its top. The shortest path to the stone is from near the second footpath sign some way beyond the car park.

After passing below Castle Crag, the valley opens out again, to reveal a rich sheltered vale, in the centre of which is the hamlet of Rosthwaite, a good halt for refreshment as here are the last inns and shop in the valley.

Rosthwaite to Watendlath by path

This makes a grand diversion, if unhindered by a cycle. Allow an hour in each direction. The path is extremely well trodden as this is a popular excursion, and there is no chance of losing one's way. Watendlath (see above) presents a most serene picture on the descent from the summit. The return may be profitably varied via the top of Brund Fell, which offers an extensive view of Derwentwater not revealed from the path. This should be regained near its highest point: avoid short cuts down to Borrowdale.

The eminent Victorian guide-book writer, H.I. Jenkinson, chided the hotel-keepers of Keswick for not constructing a carriage-road from Rosthwaite to Watendlath and so opening up a circular route for tourist traffic. One wonders at the reaction that such a suggestion would now receive!

A little above Rosthwaite the valley forks. Take the side turning on the left, which leads in a little way to the hamlet of Stonethwaite, tucked right among the fells. An alternative, recommended, from Rosthwaite to Stonethwaite is by a delightful track along the east side of the beck between the two bridges, one of the prettiest miles in Lakeland. At Stonethwaite the road ends, but a stony cart track, barely rideable in parts, may be followed up to the meeting of Langstrath Beck and Greenup Gill, below Eagle Crag. The river here is very attractive. Cycles can be taken a little further up Langstrath, but we are now in walkers' territory. A return to the main road, though necessary, is hardly an imposition.

Continuing along this road

Blencathra and Derwentwater from Catbells

for a mile, one comes to Seatoller, nestling at the foot of the Honister Pass. Unless proceeding to Buttermere, there is no need to inspect this road any further, and one should now explore the side turning to Seathwaite. Although the road has climbed less than 150ft (45 metres) in the 8m from Keswick, the valley now narrows abruptly at the confluence of its headstreams.

Seathwaite enjoys the reputation of being the 'wettest inhabited place in England', with an annual rainfall of about 125in. This is about four times that of London and twice that of nearby Keswick. This should not be taken to imply that it is always raining in Borrowdale — rather that when it rains it really rains. It should not be forgotten that it is due to this that many waterfalls are a feature of the area.

An interesting walk may be had from Seathwaite up the west side of the valley to Taylorgill Force, a fine fall. The stream may be forded higher up, and a return made via Stockley Bridge. The mountain path from Stockley Bridge over to Wasdale is given in Route 40.

From Seathwaite the road down the valley is retraced for 4m to the bridge at Grange, which is crossed to gain the road along the west side of Derwentwater. The road runs some way above the lake and offers fine views across to the wooded cliffs that flank the east of the valley. The woods of Brandelow Park stretching down from the road to the lake present a wonderful picture.

Still finer views can be obtained from an old abandoned road (marked on the map as a bridleway) running parallel but at a higher level. This starts immediately after the picturesque farm of Manesty (¾m from Grange) and follows the Newlands track for 300yd before diverging to the top corner of the wood. This initial stage is hard going, but, after passing the wood, a glorious panorama over Derwentwater is revealed. The road surface is now much better, especially where recent repair work has been undertaken, and it can be ridden almost throughout. After briefly reuniting with the present road at a little quarry, (so enabling this trickier first part to be avoided) it diverges to the left again to continue as a grassy terrace along the hillside, all rideable and free of traffic. No one who takes this upper road is likely to feel unrewarded.

Bearing in mind the recent growth of interest in industrial archaeology, particularly that of railways and canals, it is strange that the history and development of our roads has been so neglected. Along Derwentwater the present road is, in fact, the third to be constructed. The original, passing through Brundelow Park, was stopped up around 1780 and the road described above was constructed. This was soon found to be too hilly and the present motor road was built to replace it. The top road has been abandoned ever since.

32 Considering the amount of time and money spent restoring other transport relics, it is good to see that attention has been given to protecting this fine old road from further decay.

The upper and present roads eventually unite at the northern end of the Catbells ridge, near where the direct road to Portinscale and Keswick, reached in about three miles, drops down the hill. The gated road forward leads to Skelgill and the Newlands valley and may be followed through Stair to rejoin the direct road at the Swinside Inn. This road rises a little further before dropping to Portinscale. A short diversion leads to the fringe of the lake at Nichol End, a pleasant enough spot to while away any remaining time.

At Portinscale, traffic for Keswick is now signposted left, but the road to the right is the shorter and original route. A footbridge occupies the site of the historic Long Bridge, dismantled after flood damage in 1954.

Skiddaw from the old road below Catbells

Keswick to Caldbeck (circular)

Distances from Keswick: Orthwaite 8½m, Caldbeck 15m, Hesket Newmarket 16¼m, Low Row 18¼m, Mosedale 21¼m, Mungrisdale 22¾m (Troutbeck 26m), Threlkeld 27½m, Keswick 31½m.

Some distances from Caldbeck: Uldale 5¼m, Castle Inn 8¾m, Cockermouth 15½m, Aspatria 13m, Wigton 7½m, Carlisle 13½m, Penrith 15¼m, Greystoke 10¼m, Troutbeck 11m.

NB The signposted way for traffic between Keswick and Caldbeck is via the A591 to Castle Inn, then via Uldale. This road, though better for motor vehicles, is a mile longer and equally hilly.

INTRODUCTION

Scenically, this excursion belongs with the northern Pennines rather than the Lake District, the rolling lower slopes of Skiddaw and the surrounding fells having little individuality. However, the roads are comparatively quiet, and John Peel's grave at Caldbeck provides a focus of interest. The round trip, encircling Skiddaw Forest, is only 32m — a half-day's cycling which can easily be extended to suit the individual. For example, a circuit of Bassenthwaite Lake may be included, or a diversion from Threlkeld to St John's Vale and Thirlmere. The delightful back lane from Threlkeld to Keswick, along the north side of the Greta, also deserves consideration. It matters little in which direction the trip is made, though, in a headwind, the westbound climb out of Caldbeck is very dreary.

DESCRIPTION

From Keswick, the Carlisle road is taken, a pleasant road rising gently below the wooded hillside. The upper road via Applethwaite, with its terrace view, might be included. About six miles from the town, a signpost points the way to Orthwaite. From the junction, the road climbs steadily (with one steep section) around the western flanks of Skiddaw, before dropping to cross the Dash Beck, flowing down the valley

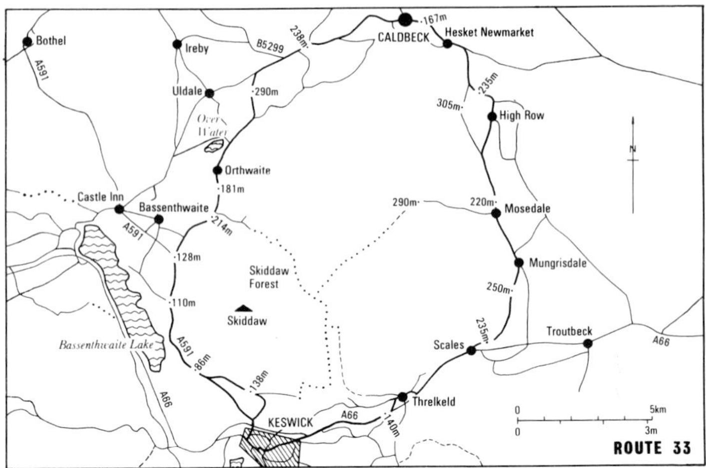

to the right. From the climb beyond the bridge, Whitewater Dash, a waterfall at the top of the valley, can be seen as a white streak. Orthwaite consists of only a few farms and the hall after which the road drops to pass Over Water, a fair-sized tarn but one neglected in this land of lakes. Despite its situation in the hills above Bassenthwaite, its outlet, the river Ellen, flows north. The road takes another steep rise and fall to Longlands, from where there is the long final climb to the junction of the road via Uldale. In the reverse direction, that is the signposted route to Keswick; there is also a confusing sign near Over Water. From the road junction it is an easy run of about four miles, nearly all downhill, into Caldbeck.

The lonely, unfenced, roads stretching across the moor were in former days of greater strategic importance than now. The principal route from Carlisle to both Keswick and Cockermouth passed this way, being joined near the Thorney Stone, midway between Caldbeck and Uldale, by the road from Penrith. This ran direct from Hesket Newmarket to Parkend, passing south of Caldbeck.

Caldbeck is the halfway point of the round trip from Keswick, and presents a welcome sight after the bare moors traversed to the west. It is famous as the home of the huntsman, John Peel (1776-1854), immortalised in song. (His grave is in the churchyard.) The village itself is rather plain and unsophisticated: it is an agricultural community first, and a tourist centre second.

Just west of the village the river has created a pretty bit of scenery, the Howk, where it has carved a gorge through a limestone step. There are some falls and rocky vantage-points, yet so poorly signposted and frequently so muddy is the path that one wonders whether visitors are encouraged.

From Caldbeck there is a gradual ascent to Hesket Nemarket, once a market town, but now a quiet and rather timeworn village. The climb resumes, now steeply, for another 1½m, before the road drops to the hamlets of Low and High Row. At the latter a new Youth Hostel was opened in 1982. From there it is an easy run across the unfenced moor to the foot of Carrock Fell, which is skirted, to the hamlet of Mosedale, at the foot of the valley of the same name. Here a deviation may be made up Mosedale to the road end at the Carrock Fell Mines, about two miles away (see Route 34).

Continuing along the road to Keswick brings one to Mungrisdale, an attractively situated village, its houses nestling under the hillside. Here turn right over the river Glenderamackin and take the narrow road behind the Mill Inn. This runs via Southerfell to the main Penrith to Keswick road at Scales and is tarred throughout, though gated. From Scales, Keswick can be reached in under half an hour by an easy run down the busy A66, but the unhurrying cyclist will have no difficulty in choosing a more interesting or attractive route.

Hesket Newmarket

34 Through Skiddaw Forest

Distances/times from Keswick: Start of track to Dash Beck 7¼m (¾hr), Skiddaw House 10¾m (1¾hr), Keswick 16¾m (2¾hr), Threlkeld 14¾m (2¼hr), Mosedale 16m (3hr).

Times to Skiddaw House direct: From Keswick 1½hr, Threlkeld 1hr, Mosedale 1¾hr.

The road encircling Skiddaw Forest through Caldbeck is described in Route 33.

INTRODUCTION

The treeless upland of Skiddaw Forest offers considerable scope for the cyclist who is hoping to find peace and solitude away from motor roads. These rolling heather-clad hills, dominated by the smooth flanks of Skiddaw, are unbroken by wall or tree, the only building being the now uninhabited Skiddaw House.

The tracks described are in surprisingly good shape and for the most part rideable, if cumulatively bone-shaking. They are appreciably less difficult than the mountain passes given in a later section of this guide, involving much less physical effort or natural hazard, but the area is remote and the precautionary points made on pages 17-18 should be noted. All the streams and water courses are crossed by footbridges.

There are four tracks into the forest: from near Bassenthwaite village, climbing up alongside the Dash Beck; the two from Keswick and Threlkeld, which unite at the head of the Glenderaterra Beck; and from the hamlet of Mosedale following the Caldew. By coincidence each of these approaches uses a tarred road to more or less the same elevation, 950ft (290 metres). Scenically, the best route is eastwards from Bassenthwaite village up to Skiddaw House, then turning south to gain the spectacular terrace path skirting Lonscale Fell, to emerge high above Keswick. The Threlkeld path provides an equally impressive conclusion. The reverse of this route involves a very long and stiff ascent out of Keswick, and the better views all lie behind. The path from Skiddaw House down the valley of the Caldew is not rideable and is a little tedious. The route described is thus from Bassenthwaite to Skiddaw House, with notes on the later alternatives.

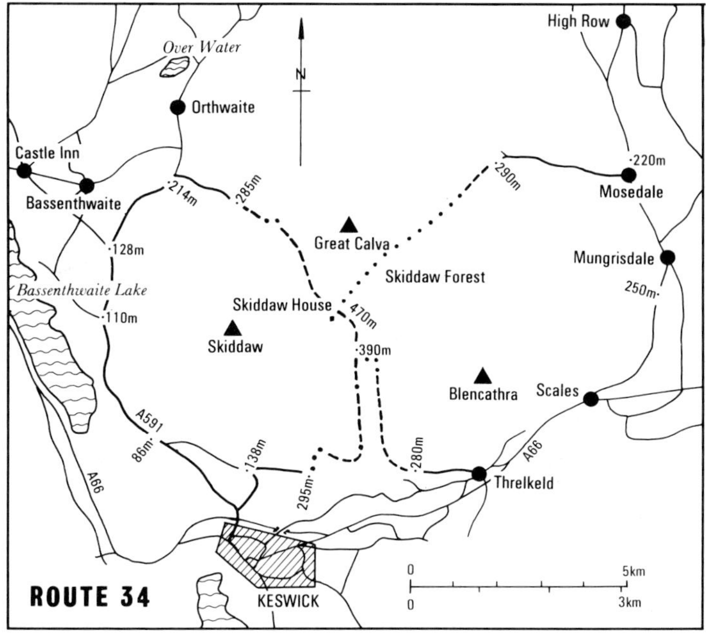

DESCRIPTION

From Keswick the A591 Carlisle road is followed to the Orthwaite turn (6m), this sideroad being followed to just before the second summit. The main road passes below the wooded height of Dodd, an outlier of Skiddaw, and it might be worth mentioning that we shall be climbing to an equivalent height. Joining from Bassenthwaite village (7½m from Cockermouth), the shortest way (if you can find it) is up by Chapel Beck to meet the road from Keswick in a dip.

From the road, the bridleway to Skiddaw House commences as a farm access road, tarred and gated, for nearly a mile until it forks right. It continues as a well-made track, surfaced with stone chippings, gradually working its way up the valley. The waterfall, Whitewater Dash, presents a fine appearance ahead, while on the right towers the lofty eyrie of Dead Crag. With a big zigzag the track winds up to the top of the fall, this steep pitch requiring care in descent. After crossing a bridge, the way ahead strikes across the heather moor to the summit level of 1,620ft (494 metres). To the south is the unbroken northern flank of

Skiddaw, the one shapely peak being Lonscale Fell, skirted by the track to Keswick. Ahead can be seen the lonely Skiddaw House, with its sheltering belt of trees. The track remains good throughout, and provides the vehicular access to the house.

Skiddaw House is in fact a short row of cottages, built to accommodate the shepherds and gamekeepers whose work was among these hills. With changing patterns of farming, they gradually fell vacant and are now boarded up and unoccupied, save at lambing time. In medieval times there was a hunting lodge on the site. There are more remotely situated buildings in Britain but few can match the sense of isolation here.

(a) Skiddaw House to Mosedale
This accompanies the infant river Caldew down to the road, skirting the eastern perimeter of Skiddaw Forest. The path drops steeply from the house to a footbridge, then rises slightly before contouring down the valley. If coming from Dash Beck the corner may be cut off by a faint path along the foot of Great Calva. The path onwards is a little indistinct in places, and, though grassy, is a little too rough for cycling. Progress is thus steady but slow for about 2½m, until the end of a dirt road is reached. Skiddaw House will still be in view behind, an hour after it was left.

The dirt-road, recently bulldozed, provides a poor cycling surface, but the tarred road is reached just below the Carrock Fell Mine. The remaining 2m down the valley are refreshingly green, and the riverbank usually lined with tourists' cars. Mosedale hamlet is about ten miles from Keswick, six from Caldbeck, the way described in Route 33.

(b) Skiddaw House to Threlkeld
This turns out of the Keswick track (see below) about a mile south of the house and, of the two, has the better surface. After dropping across the valley bottom, it continues as a well-constructed track which is easily rideable. On the descent, Derwentwater, backed by successive ranks of fells, emerges, while the sheer-sided valley of the Glenderaterra adds some interest close at hand. The tarred road is met by the entrance to the Blencathra Centre, with a steep descent from there into Threlkeld. The village is entered by Blease Road.

There is also a metalled track from Wescoe, near Threlkeld, up the bottom of the valley to the old lead mine, but there is no northern outlet.

(c) Skiddaw House to Keswick
From the house the track drops to a fence on the indistinct

watershed between the Caldew and the Glenderaterra, then bearing slightly right. A little further on it meets the top corner of a wall (coming the reverse way one should bear left here, uphill, not straight on). After a quarter mile, the Threlkeld path drops away, and can be seen contouring along the opposite side of the valley, while the Keswick path takes a parallel and equally impressive course. Just beyond the fork one execrable section, a morass of liquid mud, has to be circumvented where the path climbs a little, but then it continues in excellent shape again, a firm mat of small stone and turf. Ahead, the eye is drawn to the fine prospect up the Vale of St John to Helvellyn. After cautiously skirting the rocky outcrops on the east side of Lonscale Fell, the path swings right to a gate. The view now extends to include Derwentwater and Borrowdale, though Keswick remains concealed behind Latrigg. The firm, grassy, track continues to descend, with magnificent views. Eventually, after crossing a stream, it climbs again, to join the main footpath down from Skiddaw. The path is narrow and fenced in, and involves two stiles, but one can use the gates in the field alongside. A little further on is the terminus of the road leading down to Applethwaite which forms the best route to Keswick. This road is in poor condition — loose and potholed — and is probably the most hazardous part of the journey.

The direct way to Keswick, by the bridle path turning out of the road a little way down it, is popular with hikers and so cannot be recommended.

Blencathra from across Derwentwater

35

Around Ullswater: Patterdale to Howtown

Distances from Patterdale: Sandwick 4m (allow about 1½hr), Howtown 6¼m, Pooley Bridge 10¼m, Patterdale 19½m.

INTRODUCTION

This forms an extremely useful link along the eastern shore of Ullswater, its main advantage being that it enables the cyclist to make a complete circuit of the lake.* For the fully-laden tourist it will be found a little arduous, and for those of a nervous disposition there are one or two places where there is a steep drop to the watersedge. For cyclists who like to get away from busy roads and don't mind wheeling their bikes along the rougher parts, it will be found ideal. It will here be described starting from Patterdale, as if circling the lake this traverses the slow part first; scenically, there is little to choose between the two directions.

DESCRIPTION

From Patterdale, cross the bridge just north of the hotels, turning left in the hamlet of Rooking on the far side of the valley. The road passes through two gates and joins another that leaves the main road near the school at Glenridding (signposted to Side Farm). Continue through another gate marked 'Private road to Blowick House and camp site', and continue along the cart track. Across Ullswater are seen Grisedale and Glenridding, the latter with its old mineworkings. Between the two valleys rises the path to Striding Edge and Helvellyn.

The track onwards is dry but a little lumpy in places, and it will be found easier to wheel the cycle. A little further on, there is a beautiful view across the head of the lake, all the more attractive if there are some boats on the water. The wooded hills beyond the lake are charming, the craggy higher fells providing a fine backcloth.

* For steamer services between Glenridding and Howtown see page 16.

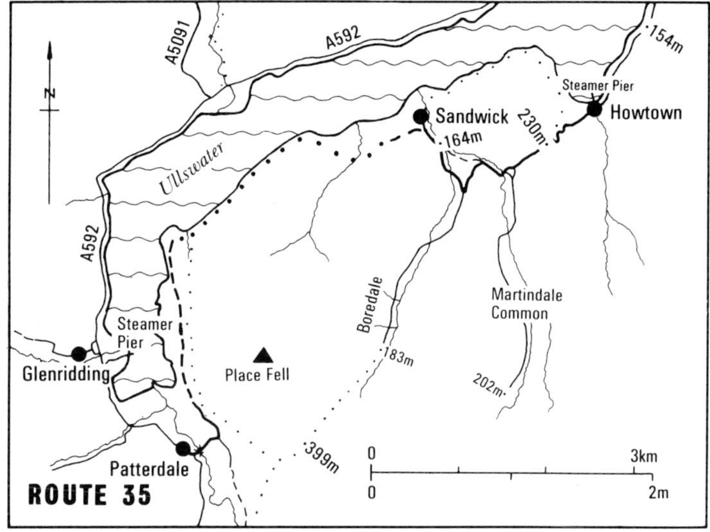

Soon a farm outbuilding is passed on the left, shortly after which the track divides into three, our route continuing along the wall to the left. The green central track leads nowhere and the rough footpath to the right ascends to the upper track from Rooking. This is passable (and affords the better views) but is not recommended as it rejoins the main path by a rough and steep descent in about ¾m.

Continuing along the bottom track the view is impeded by the high wall alongside. Where this finally bears away left, the surface, which so far has been mainly rideable, deteriorates and the cycle can only be wheeled. There are still 2m to the road end at Sandwick. The path first drops steeply to the side of a little headland (a good viewpoint) just below Silver Crag, before winding round the foot of the hillside. Ahead is the long curving middle reach of Ullswater, and there is a noticeable difference in the landscape, the hills being smoother and less enclosing. The retrospective view up the lake is dominated by St Sunday Crag.

Shortly after the headland, the upper track rejoins near a large cairn and the path continues below the wooded crags, with the lake some twenty or thirty feet below. After about half a mile the track climbs diagonally up the hillside, and there is a rather tricky spot where some boulders straddle it. The top, when reached, provides a fine picnic spot. The most prominent peak is now Catseye Cam, an outlying spur of Helvellyn, the summit of which it conceals. Across the lake the road over to Dockray and Keswick can be seen above the woods surrounding Aira Force.

Onwards the going becomes easier, and a little cycling is
35 possible. Turning a headland, there is a fine view down the lake, here looking more like a broad river. The path then climbs alongside a wall and drops to the footbridge over Scalehow Beck. Here it is very cut up but it soon improves to become a stony cart track as far as Sandwick, where the road proper is met. From here, the 2m to Howtown are hilly but very attractive, the road first following Boardale and then crossing into Martindale. The fine views up these secluded valleys, to the comparatively little-known fells beyond, are likely to encourage further exploration, roads running a short way up both dales. After crossing behind Hallin Fell, the road drops down a series of steep hairpin bends to the hamlet of Howtown. Here is the Howtown Hotel and a pier served by the lake steamers.

The 4m from Howtown to Pooley Bridge are easy, but the scenery becomes increasingly tame. If returning back up the western side of Ullswater, the details of the journey will already be familiar, but the views are completely different, with the eastern side of the lake now seen to the best advantage. The complete road from Penrith to Patterdale and beyond is given in Route 22.

NB If travelling from Pooley Bridge to Patterdale via Howtown avoid taking the wrong path, there being more than one way signposted between them.

Patterdale Youth Hostel

Coniston to Dunnerdale via Walna Scar

Distances from Coniston: Summit of Walna Scar Pass 3m, Seathwaite 5¼m, then to Broughton 7¼m, Cockley Beck Bridge 4¼m, Coniston (via Broughton Mills and Torver) 11¾m. Allow about three hours to Seathwaite.

INTRODUCTION

NB See general comments, pages 17-18. This ancient packhorse road leads west from Coniston to Seathwaite, in the Duddon valley. Its indeterminate history is presumably the reason why it is not awarded any specific status as a right of way, although there can be no objection to its use by cyclists. It involves some very rough going for about two miles on either side of the summit of the pass which will need to be wheeled; there is one very awkward section, on the eastern approach to the summit, where the cycle will have to be carried.

The Duddon valley near Seathwaite is most attractive: yet it can be reached only from Ambleside or Coniston by hilly roads —either over Wrynose or round via Broughton. The Walna Scar Road presents a central course, which, though not offering any saving of time (indeed the reverse) is a sporting route with some glorious views. If making a circular tour from Coniston, either of the two road routes mentioned above may be used for the return, or the variation described below. This brings the total ascent to 3,400ft (1,000 metres), which should be enough to please anybody. The inns at Seathwaite and Broughton Mills provide the only opportunities for refreshment until Torver, although there is a shop at Ulpha.

DESCRIPTION

From alongside the bridge in Coniston, turn up the by-road leading to the Sun Hotel, above which the road winds up to a junction. Here a finger post indicates the way up a very steep hill: cyclists coming in the reverse direction should take extreme care, this dangerous section coming unexpectedly after a sharp left-right zigzag. At the top the road continues to ascend, but less steeply, and the view up the

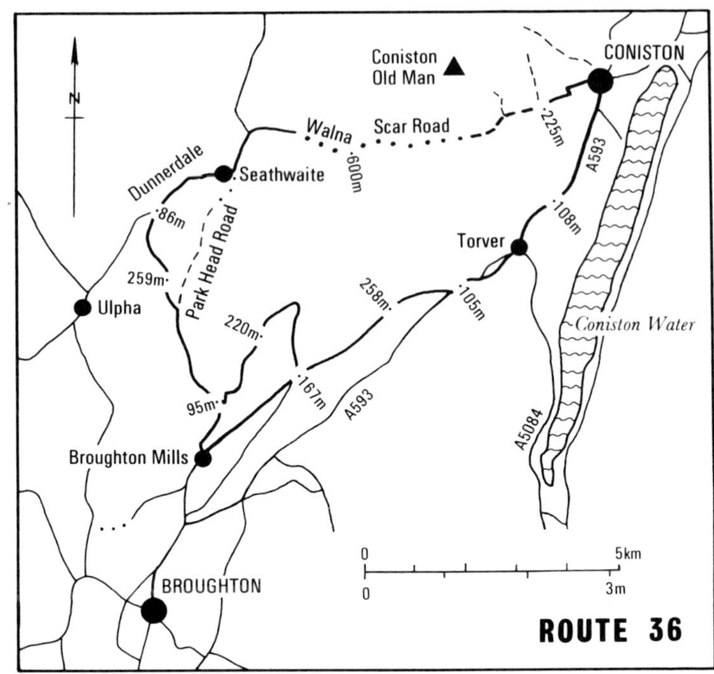

Coppermines valley, to the right, gradually opens up. The fine rocky peak at its head is Swirl How, 2,630ft (802 metres). Ahead is the great bulk of the Old Man of Coniston, the footpath to the top being conspicuous.

At a gate, a quarry track bears off right towards the mountain and the Walna Scar Road, now untarred, continues ahead across a rather bleak upland. After about a further half mile, the main track, to a quarry, climbs off to the right and the onward track shortly deteriorates into a stony, but well defined, path. From here onwards, cycles will need to be pushed to, and beyond, the top of the pass. Ignore all grassy tracks leading off to the left. In a little while the path forks, that to the right climbing to Goats Water, a fine corrie tarn overtowered by the Old Man and Dow Crag. If making the diversion, cycles should be left behind.

The main track (the left fork) continues diagonally up the hillside to a rustic bridge over the stream coming down from Goats Water. Some not-so-rustic railings are provided for you to lean your cycle against them while having a cooling paddle. The path continues to climb, though its stoniness can be avoided by taking a grassy alternative a little to the left. The two tracks unite below Goatfoot Crags. The next pitch is the steepest and roughest part of the crossing, and the cycle will need to be half dragged and half carried to get up it, though thankfully it only lasts about 200 yards. Then the track resumes a more gradual and uneventful climb, until the top of the pass is reached. This will have taken about two hours from Coniston.

The summit of the road falls just short of 2000ft, a deficiency which can be made up by pushing one's cycle a little way up the grassy hillside. The 2000ft mark is, incidentally, exceeded by one or two roads in the vicinity of Alston in the east of the county.

The view from the top of the pass, or, better still, the adjacent ridge, is very extensive, embracing the indented coastline of Morecambe Bay, the far-off Yorkshire peaks, and the readily identified flat-topped Ingleborough and man-made landmarks such as Heysham power station and Blackpool tower. The view ahead over the Duddon valley is superb. To the right is the ridge forming Sca Fell and Scafell Pike; in the centre is Harter Fell, and on its left is Sellafield. The river Duddon is not seen, having cut into its glaciated valley. Eastwards, and now seen for the last time, are the Old Man and the highlands beyond Windermere.

The descent into the Duddon valley begins steeply but soon eases, and is just rideable with care to the point where some disused quarries are passed on the left. Below these quarries the track disintegrates into a series of boggy ruts alongside Long House Beck, making the going extremely tedious. Eventually, a metalled lane is reached, and from there it is half a mile to the minor road up the valley. Following the road south brings one in about ¾m to the Newfield Inn at Seathwaite. For Seathwaite and the Duddon valley see page 82.

The route described below is the most direct way back to Coniston, but it involves further hillclimbing across the intervening fells. From Seathwaite, continue down the valley to Hall Dunnerdale; do not cross the bridge there, but follow the road which at first runs along the riverbank. It then rises steadily up the flank of the distinctive Stickle Pike. Near the top, a look back up Dunnerdale features Bow Fell.

From the road summit (840ft, 259 metres), there is a long drop into the secluded valley of the river Lickle and the hamlet of Broughton Mills. Here, a left turn gradually climbs over the ridge to Torver and the main Coniston road. An alternative road — slightly longer and involving more hillclimbing — is that encircling the head of the Lickle valley via Stephenson Ground. It is well surfaced throughout. The turning for it is easily missed on the descent from the watershed between the Duddon and

Lickle valleys, the best indication being a conifer wood on the left. A narrow lane (signposted 'Cross Hawes') turns up alongside this wood, and climbs steeply for about half a mile.
36 Then it winds around the valley side to Stephenson Ground, where it drops to Water Yeat Bridge. From here it rises to a crossroads, where it meets the road up from Broughton Mills previously mentioned.

The term 'ground' which appears in the names of many of the local farmsteads can be traced back to the beginning of the sixteenth century. In 1509 and 1532 Furness Abbey made agreements with local tenants and squatters for the sale of plots of land scattered round the fringe of the open grazing on the fells. The plot, or 'ground', each bearing the owner's name would be enclosed, cleared and a farm built.

Turning sharp left at the crossroads a steady climb follows to the top of the ridge; from here the view is disappointing, the expected sight of Coniston Water not materialising. The road drops to meet the A593 1m south of Torver and $3\frac{1}{2}$m from Coniston. The approach to the village, overlooking the lake, is most attractive.

Walna Scar Road, Coniston

The Garburn Road: Kentmere to Troutbeck

Distances from Kentmere: Top of Garburn Pass 1½m, Troutbeck 4½m, Windermere (town) 6½m, Staveley 8m.

INTRODUCTION

NB See also general comments, pages 17-18. This track, linking the Kentmere and Troutbeck valleys, provides a northern outlet from the former, but offers no saving in time over the alternative of retracing one's route to Staveley. Formerly a well-constructed and metalled road, it has suffered from lack of maintenance, particularly attention to drainage, and is now impassable to motor vehicles, though its gradients are no steeper than several minor tarred roads. It is one of the easiest hill passes to take a cycle over but it will be a fortunate cyclist who avoids getting wet feet. About 1,000ft (300 metres) of ascent is involved and the way is unmistakable throughout. Allow about one hour from Kentmere village to the top and then ¾hr to Troutbeck, 1hr to Staveley or Windermere. The description below will suffice for both directions.

DESCRIPTION

From Kentmere, the road leading past the church is taken, this rises to terminate at Nook, a pretty group of cottages from which there is a fine view down the valley. Below is Kentmere Hall, built on to a pele tower. The Garburn Road soon bears right, and this lower section, in good condition, is rideable in parts. Passing through a gate, the track climbs, and, although firm, it is often partly flooded. When a hollow in the hillside is reached, a small stream has to be forded before the track resumes its upward course. This section is very wet after rain, and the track is cut up by running water. Just before the summit (1,480ft, 450 metres), a gate is passed through after which the track winds its way across a rather bleak upland, prior to beginning the long gradual descent into the Troutbeck valley.

The view, as it opens up, is very fine, with Troutbeck village seen across the valley on the slopes of Wansfell, while to the

37

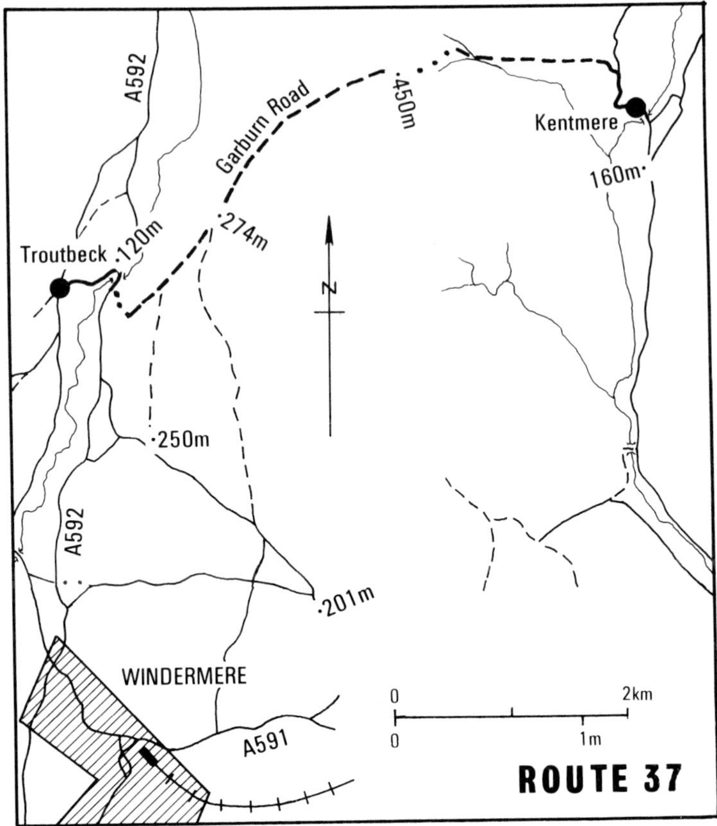

north is the long ridge that culminates in the High Street range. Ahead is part of Windermere, and beyond is Coniston Old Man and neighbouring fells. The only jarring feature is the camping and caravan site at Limefitt in the valley bottom, unscreened from this angle.

The easy downhill grade tempts one to cycle, but great care is required, as the surface quality is extremely variable. It is wiser to wheel the cycle as far as the old quarry tips, just beyond which the track forks. The left branch leads in 1½m to the Troutbeck to Ings road and though untarred may be cycled throughout; the road from there to Staveley is nearly all downhill. This left branch at the fork is also the shortest and easiest way to Windermere station and town, but cannot compete in beauty

Kentmere & the Garburn Pass

with the run down the valley from Troutbeck.

For Troutbeck the right fork is taken, bearing right again a little further on. The track is a good one but eventually becomes too steep to cycle and the last 200yd (after the gate) are very rough. A steep lane leads up from the nearby bridge to the village, where the two inns will be found at its northern end, one on each road. Troutbeck to Ambleside is about four miles, a beautiful ride on the descent to Windermere.

Lake Windermere, near Ambleside

38 Haweswater to Longsleddale via the Gatescarth Pass

Distances: Mardale Head, at the southern end of Haweswater, is 15m from Penrith (Route 21), 10½m from Shap. Sadgill, the terminus of the tarred road up Longsleddale, is 10m north of Kendal.

About two hours should be allowed between the two road ends.

INTRODUCTION

NB See also general comments, pages 17-18. The Gatescarth Pass (1930ft) forms the shortest link between Haweswater and Kendal, and of the major mountain passes is probably the most straightforward, requiring no more than simple physical effort. It is much easier than the neighbouring Nan Bield Pass and even with the Sadgill to Kentmere track (Route 8) constitutes a less exacting alternative.

As a through route it keeps mainly to the valley bottoms and only in the 2m over the pass attains any altitude; it was seriously considered as a possible route when the Lancaster and Carlisle Railway was surveyed. Had not the necessary tunnel been thought too ambitious, the peace and solitude of Longsleddale might have been lost for ever.

The way over the pass was formerly traversable for carts and wheeled traffic, but is now much cut up on its steeper parts. It is still well used by hikers wishing to gain the mountain ridges. The route will be described going south, though there is little to choose between the two directions, both involving 1,100ft (335 metres) of hard climb.

DESCRIPTION

From the road end at Mardale Head, the Nan Bield and Gatescarth routes immediately diverge, the latter a grassy cart track ascending the side valley on the left. This levels out above some old sheepfolds (1400ft), from which there is an excellent view back to the ridges of High Street. The final pull to the top is rough but presents no difficulties. The summit lies just beyond the boundary fence, on a slightly boggy section.

Sadgill, Longsleddale

The first half of the descent into Longsleddale is not as good as the Haweswater side, but is still reasonable and waymarked with cairns. Eventually a wall is reached, just where the valley bottom levels out (coming north note that the Gatescarth path, less conspicuous from below, leaves the wall about thirty yards beyond a stile to bear slightly to the right). Alongside the wall is a good cart road, leading down from some old quarries and a little cycling is possible, but the improvement is only temporary. A signpost indicates the lonely branch path over to Mosedale and Shap.

Beyond a gate, the cart road plunges at an unrideable angle, winding down alongside the ravines and falls of Wren Gill. Preserved is an interesting old form of surfacing — stones set on edge to give a good grip for animals. The wildness of the upper part of the valley is impressive and contrasts with the smoother hills and green fields ahead, slowly nearing. Only when the very bottom of the dale is reached does the track level out, and then the surface is still so rough that the mile on to Sadgill, which could be one of the most pleasant in the Lake District, is scarcely rideable.

At Sadgill, relief comes in the form of the tarred road which leads down the straight and narrow Longsleddale. The scenery is not especially remarkable but has its own quiet appeal. Like neighbouring Kentdale, it is off the main tourist routes, and its dead-end road puts off motorists. Beyond Garnett Bridge, a pretty hamlet on the river Sprint, the valley opens out, and there is a choice of the A6 or the lanes through Burneside to Kendal.

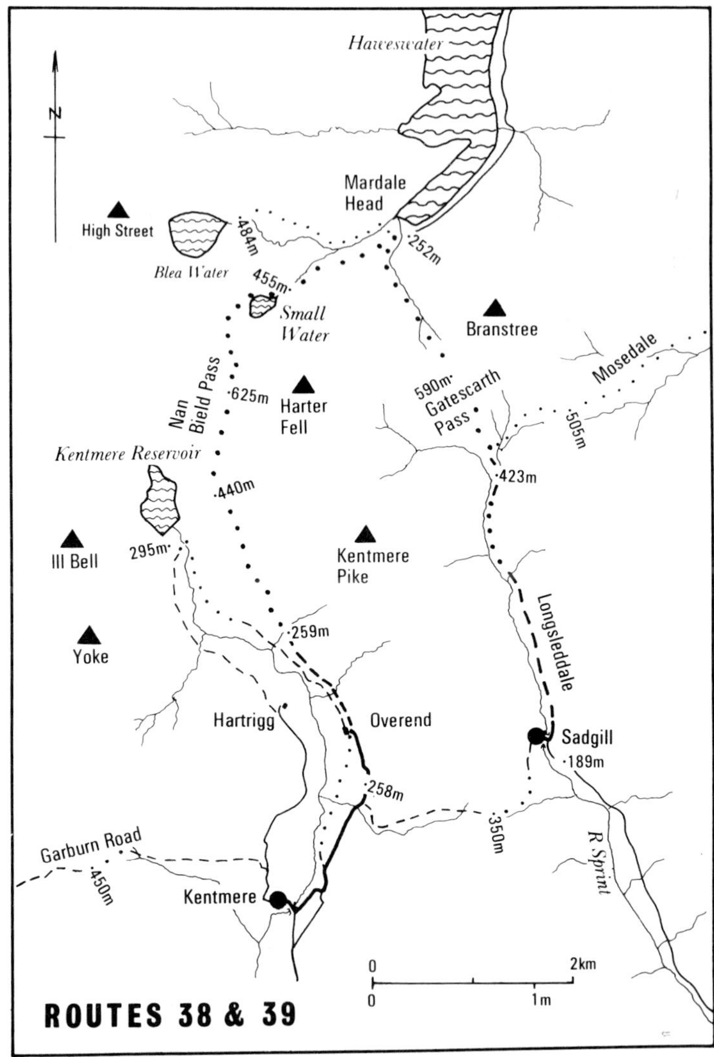
Haweswater
N
Mardale
Head
High Street
Blea Water
484m
455m
252m
Small
Water
Branstree
Mosedale
Nan
Bield Pass
625m
Harter
Fell
590m
Gatescarth
Pass
505m
Kentmere Reservoir
440m
423m
Ill Bell
295m
Kentmere
Pike
Longsleddale
259m
Yoke
Hartrigg
Overend
Sadgill
189m
258m
Garburn Road
350m
R Sprint
450m
Kentmere
0
2km
0
1m
ROUTES 38 & 39

Haweswater to Kentmere via the Nan Bield Pass

Map — see Route 38

Distances: Mardale Head, at the southern end of Haweswater, is 15m from Penrith (Route 21). Kentmere is 8½m north of Kendal and about a mile less from Windermere (Route 7).

About three hours should be allowed between the road ends at Mardale Head and Overend, a little north of Kentmere.

INTRODUCTION

NB See also general comments, page 17-18. This is one of the most magnificent passes in the Lake District, traversing splendid mountain scenery in linking the northern and southern halves of the area. Its practicality for cyclists is rather dubious, yet, considering the nature of the terrain, the path is a good one, well thought out, with no awkward or dangerous spots *in dry weather.* In wet conditions the steepness of the upper sections is certainly hazardous. The neighbouring Gatescarth Pass, only 120ft (35 metres) lower, is much easier, though scenically there is no comparison.

The route is equally difficult in each direction, but as the worst underfoot conditions are likely to be found on the northern side, it is best approached from that side, as described below. Several hours of hard work are involved.

DESCRIPTION

A good view of the route is obtained from the road along Haweswater, before the final drop to Mardale Head. From the road end, the path leads forward unmistakably, with the branches to Longsleddale and back round the lake heading off left and right respectively. The ascent is a very steady one, a little wet in places, with the summit ridge of High Street dominating the view up the valley. Eventually, the stream emanating from Small Water is reached near some falls and is later crossed at the outfall of the tarn. The tarn, at 1,480ft (450 metres), is a natural stopping place before tackling the steeper upper half of the ascent. From it, the summit may be discerned as a slight nick in the seemingly impregnable line of crags ahead.

The path skirting the tarn is good, passing some crude stone shelters. A little further on, the path turns away from the waterside and winds its way up the fell in a series of small zigzags which should be faithfully adhered to. Although much steeper than before, the going is generally good, without any hazardous stretches — it is simply arduous.

The summit (2,050ft, 625 metres), marked by a windbreak shelter and the ridge path, is a narrow defile with a few paces separating one valley prospect from another. The views are grand — back over Haweswater to Penrith and the dull outline of the Pennines, forward to the distant shores of Morecambe Bay. Below is the ink-black Kentmere Reservoir, in the shadow of Ill Bell. For abruptness, the pass is unrivalled in the Lake District, even among purely hikers' routes. The name Nan Bield, incidentally, signifies Deer Refuge. By following the ridge path eastwards, a five minute stroll will reveal the whole of Haweswater, and also a patch of Windermere.

The descent to Kentmere starts with another very steep section of zigzags, soon easing to a more gradual fall down the grassy flank of the valley, undemanding but rather tedious. There follows a spectacular terrace, high above the reservoir, before the path turns away and drops to a broad hill shoulder. Here most maps indicate a path down to the old quarries in the valley bottom, but this is no longer traceable. Dropping into a subsidary valley, the way is a little indistinct, but is marked by frequent cairns, as it winds down to the ford on Ullstone Gill. Coming north the track is harder to pick out, but by maintaining one's previous direction the cairns will be traced. Bear just to the right of the crags ahead.

Beyond the ford, the path is clear and partly rideable, running parallel to and a little above a lane coming down the east side of the Kent. From Overend, either the tarred road or a somewhat boggy bridleway may be taken for the mile or so on to Kentmere, the former will probably be the preferred choice. Northbound, remember that the signposts refer to Mardale rather than the reservoir which now floods it.

Kentmere is more of a cluster of small settlements than a single village, situated in the prettiest part of the valley. The nearest shops and inns are at Staveley, 4m further on.

Borrowdale to Wasdale via Sty Head

INTRODUCTION

NB See general comments, pages 17-18. The 4m by path, compared with the forty-odd miles by road, between the heads of Borrowdale and Wasdale will tempt many cyclists into taking the hill route via Sty Head. The path, although a good and unmistakable one, is extremely rough and arduous and its difficulties should not be underestimated. Decent hiking boots should be worn.

As a through route from Keswick to Wastwater and the coast, it cannot be recommended, the alternative way via Loweswater and Ennerdale Bridge offering some of the finest Lake District scenery, and, after all, cycles are meant to be ridden rather than pushed. Also, although it is something of an accomplishment to reach Sty Head, it must be admitted that the top of the pass is, in hiking terms, only 'first base', and the glimpses afforded into the remoter corners of the mountains provide insufficient compensation for the effort involved. About 3-3½hr should be allowed between the two valleys, about 1¾-2hr up and 1¼-1½hr down. Westbound is perhaps slightly easier.

There have been proposals at various times for the construction of a proper road over Sty Head, principally toward the end of the last century (ie even before the advent of the motor car) and in the 1930s, when a number of minor roads were being improved. From this latter period date the motorable roads over the Honister and Wrynose passes, but anyone who has witnessed the procession of traffic over these narrow routes on a summer weekend will be thankful that Sty Head was, by public pressure, spared the same treatment.

In view of the route's relative complexities, it is described fully in both directions. In addition there is a choice of paths on the Wasdale side of the pass; the main route, direct but tedious, or the valley route, a little longer but more varied. There is little to choose between the two routes in journey times, the one thing they have in common is that from each the alternative path *looks* infinitely easier. The valley route might be described as the less unpleasant; however, in mist, its upper stages could be rather difficult to follow.

40

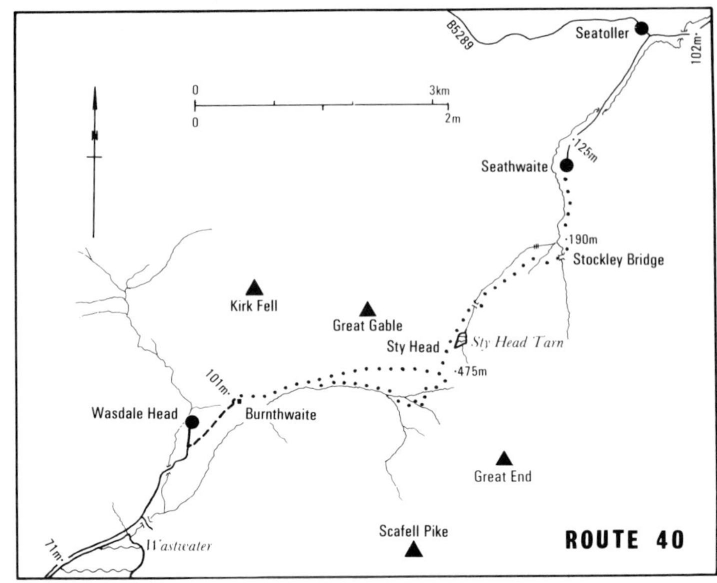

DESCRIPTION - *WESTBOUND*

The track from Seathwaite to Stockley Bridge is mostly not fit for cycling. Ahead can be seen the steep path up Grains Gill to Esk Hause and, across the valley, the white streak of Taylor Gill Force. Crossing Stockley Bridge the track is then sheer purgatory — very steep and uneven. The National Trust has recently done a considerable amount of erosion repair work to the track and part of the original stone paving has been extended with similar materials. Please keep to the path. A gate in a wall marks the halfway point of this initial, and worst, part of the climb. By cutting through the trees on the right, a good, if somewhat precarious, view of Taylor Gill Force can be obtained. Above the trees the gradient eases somewhat but the path remains very rough. Presently a footbridge comes into view, to be crossed unless the easier western bank of the stream has already been gained. Shortly after the bridge, Sty Head Tarn suddenly comes into view and, beyond it, the top of the col. The going alongside the tarn is good, after which there is one steep pull before the top (in mist, avoid taking a track bearing left — leading up to the Sprinkling Tarn path — at the start of this last climb).

From the First Aid box at the top of the pass a number of paths diverge — to Sprinkling Tarn and Langdale, to Scafell Pike via the Corridor route beneath the crags of Great End, to Great Gable, either direct or via Nape's Needle, and down to Wasdale. Only in thick mist is there any chance of going wrong, and there are always plenty of walkers to put you on the right path.

From the top of the pass (1,580ft, 480 metres) two routes lead down into Wasdale:

(a) Main route, westbound

This continues in the direction already followed, passing a large cairn and initially not dropping down the valley. Soon a steep slope opens up on the left, across which is seen the deep cleft of Piers Gill running down from Scafell Pike. A few hundred yards from the top, the path begins to drop, with an awkward rocky step to begin with. The way down into Wasdale is then straightforward, although the Wasdale Head Inn never appears to be getting any closer and the path — loose scree all the way down, with some rocky steps to negotiate — is extremely monotonous and hard on the feet. Eventually, the bottom of the valley is reached, and, on crossing a narrow footbridge, a field of springy turf offers the first opportunity to cycle since Borrowdale. Then, after skirting the farm of Burnthwaite, a cart track leads to the tarred valley road.

(b) Valley route, westbound

From the First Aid box, follow the Sprinkling Tarn path for a few yards across a peaty hollow, and then bear right over grass in the general direction of the col between Lingmell and Scafell Pike, following a faint path with a few cairns. After 80yd a deep stony hollow, Spout head, appears, through which the path down can just be traced. From this point, the track drops to the left, skirting a rocky knoll and fording a stream, which is then kept on the right to the lip of the hollow, where another stream, coming in from the left, is crossed. Now dropping more steeply, the path winds carefully down the hillside with a steady gradient, crossing a stream about half way down. At the bottom, it fords the main valley stream just above its confluence with Piers Gill and crosses an awkward rocky outcrop alongside some little waterfalls. The path then picks its way through a boulder field to a gate in a wall, beyond which it improves to meet the main track, long visible above on the right, about ¾m before Burnthwaite.

DESCRIPTION - *EASTBOUND*

For Sty Head, follow the cart track that leaves the road about 200yd short of the inn and leads to the last farm

in the valley, Burnthwaite, where it passes through a gate on the left. Beyond Burnthwaite there is only a stony footpath, initially rough, but with a little cycling possible to the narrow footbridge
40 over the beck coming down between Kirk Fell and Great Gable. Here it is worth stopping to decide which way to take up to Sty Head.

(a) Main route, Eastbound
This is plainly visible running up the southern flank of Great Gable to the head of the pass. The going is stony throughout and extremely gruelling — a monotonous slog with no respite. The only interest lies in the view across the valley to the fine crags below the Scafell Pike ridge and the deep rift of Piers Gill running down from the direction of the summit. There are one or two awkward rocky steps requiring care. Directly opposite Skew Gill, the deep gully below Great End, after crossing some scree there is a most tricky step to be negotiated. It is better not to attempt this with a bicycle without first examining it. After this, there are only a few hundred yards of uneven, but generally level, path before, on bearing left, the top of the pass is reached.

(b) Valley route, Eastbound
This leaves the main path about 400yd beyond the footbridge, bearing right to follow a wall alongside the stream; (avoid turning too soon across boggy ground: the correct path is distinct). Presently a gate in a wall is reached, beyond which the path at first appears to be lost in a sea of boulders, but, once found, is unmistakable. The going is slow, and in places wet. Nearing the stream some fine rocky pools are seen, their beds a lovely deep blue. A little further up is a small waterfall, alongside which the path practically disappears as it picks its way over the rock outcrop on the left. This part is the worst of the ascent. The stream is forded just above its confluence with Piers Gill, to reach a grassy tongue, where the smoother going is most welcome. The path continues to climb steeply, but steadily, up the bare hillside towards the valley head. In places where the original grassy track remains intact it is fairly easy, but where this has been eroded to a stony rut, it is extremely rough and hard work. On reaching the top it proves, as probably expected, not to be *the* top but the lip of a rounded hollow, Spout Head. From here there is a good retrospective view of the deepest part of Piers Gill, below Lingmell. The path crosses a stream coming down from Skew Gill, a narrow gully above on the right, and continues up the hollow with the main stream on the left. The path is indistinct and marked only by small cairns. In about 250yd, the stream is crossed near a large cairn after which the path turns left

Seathwaite

to run beneath a rocky knoll. A few tricky patches are crossed, after which the cyclist emerges on to a level area of grass to reach the track coming down from Sprinkling Tarn. Here, bear left for the First Aid box that defines the top of the pass, reached in a few yards.

NB There are some variations on the top section of this path, but all lead up to either the main route (on the left) or the Corridor path from Scafell Pike (on the right).

From the top of the pass, the view ahead down the valley is bleak and a little disappointing. The mountain seen in the distance is Blencathra, beyond Keswick. The path down beside the tarn looks deceptively good from above, but will be found mostly too rough for cycling. A short way below the tarn, a footbridge is reached and this must be crossed; the path continuing along the left bank of the stream *must not* be taken, as it leads to some very steep scrambles down by the side of Taylor Gill Force. The path follows the right hand of the stream and remains rough, although the gradually-enfolding view over Borrowdale is some compensation. On reaching the top corner of a small wood, the path steepens and becomes much rougher from heavy use. Where the trees thin out it is possible to walk across to the side of Taylor Gill Force, a fine waterfall. The path continues to drop towards Stockley Bridge, seen below, but still a considerable time off. From Stockley Bridge the track improves considerably but is still mostly not rideable. Not until the hamlet of Seathwaite is a decent road reached; then it is 8½m on the level to Keswick (Route 32).

41 Ennerdale to Buttermere via Scarth Gap

Approximate times: Northbound 30min up, 45min down; southbound 75min up, 20min down. Times are between Black Sail and Gatesgarth on B5289.

INTRODUCTION

NB See also general comments, pages 17-18. Of the two mountain passes out of Ennerdale — this and the Black Sail Pass to Wasdale — this is the easier, chiefly because of its lower summit level of 1,450ft (447 metres). The total climb out of Ennerdale is thus only about 540ft (160 metres), compared to 1,100ft (330 metres) from Buttermere, and so the pass is best taken northbound. Coming in the reverse direction there is also the fact that, if any mishap occurs, Ennerdale is not a very useful place to aim for. The path, it need hardly be said, is extremely well defined.

DESCRIPTION

The path turns up at the end of the Forestry Commission plantations, ¼m short of Black Sail Youth Hostel, and begins as it intends to continue. This path is really a number of parallel routes, all equally stony, requiring hard work, but presenting no problems unless the midges are biting. Beyond the top of the wood, the path separates into various strands, the best course being to cross the stream here, though eventually all the tracks reunite. Across the stream the going is steeper but now less rough. Before long the boulders give way to a grassy saddle separating the rival crags of Haystacks and Seat and the hard work is now over. The confusion of cairns may cause some anxiety in mist, but there is no risk of going wrong. The actual top is marked by a mammoth cairn, the remains of an old iron fence, and some wandering sheep.

The path on to Buttermere bears away left, dropping only gently at first, but working its way round the crags to enter a shallow gully. This part of the crossing, as far as the old wall, is by far the roughest, a wearying succession of bumps and jolts, half streambed, half scree. On the left, High Crag, the first peak on

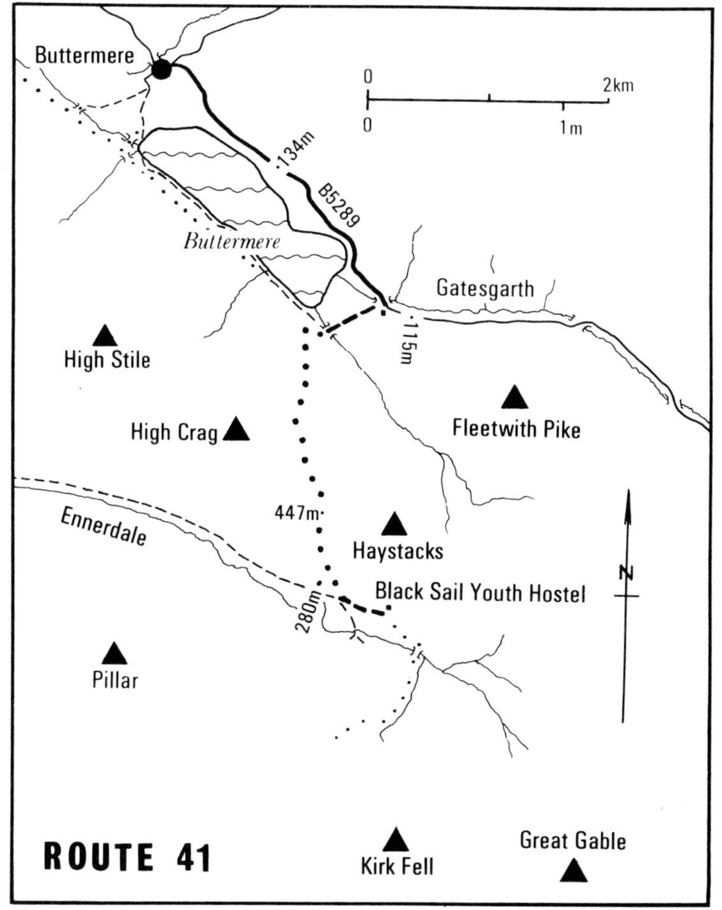

the ridge to Red Pike, presents a shapely profile as does Fleetwith Pike across the valley. Buttermere lake and the green vale backed by Grasmoor together make a fine picture.

After crossing the old wall, the going improves somewhat, as the path falls steadily towards the lake. A steep and badly-eroded section leads to the junction of the lakeside path to Buttermere (see page 131) and the lane across the flat valley bottom to Gatesgarth on the Honister road, 2m from the village. The views from this road back across the lake are delightful.

42 **Ennerdale to Wasdale via the Black Sail Pass**

Times: Southboud $1\frac{1}{4}$hr up, 1hr down; northbound 2hr up, 1hr down.

INTRODUCTION

NB See also general comments, pages 17-18. This provides a convenient, and not over-difficult, valley to valley route for the suitably equipped and not overloaded cyclist. It is much preferably taken from north to south; the total climb out of Ennerdale being 850ft (260 metres) compared to 1,500ft (460 metres) out of Wasdale and the steep section alongside Sail Beck less of a hazard going up than coming down. Another and important point is that Wasdale Head offers refreshment, shelter, and, if need be, assistance, whereas Ennerdale is inhospitable to all but Youth Hostellers with the nearest village, Ennerdale Bridge, 9m down the valley. The road distance between the two valley heads is 28m. The path is unmistakable and well used.

DESCRIPTION

The path passes the Black Sail youth hostel and winds down to the footbridge over the Liza. The way at first runs across springy turf up to the top corner of the plantations. The character of the ascent here changes abruptly for the worse, the path making its way up the side of the rocky gorge containing Sail Beck. There is no alternative to shouldering the bicycle and carefully making one's way over the bare rock, stopping at intervals to reconnoitre the path. This section, although only about 250yd in extent, is the real bugbear of the crossing, and is extremely hard work. In wet weather, or coming in the other direction, there is a real risk of a fall. It is best to keep well to the right of the stream. Below, in the valley, is seen the lonely youth hostel and the ranks of smooth moraines.

Eventually, the open fell is reached and the summit col seen ahead. There is still a lot of climbing to do, but the path winds up at a reasonable gradient. The top of the pass, 1,780ft (545 metres), is crossed by the remains of an old iron fence. Coming

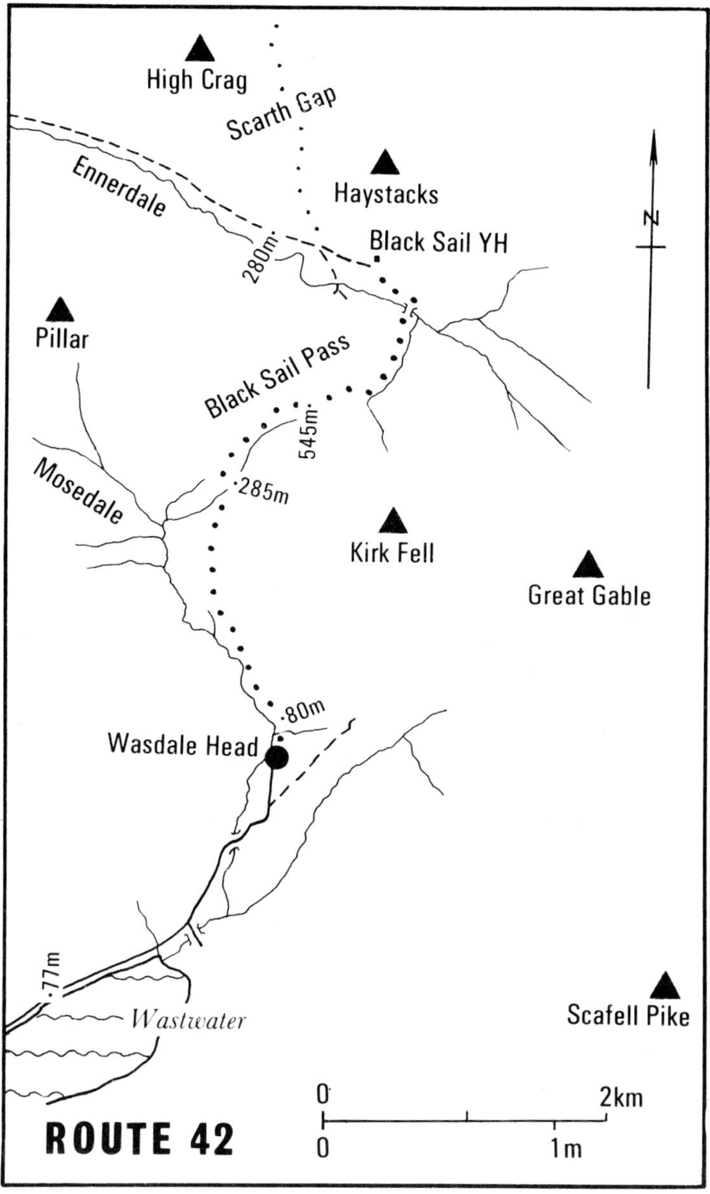
High Crag
Scarth Gap
Ennerdale
Haystacks
Black Sail YH
280m
N
Pillar
Black Sail Pass
545m
Mosedale
285m
Kirk Fell
Great Gable
80m
Wasdale Head
77m
Wastwater
Scafell Pike
0
2km
0
1m
ROUTE 42

42

Wasdale Head

into view on the Wasdale side are Red Pike and Yewbarrow, across the deep hollow of Mosedale.

Having reached the ridge, one should make the most of it, and an easy walk may be taken westward to Looking Stead, a superior viewpoint (first remember to lock you cycle). The Derwent Fells now appear over Haystacks, to the left of which is the Scarth Gap route to Buttermere. In the other direction, Mosedale sweeps down to Wasdale Head, south of which a glint of light indicates Burnmoor Tarn.

The descent, it may be said, is surprisingly easy, the path is stony but regular, and in places paralleled by grass; nowhere is it oversteep or rocky. The only thing to bear in mind is that it is over two miles from the summit down to Wasdale Head, much further than the climb up from Ennerdale. The track first drops steadily into Mosedale, eventually zigzagging to a ford over Gatherstone Beck at 950ft (290 metres). A rougher section follows as far as the first wall. Then, an unexpected treat, the gradient eases and the path is partly rideable, which enables one to impress the walkers by casually cycling past them. A few fords — not difficult — need to be crossed before the path accompanies the wall to Wasdale Head. The last half mile, above and alongside the stream, is delightful, with Sca Fell towering ahead.

CYCLE DEALERS AND CYCLE HIRERS

This list covers the parts of Cumbria and north Lancashire included in the book. It is believed correct at time of publication but is of course liable to alteration. A useful leaflet, regularly revised, is 'Cycling in Cumbria' obtainable from Tourist Information centres or The Cumbria Tourist Board, Ellerthwaite, Windermere, Cumbria.

Please note that, although certain shops will undertake repairs, work may not be able to be handled immediately. Where advertised, cycle hire is usually available at part-day, daily, or weekly rates. A deposit will be required.

There are a few organisations offering package tours of cycle hire and accommodation. These usually advertise in the cycling press.

Ambleside
Ghyllside Cycles
The Slack
Tel: 0966 33592
Spares and accessories, repairs.

Arnside
South Cumbria Cycles
Tel: 0524 761929
Cycle hire (Easter - end October). 8 cycles.

Barrow in Furness
Halfords Ltd
72 Duke Street
Tel: 0229 20164
Spares and accessories.

E. & E. Roberts
162 Rawlinson Street
(off Abbey Road)
Tel: 0229 21104
Spares and accessories, repairs.

Bowness (see also Windermere)
Rentabike
117 Craig Walk
(off Lake Road)
Tel: 09662 3270
Cycle hire (all year round), some spares.

Broughton in Furness
Mountain Centre
Market Street
Tel: 06576 461
Spares and accessories, repairs.

Carlisle
Border Cycles Ltd
133 Lowther Street
Tel: 0228 36872
Spares and accessories, repairs.

Halfords Ltd
62 English Street
Tel: 0228 22744
Spares and accessories.

Palace Cycle Stores
122 Botchergate
Tel: 0228 23142
Spares and accessories, limited repairs.

K. Whitehead
104 Botchergate
Tel: 0228 26890
Spares and accessories, repairs.

Cleator (2m north of Egremont)
Ainfield Cycle Centre
Jacktrees Road
Tel: 0946 81247
Spares and accessories, repairs, cycle hire (all year round), 12 cycles.

Cockermouth
Derwent Cycle Sports
4 Market Place
Tel: 0900 822113
Spares and accessories, repairs, cycle hire (all year round) cycling clothing.

Kendal
Askew Cycles
Kent Works, Burneside Road
Tel: 0539 28057
Spares and accessories, repairs, cycle hire (all year round).

Brucie's Bike Shop
187 Highgate
Tel: 0539 27230
Spares and accessories, repairs.

Halfords Ltd
54 Stricklandgate
Tel: 0539 20467
Spares and accessories.

Lakeland Cycles
Stricklandgate
Spares and accessories, repairs.

Keswick
Keswick Cycle Hire
Pack Horse Court
(off Main Street)
Tel: Braithwaite (059682) 273
Spares and accessories, repairs, cycle hire (all year round), 80 cycles.

Lancaster
Ron Davies Cycles
1 Westbourne Road
(near railway station)
Tel: 0524 34622
Spares and accessories, repairs.

Alan Dent Cycles
4 China Street
(northbound A6 in town centre)
Tel: 0524 39755
Spares and accessories, repairs, cycle hire.

Halfords Ltd
22 Cheapside
Tel: 0524 64553
Spares and accessories.

Smalleys
30 Parliament Street
(near bridge)
Tel: 0524 63478
Also 105 Higher Penny Street
(in town centre)
Tel: 0524 64864
Spares and accessories, repairs.

Millom
Charles McIntosh
54 Queen Street
Tel: 0657 2294
Mainly repairs, some sales.

Morecambe
Armitage Accessories
1 Bare Lane
Tel: 0524 410836
Spares and accessories, repairs. Open: 7 days a week.

Smalleys
104 Euston Road
Tel: 0524 412446
Spares and accessories, repairs.

Wrights
92 Clarendon Road
Tel: 0524 411344
Sales and accessories.

Penrith
Harpers Cycles
1-2 Middlegate
Tel: 0768 64475
Spares and accessories, repairs, cycle hire (all year round), 30 cycles.

K. Whitehead
35 King Street
Tel: 0768 62910
Spares and accessories, repairs.

Pooley Bridge
Tree Tops Ltd
Tel: 08536 267
Cycle hire (all year round), 19 cycles.

Ulverston
Harvey Jackson
Market Place
Tel: 0229 52247
Spares and accessories.

Whitehaven
Mark Taylor
20-21 King Street
Tel: 0946 2252
Spares and accessories, repairs.

Wigton
Wigton Cycle & Sports Shop
23 West Street
Tel: 09654 2824
Spares and accessories, cycle hire.

Windermere (see also Bowness)
Rentacamp Leisure Hire
Station Buildings
Tel: 09662 4786
Spares and accessories, repairs, cycle hire (all year round), 41 cycles. Also inclusive holidays.

Workington
Halfords Ltd
29 Murray Road
Tel: 0900 2210
Spares and accessories.

Smalleys
Traffic Light Bike Shop
35 Washington Street
Tel: 0900 3283
Spares and accessories, repairs.

Mark Taylor
4 Murray Road
Tel: 0900 3280
Spares and accessories.